MAKING COOPERATIVE LEARNING WORK

Student Teams in K–12 Classrooms

PAUL J. VERMETTE

Niagara University

Merrill,
an imprint of Prentice Hall
Upper Saddle River, New Jersey   Columbus, Ohio

Library of Congress Cataloging-in-Publication Data
Vermette, Paul J.
     Making cooperative learning work : student teams in K-12 classrooms / Paul J.
Vermette
       p.   cm.
     Includes bibliographical references and index.
     ISBN 0-13-206392-1 (pbk.)
     1. Team learning approach in education—United States. 2. Group work in
education—United States.   I. Title
   LB1032.V39   1998
   371.3'6—dc21   96-53392
                                       CIP

Cover art: Diana Ong/SuperStock
Editor: Debra A. Stollenwerk
Production Editor: Patricia S. Kelly
Design Coordinator: Karrie M. Converse
Text Designer: Mia Saunders
Cover Designer: Russ Maselli
Production Manager: Patricia A. Tonneman
Electronic Text Management: Marilyn Wilson Phelps, Matthew Williams, Karen L. Bretz,
    Tracey B. Ward
Illustrations: Tracey B. Ward
Director of Marketing: Kevin Flanagan
Marketing Manager: Suzanne Stanton
Advertising/Marketing Coordinator: Julie Shough

This book was set in Galliard and Eras by Prentice Hall and was printed and bound by
Quebecor Printing/Book Press. The cover was printed by Phoenix Color Corp.

© 1998 by Prentice-Hall, Inc.
Upper Saddle River, New Jersey 07458

Printed in the United States of America

10 9 8 7 6 5 4 3

ISBN: 0-13-206392-1

Prentice-Hall International (UK) Limited, *London*
Prentice-Hall of Australia Pty. Limited, *Sydney*
Prentice-Hall of Canada, Inc., *Toronto*
Prentice-Hall Hispanoamericana, S. A., *Mexico*
Prentice-Hall of India Private Limited, *New Delhi*
Prentice-Hall of Japan, Inc., *Tokyo*
Editora Prentice-Hall do Brasil, Ltda., *Rio de Janeiro*

PREFACE

Making Student Teams Work: Cooperative Learning in the K–12 Classroom is the result of more than a decade of intensive analysis and observation of teachers' attempts to put cooperative learning into practice. On the surface, cooperative learning seems to be a simplistic concept: Let groups of students get together during class time to help each other learn. Yet successful practice of cooperative learning has become a some-what elusive phenomenon. Many teachers deemed it to be "old-fashioned" group work, so they implemented it as such—and failed. Others rejected its use because of previous bad experiences with groups, either in their own classrooms or as students themselves. Still others simply paid little attention to it, deeming it inappropriate for their students. This last group, interestingly, includes people who rejected it for the following, paradoxical reasons:

"My students are too young to work together."

"My students are too old to benefit from working with others outside their cliques."

"My subject is too individualistic . . . the students need to work alone."

"My subject is too broad . . . peers won't provide a wide enough sampling of perspectives or ideas."

"I need my students to learn about diversity . . . and my classes are too homogeneous to build meaningful groups."

These concerns, though, are unsupported. The research base is heavily supportive of cooperative learning, and thoughtful teacher practice has convinced many teachers that cooperative learning is the best way to go if one is concerned with educational goals such as critical thinking, the development of empathy, meaningful understanding, racial tolerance, the ability to use the computer, and/or the ability to do successful self-reflection. This list of goals provides a contemporary agenda for schooling, and since cooperative learning works for all the items, it offers an overriding rationale for its use. The development of an accurate and useful conceptualization of cooperative learning is the purpose of this book.

ORGANIZATION OF THE TEXT

It is clear to me after years of study that teachers need to develop a deep awareness of several aspects of the cooperative learning experience: First, they must realistically analyze their own starting points, their own preconceptions, and their own current understandings of cooperative learning. The Introduction and **Chapter 1** introduce the concept of team learning and provide the experience necessary for the reader to begin incorporating the strategic suggestions that follow.

Second, teachers should be aware that cooperative learning is more than a "good idea" or some new "innovation." It is the most thoroughly researched instructional strategy available, and the research cries for its implementation across subjects, grades, and all student populations.

The research base, extending across two decades and across all types of boundaries, provides support and information relevant to a new teacher's implementation. **Chapter 2** describes relevant exemplary research studies from diverse scenarios and from different theoretical perspectives and does so in a manner that makes it comprehensible and interesting for all readers. *Research* is a term that teachers often do not like to hear and one that they seldom use. The discussion presented in Chapter 2 is meant to change that pattern and to help teachers understand why those of us who are excited about cooperative learning feel the way that we do.

My own work has shown that successful practice of team learning usually involves the effective use of three structures, which form the heart of the model that is developed in Chapters 3, 4, and 5: (1) the intelligent and defendable practice of grouping students, (2) the formulation and articulation of an acceptable grading strategy, and (3) the thoughtful and comprehensive use of a governing system. **Grouping**, **grading**, and **governing** are thus the fully developed topics, replete with ideas and suggestions, that make up most of the text.

Unlike Spencer Kagan's (1989) structures, mine are not the differing types of lessons for different knowledge; instead, they are the three separate components that

form a unified policy governing a teacher's implementation. Culled from the hundreds of research studies since the 1970s, these structures boil down to the following ideas:

1. the building of teacher-constructed groups that maximize the advantages of heterogeneously mixed, small, semipermanent teams and that have a team philosophy of interdependence;

2. the construction and dissemination of an acceptable and well-articulated grading system that motivates interdependence and yet fails to be divisive and punishing; and

3. the monitoring or governing of team efforts by the teams themselves and the teacher so that students are aware of how they are doing and what needs improvement.

These three structures—*grouping, grading,* and *governing*—are the foci of **Chapters 3, 4, and 5,** respectively. These structures, along with a well-articulated set of classroom activities and projects, provide the means for teachers to establish and implement a successful cooperative learning system in their classrooms.

The final component of the model I present is the development of instructional strategies that can be used effectively with teams of learners. Many ineffective teachers build interesting teams that do little of value together. Some teachers send all teamwork home, which is a self-defeating system. Some teachers build a team that spends its time trying to memorize useless facts and ends up frustrated and no farther ahead. Still others create teams that engage in critical analysis of members, which often produces feelings of anxiety and hostility, defeating one of the key reasons for putting the students together in the first place! Finally, some teachers put teams together in a way that either allows one person to do all the work (because of apathy, laziness, absenteeism, or domination) or everyone does his or her own work separately. Both of these scenarios are devoid of the positive benefits to be gained by effective cooperative learning practice.

Chapter 6 attempts to solve this problem by offering learning practice conceptualization for inventing or modifying good classroom strategies. The first is simple, yet profound: task versus object. Often teachers do not distinguish between the demands of these two types of activities. They must recognize the characteristics of both if they are to weave them effectively throughout the course of a year's work.

The second strategy offered follows Bloom's taxonomy and provides many examples of sound classroom activities at each level of the taxonomy.

The third strategy presented provides a new categorization schema, called CREEEPP (construct, rehearse, examine, elaborate, evaluate, predict, and personalize), and gives examples of numerous activities for all levels of schooling. This schema, designed specifically for team learning, has proven useful to the student teachers I have worked with at Niagara University for the past few years.

Finally, the last part of the final chapter describes a system by which Howard Gardner's concept of multiple intelligences can be used to invent classroom strategies that involve a variety of student talents (or potentialities) and that have differential appeals to diverse populations. Using this approach in combination with Elizabeth Cohen's call for complex team instruction, teachers can produce thoughtful and meaningful projects that take great advantage of the diverse strengths found in groups of youngsters—strengths that are not often (if ever) found in a youth working alone.

FEATURES

This book has several features that mark it as a very special text for new teachers and for veteran teachers learning a new system. Each of these has been field tested and holds great potential for success.

The book is **interactive** in nature. It regularly calls for the reader to complete an activity before it delivers new content, thus creating a "set" by which new information can be effectively processed. These **activities** occur throughout each chapter and are an integral part of the book. Readers are encouraged to work together (or in teams) to compare answers and responses both prior to reading and after the new ideas have been presented. Readers are expected to make decisions and predictions *and* test their responses against those of others.

The book is filled with **examples** that run across diverse populations, across subject areas (including bowling and college writing), across grades K–12, and across social class lines. It is meant to be comprehensive without being cumbersome. The successful examples are so numerous and informative that they create a valuable resource in themselves.

Treatment of **gender issues, ethnic realities,** and contemporary issues such as **inclusion,** learning to use **computers,** and dealing with **parents** is integrated throughout various sections of the text, providing reinforcement and offering multiple viewpoints of their interconnections with cooperative learning. Likewise, portfolios and alternative assessment are *not* seen as separate phenomena but as related components of the instructional package. When they stand alone, topics such as those just mentioned get easily overlooked or forgotten by readers. When integrated fully into the development of the larger conceptual model, they become more deeply understood and practiced more effectively.

One other component of the book makes it a powerful resource for those helping others learn about cooperative learning. Every chapter finishes with a **summary** and a set of **reflection questions.** The summaries present developed ideas and stand as a statement of the chapters' content. The reflection questions provoke further elaboration and analysis of the ideas presented. They do more than review; they extend thoughtful practice to new situations and they seek to develop in readers a reflective attitude toward their own understanding of the content. Many questions offer new data and advice and seek to have the reader connect them to their developing conceptions. All in all, they provide a meaningful and valuable set of activities to help readers make sense of all their new constructs.

ACKNOWLEDGMENTS

This book is the culmination of more than a decade of reading, experimenting, observing, analyzing, and discussing cooperative learning strategies with thousands of people. This group includes Niagara University students, professional faculty and administrators across North America, K–12 students in our schools, and college faculty at many institutions. I have had enormous amounts of help in making this work come to life, and I thank everyone who has touched my life and my work over that time.

I cannot possibly name everyone who has contributed to my ideas and my suggestions but I wish to name a few who were essential to this enterprise. I offer my thanks to my wife, Kit, whose patience is unmatched anywhere, and to my son, Matt, who has shared many "opinions" about schools and classes as he has worked his way through his school years; to all of my Niagara University colleagues, including Tom Sheeran, Deborah Erickson, Shirley Wisniewski, Carm Sapone, Chandra Foote, and Dan O'Leary, who have pushed and driven me with ideas, suggestions, experiences, and threats; and to my students, who have magically turned good ideas into brilliant applications as lesson plans. They are a gifted lot and most have gone on to become superb teachers in their own right. Several, including Michele Pope, Julie Gladman, and Lori Ann Aaviku, went out of their way to help me with the writing and three others, Brian Carlson, Julie Grando, and Rose Mastroianni, contributed some of their own theories to the text.

Thanks are also due my colleagues in the schools who have contributed so much to this project, including Mary Murray and Wayne Ginty (Lockport, NY), Dan Johnson (Wilson, NY), Herb Wilkinson (Millbrook, NY), John Myers (Toronto, Ontario), Sharon Sorensen (Toronto, Ontario), Kathy Gedeon (Pendleton, NY), Tina Asklar (Niagara Falls, NY), Sue Janssen-O'Leary (the best student teacher in Western history and now a teacher in Putnam Valley, NY), Doug Van Vliet (Averill Park, NY), Diana Tyler (Hamburg, NY), Brenda Giffen (Toronto, Ontario), Rob Touchette (Niagara Falls, NY), Deborah Asklar (Niagara Falls, NY), Diane Havens (Niagara Falls, NY), Georgia Peach (Skaneatles, NY), and Terry Serviss (Montreal, Quebec) and to Kristina Martinez Herr, who has painstakingly put these ideas to print and has been a constant editor-in-practice since the book's inception.

I also thank the book's reviewers for their helpful comments: Cynthia G. Kruger, University of Massachusetts; Betty Jo Simmons, Longwood College; Norma J. Strickland, Rust College; and James E. Watson, Trinity Evangelica Divinity School.

Truly, this text could not have happened without these special people, to whom I will be forever indebted.

BRIEF CONTENTS

CONTENTS

THE IMPORTANCE OF TEAM LEARNING

AN INTRODUCTION TO COOPERATIVE LEARNING

"Oh, right . . . another book on cooperative learning . . . just what I need."

As I have traveled around the United States and Canada teaching teachers about cooperative learning during the past several years, I have felt the sting of sentiments similar to the one expressed in the preceding quote. To many teachers, the use of learning in teams from kindergarten to high school is just another passing fancy destined for the scrap heap of educational innovation history. Yet, in other ways, cooperative learning seems to be special and different from other "fads" in education:

1. It does have a huge and well-established research base and has been subjected to many trials.
2. It has been successfully used by teachers at all levels and in all subjects across many districts.
3. It appears to have the staying power lost to other innovations. Each year cooperative learning picks up more advocates.

Since the publication of *A Nation at Risk* (NCEE, 1983), many changes have occurred in educational systems. In fact, change seems to be the order of the day. However, only cooperative learning has changed what students do in class and has transformed the traditional "teacher talk, students listen" pattern that has transcended all of educational history (Goodlad, 1984; Cuban, 1983; Sirotnik, 1983).

It seems, then, that there is a continued huge interest in cooperative learning and in its effective implementation. The very fact that you continued reading beyond the bizarre opening line of this chapter suggests that you are curious and you feel there is something to be gained by reading another book about this topic. As I will explain, this book is different from others about cooperative learning. In it, I will attempt to explain the central tenets of the team technique and provide practical and immediate advice for its implementation.

In short, this book is needed because it provides a reader-friendly and practical system that can help all teachers use team learning effectively. It is different from other books on cooperative learning because it is designed to engage the reader in reflective activities that help restructure and broaden his or her understandings. To a large degree, it is a "workbook" to be read with a pen or pencil at hand. It has been designed to challenge learners actively at various points, both to raise perspectives and refresh memories, but also to assess learnings and to evaluate ideas. It can be used alone or in tandem with a partner or partners. Done with others, the text's activities provide rich contexts for the analysis of the ideas called for by modern constructivist theories. The activities simulate cooperative learning exercises. Done individually, they are useful as motivators and as assessments.

The first such activity is the three part pretest offered in the next section; it includes one self-examination question and two knowledge analysis questions.

THE THREE-PART PRETEST

I once had a psychology professor who advocated that teachers should always begin a new unit of study with a pretest so that an accurate measurement of learning could be made. The idea seemed to make sense to me then; after all, such a practice would make growth all that much easier to spot! However, I always worried about several things that could go wrong with a pretest: (1) The students who scored poorly or who simply recognized that they did not know anything at all about the topic would simply give up, think of themselves as "dumb" or lose face. (2) Would I really change my teaching approach based on what the pretest scores revealed about students? (3) Would I be able to handle whatever else the pretest score revealed about my students? This final concern, by the way, included the fact that if they scored low would I lower expectations for them? If they scored high, would my sense of efficacy drop . . . knowing that I was not responsible for their eventual high grades?

These concerns were grave enough for me that I usually rejected pretests. For several reasons, however, I have chosen to start you off with one. First, I will never know how you do on it, so I cannot lower my expectations and cannot adjust the methodology anyway (the finished book is in your hands). Secondly, I have structured the pretest in a way that I think will prove to be most helpful to you. It asks for your personal reflections and activates your prior knowledge, so low scores should not affect your self-esteem or drive. As a matter of fact, there will not be any low scores!

The benefits of a good pretest should be met here. The reader probably has a well-established starting point to allow reflective analysis of his or her own knowledge growth. Secondly, familiarity with the topics in the book ought to increase and serve as a good anticipatory set (Hunter, 1994) that will both hook and motivate the reader and call up relevant prior knowledge. Finally, the pretest serves as an example of the activities built into the book so that the reader can get an idea about the book's style and its way of informing. With these thoughts in mind, let's move on to the pretest.

Part 1: Recognition Items

In this first part of the pretest, 12 statements about cooperative learning are offered. These maxims or truths about cooperative learning have been culled from the research and are generally known by practitioners. However, experience indicates that they are often forgotten in practice and thus should serve as valuable reminders to all practitioners.

Readers are asked to *rate themselves* on each of the 12 items on a familiarity scale, with a zero (0) indicating no familiarity and a five (5) indicating that the item is both familiar and often thought about. At the end of these important generalizations, the reader ought to have a good sense of where he or she stands regarding knowledge about cooperative learning.

Please pencil in your own estimate of your familiarity with the following true propositions:

_____ 1. Simply having students work together on a task or a project does *not* mean that they will realize the gains offered by cooperative learning.

_____ 2. *Teams* are not just groups: generally, it is recognized that teams have common purpose, work together, share a similar fate, and will be together for awhile. Teams work better than do groups.

_____ 3. One of the strengths of cooperative learning is its power to help different types of students and its use of diversity as a strength, not an obstacle. Heterogeneous groups maximize the gains that can be realized.

_____ 4. Students differ on many variables. Gender, ability, interests, past experiences, ethnicity, social class, handicapping conditions, and religion can all be meaningful indicators for arranging effective teams.

_____ 5. Most teachers have not experienced true cooperative learning; instead they have had experience with *bad* group projects, assignments, and experiences. One's own past (ineffective) history should not be the model for emulation but a source for reflective analysis of the effects of working together.

_____ 6. The data indicate that students of all ages can be made to feel that they have a shared responsibility to help others and they can experience helping others. For very young children, perhaps stable pairs make the most sense, and for older students, fours seem to work the best.

_____ 7. Teams of students can work for a very brief period or on an entire project. Teachers are advised to start small to send a message that students need to work together and to give them a chance to experience a success. Later, projects can include long, complex and difficult multiple-part projects.

_____ 8. Teams do not have to compete (that is, create winners and losers) in order to maximize the effect of working together. Some models of cooperative learning involve team competition, but it is not a necessary component.

_____ 9. When students share their theories and learnings, they are likely to get feedback, encouragement, a sense of belonging, more ideas, pride, enjoyment, a chance to experiment, and a chance to personalize new knowledge. All of these are positive factors in the learning process.

_____ 10. Teams do not need to spend every minute of every day together, nor do all the learning activates that a particular student is assigned have to be done cooperatively. About 50% of class work is probably the right amount for teamed activities for youngsters K–12, although different models (and theorists) disagree on this issue.

_____ 11. Contrary to many complaints about cooperative learning, the time available to teachers while teams study together is not a vacation or downtime for teachers. They have to monitor, evaluate, and give feedback to the groups and help teach and reinforce the development of social skills. Teachers can provide enrichment learning or remediation to students who need it, and also make judgments about students. Team time is *not* a time for teachers to correct papers or read the newspaper.

_____ 12. Cooperative learning is not just a strategy, part of a bag of tricks. It is also a philosophy, one in which the teachers see the class as a learning community that serves itself as it helps each and every member. Treating team learning as just one technique ("Hey, it's Tuesday, let's get in discussion groups.") fails to produce gains and also hurts other teachers' attempts at building the successful structures elsewhere.

Part 2: The Teaching Analysis

As you may have noticed, Part 1 was designed both as an introduction to the main ideas of cooperative learning *and* as a review of these ideas for some readers. In any case, the task involved was simple recognition and a self-judgment about familiarity. Part 2 presents a far more complex task, at the analysis level of Benjamin Bloom's famous taxonomy. You will be given an account of a teacher who was moved by his peers to try cooperative learning in a high school social studies class but one who was not moved hard enough to do it thoughtfully or carefully. The session fails miserably and the teacher later complains that "this group stuff stinks! I'm never doing that again." Of course, he blames the technique and places no responsibility whatsoever on the fact that he implemented it poorly and that the design was disastrous. As you read, identify 10 mistakes that were made in his teaching—mistakes that doomed the class to failure.

Once again, you are encouraged to do this section with a partner; as with a cooperative learning session in school, such collaboration is not cheating but sharing and comparing.

Fran Jones's Lesson

On entering the room, Fran Jones, a 10-year veteran social studies teacher, writes on the board: "TODAY: Group Work," then in small letters below, "Tomorrow: Back to regular work."

Jones turns to the class and, at the bell, announces: "I've just been to a workshop that told us all about the advantages of working in groups. Even though you guys are big kids . . . ninth graders . . . there are still some advantages when we do our work together. Right now, open your notebooks to get today's notes about the Japanese economic system, then we'll get in groups."

After about 12 minutes of teacher presentation, Jones announces: "OK, put those notebooks away. It looks like you guys understand how the Japanese economy got so strong. Now, we're going to do a group project. I'm gonna let you form your own groups . . . pick those who you want to work with. Nobody can work alone, and don't make your group any bigger than six or seven kids.

"Now, I'd like you to pick one of the seven countries listed on this board. For that country, you are to make a report that contains as many parts as you have workers. I'd like you to set up some meeting dates so you can get together after school. There will be one grade that everybody in the group gets. Any questions? You can use the rest of the period to set up the groups, get organized and then start your homework. Oh yes, remember, the project is due two weeks from today."

Twenty minutes later, just moments before the bell is to ring, Jones pushes to the front of the room: "You know, I have some doubts about this group stuff, but apparently some teachers really like it. I don't have too much confidence about some of you doing it, but what the heck, it's worth a try. Maybe the others will help you. Now remember, homework is due every day . . . but the project will count for a test grade" (Vermette, 1994).

Part 3: The True/False Assessment

Having completed the other two parts, you are now faced with the dreaded true/false test. Since I am trying to convince you that you need to read the entire book, many fellow teachers would advise me to make this part as hard as possible so that you won't be overconfident and not feel any pressure to read on. However, the fears of pretesting rise again. If you sense that you do not know very much, you may simply quit on the whole thing; this is, of course, a common response to those first learning to dance, golf, or use a computer (and maybe drive standard shift cars).

However, if you were to give up, *we would both lose* (and so would the students we teach). Thus I suggest that you do your best on these items and trust that those items missed will be "taught" in the book and those items correctly answered will be further explored.

T F   1. The research on cooperative learning has been done mostly in the laboratory, not in real classrooms with real kids.

T F   2. When students get to pick their own teams, they are happier, work harder, and learn more than when they are placed in assigned teams by the teacher.

T F   3. Teams of size 5 are better with younger children (grades K–5) and smaller groups (such as pairs) work best with older students (grades 10–12).

T F   4. In effective cooperative learning systems, the students spend upwards of 90% of school time in their teams.

T F   5. The best way to convince high achievers to like cooperative learning is to begin with group-graded projects that they can lead.

T F   6. Middle-level youngsters achieve more in strictly same sex, same race, and same social class groupings than they do in more mixed groups.

T F   7. Some of the famous cooperative learning theorists are Groucho, Chico, and Harpo and Tinkers, Evers, and Chance.

T F   8. It is difficult to get grade 3–8 youngsters to work in groups; teachers *must* use threats or rewards (bribes) to get them to do so.

T F   9. Most parents dislike student teams and see them as either a waste of time or busy work that substitutes for real teaching.

T F 10. Cooperative learning has only been successful in courses such as English and history but not in science and mathematics.

T F 11. In general, the use of teams increases learning of the material taught, but severely restricts the amount of topic coverage that can occur in any one course.

T F 12. Cooperative learning damages the achievement of the highest scoring learners more often than not.

Answer Key

Please note that if you worked with a partner, you have already received some feedback for your ideas and answers. I have always seen that feedback loop as one of the fundamental strengths of teamed learning: It helps us to determine how our ideas have been received. In a real schooling situation, it often takes a long time to get any feedback whatsoever about one's thinking. Witness the never-get-feedback reality of SAT and CTBS tests! As a student, I see that feedback from a writing partner or from a cooperative teammate helps me, especially if (1) we sense a mutually helpful relationship, (2) I am comfortable with that person, (3) we have had previous successes, and (4) we have discussed related material previously. These four conditions are precisely the conditions that we teachers seek to establish within effective cooperative groups.

For the record, I wish to have you score your test in this way: On Part 1, the familiarity test, you got all items right because you alone can be the judge of how familiar some fact is to you. The point of that component was to have you assess your starting point for the book's detail.

Part 2, the identification task, has many possible right answers. Jones, of course, dooms the session by his negative expectations at the start; he also lets them pick their own teams and demeans the project by negatively comparing it to "regular work." Make note that the real answer key for this component *is* the text of the book. I ask that you reassess the lesson in Part 2 after reading the entire book and compare your two lists.

Part 3 is the tricky part, because true/false questions are supposed to have unambiguous right answers. To avoid angering you by sending you ahead into the pages of the text, I will simply say that *all 12 items are false* and that they contain a great deal of information that would have been helpful to Fran Jones (in Part 2).

If you scored a perfect 12 correct on Part 3, you will have perhaps the *most to gain* from reading the book. Designed for both novice and veteran practitioners, it distills 10 years of study, practice, and observation of student teams at all levels and it should deepen the already strong base of the high achiever. The more one knows about a topic the more one can learn from actively engaging in it (Bargh and Schul, 1980) and the perfect 12 should gain a great deal (especially if she or he serves as a mentor with a partner also reading the book).

If you scored a zero, none right, you are a statistical anomaly! However, if you really scored "low" in a traditional sense you probably missed question 7. Make note that Groucho et al. were loving brothers and great funny men of the 1940s and Tinkers et al. comprised the most cooperative baseball infield of all time. Interestingly enough, the latter trio could work superbly together *but* never enjoyed or liked each other, a lesson for all cooperative learning practitioners to mull over. As a teacher, I hope—but never demand—that teammates *like* each other, and only expect that they show respect and do work together. Also, note that the remainder of the 12 items will be explored in the various sections of the book and that you will be given more practice opportunities to strengthen your knowledge and assess your growth on these items.

REFLECTION QUESTIONS

1. This chapter has asked the reader to do some serious self-reflection, but several other questions are best considered right now, before more of the book is read. Please briefly jot down your "current" answers to these questions, save them, and look at your answers again after you have finished reading the whole text.

    a. How much can students be trusted to actually "work" when left alone *with* peers?

    b. Is cooperative learning really more suited for younger grades when students are apt to do what they are told and have not as yet decided who their friendship possibilities could include?

    c. Is all the time "wasted" by having students work together really costing the bright students a great deal of learning time or opportunities to learn so much more?

    d. Does a teacher need an "interactive" style of his or her own to make teamed learning work? Could an introverted or individualistic type teacher actually make a student-to-student style work?

    e. Cooperative learning is just another fad, is it not? Bottom line: Will it go the way of "open classrooms," maybe even before this book is published?

    f. North American societies are not really communities but aggregations of individuals. Is there any way that a system that calls for unity and sharing could work under such conditions?

    g. There is some evidence that female teachers prefer the use of the term "group," whereas males prefer "teams," the term of choice of the author. Do these distinctions matter?

2. There is a great deal of research support for the use of visualization in learning. Here are two brief visualization activities that may help the reader effectively process and understand segments of this chapter.

    a. Vermette offers three reasons why he should not use a pretest and, in effect, suggests that the reasons are actually dangers. They are not equally dangerous in the eyes of all practitioners, however. On a separate sheet of paper, draw illustrations that identify the three dangers and graphically demonstrate the importance that *you* place on each.

    b. As you read through Fran Jones's teaching segment, images probably danced through your mind. Choose one of those images and *draw* it as best you can, keeping the written labeling to an absolute minimum. Moreover, as you finish the sketch, imagine that a Hollywood movie is being made and it includes the part you drew: Identify the most appropriate music that would serve as background for your drawing.

3. If you have not been able to take my advice and work with a partner on any of the previous activities, please try to do so for this question.

    a. Look back at Question 2(b). It called for a drawing. Have your associate study your drawing and then identify the written passage corresponding to it. Discuss the "cues" in the drawing that either worked or did not work in the identification process.

    b. Partners should share the pieces of music that they would have used in the hypothetical movie of Question 2(b) and explain their rationales for the choice. Make sure that the partners can paraphrase *each other's* words.

    c.   Hypothesize as to which will stick longer in memory, (1) the drawing constructed, (2) the drawing analyzed, (3) the music planned, or (4) the music heard described. Hypotheses can also be generated about the effectiveness of those activities done alone or in pairs, and the influence personal preferences might play (i.e., "I hate to draw so I probably won't remember the drawing I did about Jones's class").

        Please make a personal plan to check on your responses to Question 3 after you have read this entire book, especially Chapter 6 in which direct discussion of the integration of teamwork and type of activity is forthcoming. In this particular case, we have tried to explore two of Howard Gardner's multiple intelligences (musical, visual/spatial) in relation to cooperative learning at a very brief and personal level.

4. When originally published by the *High School Journal,* I had titled Fran Jones's teaching as "The Vignette," perhaps one of the worst titles of any passage in history. Please retitle it and explain your title to another professional. Carefully *note* his or her body language on receiving your design. You cannot help but analyze it as well: Was it supportive? Interested? Did it convey reinforcement or curiosity? If this associate were a student in your classroom, would you have to teach him or her the social skills necessary for effective participation in groups?

A DESCRIPTION AND A RATIONALE FOR COOPERATIVE LEARNING

WHAT DOES TEAM LEARNING LOOK LIKE?

On the second floor of Happy Valley Elementary School six fourth-grade classrooms sit across from each other in a very typical pattern: A central hallway has parallel rows of quasi-identical rooms falling away from it in egg-crate fashion. In each of the six rooms on this day, the teacher believes that she or he is doing "cooperative learning." Truly, each does have some sort of group activity going on, yet each activity has a different structure and a different feel to it; some of these activities meet the basic conditions of cooperative teams and some do not. Take a minute to read them and decide whether you would classify it as cooperative learning or not. (Please circle Y or N after you have read the vignette.)

Y N 1. In Ms. Jones's room, the class is working on the writing process. Students are sitting in pairs, working on their own personal drafts of a paper in which they are to argue for or against a new school dress code. The finished papers are due in two days; students are encouraged to have their partners "edit" them if they wish to do so. Moreover, all students are encouraged to have many class members give ideas and feedback as well.

Y N   2. Mr. Kirkner's class is sitting in the four-student groups he has built; they are studying for a quiz on their history assignment, the Roman Empire. The students have been working on group-graded teamed collages of events during that time in history and have written individual papers about one topic. (For example, Parvinder wrote a piece titled "Bread and Circuses" and related his learning to modern day professional football. His teammates, Silvio, Juanita, and Lucy have written papers on other topics.) Finally, the individual test will be given in half an hour and the review session helps the students prepare each other. The teacher uses a bonus system based on each member of the team getting 75% or better on his or her individual test.

Y N   3. In Julian Johns's class, it is science time and pairs of students have just finished reciprocal reading. They are now going to be spending 25 minutes doing a structured experiment; each partner has a clear role (demonstrator and recorder) and each will be held accountable for explaining the process and result at the close of the session. These partners are working together for the first time today, but this is the fourth partners situation students have been assigned this year, the previous partnerships lasting about two weeks each.

Y N   4. In Ms. Washington's class, it is math time. The students have formed some groups to do practice problems. As Washington leaves the students alone to discover their own abilities, her work at the desk distracts her from observing several things: One group has six students sitting around or near Lisa Bright, who has a 99 average and is quick to answer the questions. As Lisa finishes, the others copy down her answers on their papers. In another group, Tony and Jamil are competitively coloring in the pictures in their English textbook. Finally, a group of 12 students is sitting near the back, doing nothing in particular; however, three students do have their math books with them.

Y N   5. In Dr. Burden's class, the students are split into two teams, the boys and the girls. They are playing a kind of a Jeopardy game that the teacher has invented to review facts about trees. At this moment, the two spokespersons, Andre and Tanashwanda (the top two students in class), are answering the questions for their teams. The team that gets the highest number right today gets an A for the day and the lower scoring team gets a B in the teacher's book.

Y N   6. In Mr. Giardre's class, the students are doing their daily practice on the computer. His 24 students are divided into groups of 3 each at the eight computers. These groups have been working with a piece of software, exploring some science concepts. Every day one student rotates into the role of keyboarder while the other two serve as problem-solver and recorder. They are writing a journal about their experiences with the program (in total, 22 days!) and it will include both group entries and a section for individual reflections. At this moment, Giardre is helping

Amy, Binky, and Thomas because they cannot seem to get by their current difficulty. Other groups are attentively working at their PCs.

For Reflection and Conceptualization

Research on cooperative learning has a long and intense history. The leading proponents of it, David and Roger Johnson and Robert Slavin, have defined it differently and therefore have conducted different kinds of research to investigate its power. The very dilemma that you just faced—classifying class activities as cooperative learning or not—has been a bit of a sore spot for advocates and examiners who wish to study and/or adopt its principles. Yet, commonalities have been identified and a synthesis of the research and practice has lead me to define cooperative classroom teams as follows.

A cooperative classroom team is a relatively permanent, heterogeneously mixed, small group of students who have been assembled to complete an activity, produce a series of projects or products, and/or who have been asked to individually master a body of knowledge. The spirit within the team has to be one of positive interdependence, that is, a feeling that success for any one is tied directly to the successes of others. Moreover, these groups have to have been assigned by the teacher and they have to include regular direct face-to-face interaction in the classroom setting.

Imbedded in this definition are several vague concepts that need to be briefly described at this time. Each seems to be a relative concept, one that has a range of exemplars and is open to less precise definition.

Let's look at the phrase *relatively permanent*. A "team of the day" has no permanence and therefore fails to qualify as a cooperative learning team. Part of the philosophy behind cooperative learning is that routine exposure to differences makes them less unusual and more acceptable, common, tolerable, and available for modeling purposes. Students that work together often prosper academically and socially by the comfortable interactions that develop with familiarity. From a learning styles perspective, working with a partner with different modality strengths for 5 minutes is nowhere nearly as helpful as working with him or her for an hour a day each day for a month. Thus, groups can only become teams over an elongated and distributed period of time. (Note the use of the term *regular* interaction, not sporadic or infrequent.)

If team members are helping each other learn something (as opposed to producing or constructing something), *each* individual student must be held accountable for his or her *mastery* of the subject. If the team is constructing, each member is responsible for a part and for the whole. Having one member get an A is not the goal of working together; more likely, having them all get A's is the goal. Likewise, mastery for a school program is far more likely to be seen in having all the students pass a New York State Regents Test than having four students get 100s and two become National Merit scholars. In any case, conceptually speaking, cooperative teams need to attempt mastery of the material by all teammates, not just by one or some.

The term *positive interdependence* essentially refers to the attitude *within* the group that as a team, their fates are intertwined and one's success is tied inexorably to that of others. Just like a basketball player who scores 50 points for a losing team is often reluctant to speak about his or her own accomplishments, there is a feeling that for him or her to do well, the whole team needed to succeed. Interdependence recognizes that we all benefit from each other's gains and are hurt by each other's failings. In complete contradiction to both (1) the bell curve theory and (2) a zero-sum game theory, this approach says that as all students learn more, the environment becomes more positive and richer for all individuals, including the brightest ones who may well stand to learn the most.

An old story fits well right here: Gus was very happy to see his firm hire a bunch of bad fellow salespeople, because he looked better when compared to them. Gus sold well and did not share any of his ideas with his associates. When the firm inevitably folded, he of course lost his job along with the others *and* was forever branded as being at the company when it went "under." You see, the fates of all salespeople were interrelated despite Gus's belief that he was operating as an individual alone in the world. His comparative success came at the expense of his associates and, in the end, they all lost.

A special note for football fans who think that Gus will simply move on to successes elsewhere despite the firm's failure: Jim Kelly, my favorite football player, is a Hall of Fame quarterback who will be branded forever as something of a "failure" because *his team lost* four Superbowls (at this writing). People have already forgotten that *his team won* four AFC championships; the team losses override both the personal and team successes. Kelly, like Gus and each of us, is perceived as part of a work group and his success is only as great as his team's.

The real world interrelates us all the time and if the classroom does not explicitly develop a sense of interdependence in youngsters, I am afraid that they will be shocked by the realities of the real world when they leave school. Teaching youngsters to "go it alone" is sending them false messages.

Just as the entire class can profit from the public question of one student in a traditional classroom (does the teacher answer such questions privately or to the whole class?) students need to understand that they are not benefiting from competing for the right answer but do prosper when they share their knowledge bases.

Positive interdependence can take many forms and can range in strength from strong to weak. For example, a strong form may involve four students studying together and then having one randomly selected by the teacher to take the test for all four. Another strong form is an interview session in which both members of a pair have to be active or neither can succeed. Another strong form involves the jigsaw technique in which content is split up into component parts, with each member responsible for mastering and teaching his or her part to the others. Weaker forms involve a team constructing a map of the room in which every member has been required to contribute something. Another weak form of interdependence is one in which four students study together and receive a bonus if all four meet standard criteria on their individual tests.

Although it can take many forms, interdependence is a necessity for successful use of cooperative learning teams.

Answer Key

Utilizing the definition (conception) provided earlier, let us return to the six fourth-grade examples. It seems to me that the evidence we have suggests the following classifications:

N   1. Ms. Jones appears to have encouraged but not demanded or expected cooperation and interaction. Many students may simply hurt themselves by working alone and ignoring the potential benefits of teammates. Moreover, we are not clear about the permanence of the pairs and we are not positive about the probability of a spirit of interdependence. This is probably *not* a teamed classroom.

Y   2. It is clear that the teams in Kirkner's class have been together awhile, completing several stages of the Roman Empire unit. The upcoming test has interdependent overtones and they are in face-to-face interaction. This *is* cooperative team learning and the students should realize the benefits of their efforts.

Y   3. I get the impression that Johns uses partners very often and that they are somewhat stable. Moreover, this activity requires that they work together because each has several roles that could not be done easily by an individual working alone. Since they are both accountable and therefore no free-riders or parasites can exist, this *is* a cooperative team approach.

N   4. Just because Washington's class is a totally useless waste of instructional time (and the taxpayers' money) it may still be cooperative learning. Alas, it simply *does not* fit the conception of cooperative learning (even if the teacher claims that she is using it!). The groups are haphazard, there is no sense of stability, and there is no interdependence. This is simply a pedagogical disaster.

N   5. Burden's class often gives novice classifiers trouble because to a certain degree, it appears to be teamed study. However, the importance of classroom behavior fitting the definition is not just an academic exercise: The classrooms that do seem to fit stand a far greater chance of realizing the research based advantages than do those that fail to meet the criteria. I do not think Burden's class will do too much good for anybody except Andre and Tanashwanda. As in a spelling bee, only the winners care—and they probably do not *learn* anything in the process because they already know how to spell the words! The arbitrary assignment of winning and losing scores is silly, putting marks in the book that are not substantiated at all by individual student performance. (Do the absent boys get the same grade as Andre? What about Juan, who was there but spent the whole day looking out the window?) Moreover, pitting males against females perpetuates many of the factors that have produced hostile classrooms and certainly predicts a long-term permanent cross-gender hostility if Burden uses this structure often. Despite its appearance of a "team kind of thing," I would be thrilled if this teacher returned these kids to straight rows and let them read the books quietly to themselves; this would maintain a similar low level of achievement but at least it would not damage attitudes as much as this strategy suggests. This one is clearly *not* team learning.

Y   6. Finally, Giardre's class seems to be a classic example of cooperative learning at work, this time in an instructional session dealing with the mastery of technology. The teams are relatively stable and somewhat permanent. They are all engaged together and each must show individual growth for the entire group to succeed. The structure assigns responsibilities (or roles) to help keep the group focused and functioning, and the teacher's role seems to be that of facilitating and helping the learning, not just transmitting the content.

DIVERSITY AS A STRENGTH

If you were to recall those six fourth-grade classrooms for a moment, you might want to focus on the amount of heterogeneity built into the various groupings that had been created. The major advocates of cooperative learning methods, David and Roger Johnson, Shlomo Sharan, Robert Slavin, and Eliot Aronson, based their early work on elements drawn from social/psychological research, studies that indicated that humans grow to understand, appreciate, and actually like people different from them when they are engaged in mutually supportive activities. Thus, in schools where tolerance and cross-difference affective goals are important, students working in interdependent teams makes a lot of sense.

Secondly, researchers studying aspects of cognitive development, such as Vygotsky (1962), Piaget (1963), and Kohlberg (1963), have discovered that exposure to differences in style, thought patterns, experience, and opinion helps individuals make the cognitive adjustments necessary for growth. Thus schools that have purely cognitive goals for their students ought to look at the frequent use of discussions, peer tutoring, and pair sharing sessions.

Without too much trouble one can make the leap that the type of verbal interaction (i.e., sharing, comparing, modifying, rehearsing, and evaluating) done in cooperative groups is theoretically productive in school. Moreover, because cultural and physical differences can motivate *and* stimulate, the teams being used should be heterogeneous teams, mixing different types of individuals in varying ways.

With this in mind, let us return to the six fourth-grade classrooms to analyze the makeup of the teams. Recalling that diversity is a strength, note that Burden's class attempts to use single-gender groups to maximize motivation and it fails. Jones does not construct the teams to build on student strengths, she leaves their use optional. Washington's class also uses self-selective groups: To no one's surprise, students select dysfunctional groups that are actually play groups that do not provide them with challenging ideas or peer pressure to work. Finally, although the evidence is sparse, it appears that Giardre, Johns, and Kirkner have developed heterogeneous, cross-gender teams.

BASIC MODELS OF COOPERATIVE LEARNING

Many of us who teach engage in a never-ending search for the "one best model"; we hope to find a panacea for all our ills or a surefire recipe for success. Unfortunately, there is none. However, I believe that cooperative learning in its various forms is the most important instructional innovation available to us as practitioners—outdistancing computers, Keller plans, Skinner boxes, and just about everything except individual home one-on-one tutoring (Bloom, 1984); and yet I am hesitant to suggest that teachers master one cooperative learning model and use it for ever and ever and ever. Each of the models presented here has sound research histories, but studies like that of Popkewitz (1981) indicate that teachers adapt and modify models as they put them into practice. Moreover, to a large degree, there is no one typical classroom, but many classrooms with their own structures, influences, and statuses and therefore these teacher modifications can be seen as rational. Thus, teachers should be conceptually aware of their decisions within the usage of models so that they are able to maximize the effectiveness of particular strategies.

With that caveat out of the way, let me say that I offer you some detail about the models of eight important cooperative learning theorists. While the intent of this book is to come to a new synthesis, each of these models has contributed mightily to the underlying thinking and analysis. Taken individually and implemented thoughtfully, each of these approaches offers the reader a superb alternative to the traditional classroom.

The Five Main Strategies

In 1987, during the heart of the innovational period of classroom reform, Newman and Thompson did an exhaustive review of the available studies on the use of teams. They developed brief summaries of the major cooperative models; this summary is given in Table 1.1. I have chosen to present their findings in this form for two reasons: The models presented are the "classic" ones and the thumbnail descriptions are accurate and well reasoned; their brevity is a strength. Secondly, displaying them in chart form makes comparative analysis very easy, an important point for novices who wish to find contrasts between models and similarities across models.

Along the lines of comparison, several questions arise. Take a moment to answer each of the following questions:

1. Which models tend to incorporate the most old fashioned teacher telling, front-of-the-room type of instruction?

2. Which models require the most autonomy from the students?

3. Several models adhere to competitive formats and several seem to abhor competition. Why?

4. How is interdependence accounted for in the various models ?

TABLE 1.1   Five Main Cooperative Learning Strategies

STAD	Student Teams–Achievement Divisions (Slavin, 1978, 1983, 1995): The teacher presents a lesson. Students meet in four- to five-member teams, helping one another to master a set of worksheets on the lesson. Each student takes a quiz on the material. The individual scores, based on the degree of individual improvement over previous scores, contribute to a team score. Teams with high scores are recognized in a weekly class newsletter.
TGT	Teams–Games–Tournament (DeVries and Slavin, 1978): Instruction is similar to STAD, with students trying to help one another learn the material. But instead of taking individual quizzes, students compete with classmates of similar achievement from other teams. Based on their relative success against competitors from other teams, students earn points for their own team and teams with high scores are publicly recognized.
JIG	Jigsaw (Aronson, Blaney, Stephan, Sikes, & Snapp, 1978): Each student in a five- to six-member group is given unique information on a topic that the whole group is studying. After reading their material, the students meet in "expert groups" with their counterparts from other teams to discuss and master information. Next they return to their teams to teach it to their teammates. In a variation called "Jigsaw II" (Slavin, 1986), all students are first given common information. Then the "experts" teach more specific topics to the group. Finally, students take tests individually, and team scores are publicized in a class newsletter.
LT	Learning Together (Johnson and Johnson, 1987): Students work in small groups on assignments to produce a single project. Teachers use various methods for nurturing a philosophy of cooperation based on five elements: positive interdependence, face-to-face interaction, individual accountability, social skills, and group processing. Students are instructed to seek help from one another before asking for teacher assistance. Students are usually rewarded based on a combination of individual performance and the overall performance of the group. Rewards include teacher praise, tokens, and privileges, but neither individuals nor groups compete against one another.
GI	Group Investigation (Sharan and Sharan, 1976): Students work in small groups, but each group takes on a different task or project, and within groups, students decide what information to gather, how to organize it, and how to present what they have learned as a group project to classmates. In evaluation, higher level learning is emphasized.

Reprinted with permission from Newman, F., & Thompson, J. A. (1987). Effects of cooperative learning on achievement in secondary schools: A summary of research. Madison, WI: National Center on Effective Secondary Schools, Wisconsin Center for Educational Research.

Slavin's two most famous models, TGT and STAD, have been shown to be effective in increasing achievement. [He has authored two other powerful variations, Team-Assisted Individualization (TAI) and Cooperative Integrated Reading and Comprehension Instruction (CIRC); see Stevens and Slavin, 1995a.] TGT requires a team competition in which equal-ability students are matched with each other. Moreover, his formats begin with teacher-led instruction, including versions of his Jigsaw II.

Nowhere else in cooperative learning does a theorist advise student-to-student competition and, in my judgment, there appears to be little gained by such competition. Most teachers exposed to cooperative learning seek to get away from structures that force competition and they can be assured that they are not damaging their students' achievements when they do so. (For an absolutely complete discussion of the affective damage done by competition, see Kohn, 1994.)

As for frontal teaching, the other models do *not* prohibit such teacher behavior at the outset or during the classroom activities, but they all truly emphasize the teachers' role as facilitators of learning. One estimate of Sharan's model sets the percentage of student time in group work at about 95%, a vast difference from Slavin's 30% to 35%. Jigsaw and LT also assume that the students spend their time working independently of direct teacher transmission of knowledge and also force heavy responsibility on learners.

In fact, the amount of student autonomy in Jigsaw makes it very difficult to implement well and Newman and Thompson (1987) suggest that even when it is done well it has the smallest cognitive benefit of these five models. (It does, however, show great affective and social/psychological gains for students.)

Finally, there is positive interdependence in each of these five models. In Jigsaw the only way that Juanita can get the information for the test is from her teammates Shilpa, Liz, and Perry. In LT, students are creating the knowledge together and each needs to contribute ideas and information as the project is prepared. In STAD and TGT, team scores are built on the accomplishments of individuals directly (like a swimming meet, each event counts to the team score) and in GI the whole project is broken down into component parts that are the responsibility of each member.

In each of these classic models, individual success does require some amount of team success and vice versa; the more built in, the higher the level of positive interdependence.

Three More Effective Cooperative Learning Strategies

Whereas the previous five models are often thought of as *the* cooperative learning by many practitioners, there are several other strategies and structures floating through the literature and through teacher practice that need to be described and reflected on. Although less well known than the first five mentioned, each of these has been formed to meet the needs of students and educators. They attempt to implement the philosophies and techniques of cooperative learning and each has a great deal of inherent value.

Unlike the material in Table 1.1, I have not gone outside to find capsule summaries of these less well-known approaches. Each of the following summaries is my best attempt at capturing the essence of these models.

Dansereau's Dyads

For more than a decade, teams of researchers from Texas Christian University led by Donald Dansereau have been studying various combinations of paired student learning structures (for example, see O'Donnell, Dansereau, Hall, and Rocklin, 1987). The format, here dubbed "Dansereau's Dyads" (see Table 1.2), is basic and easy to implement.

TABLE 1.2   Dansereau's Dyads: Cooperative Learning Instruction

Two heads are better than one for learning complex textbook material. In this strategy, both you and your partner study approximately two pages of a textbook. (If one finishes first he/she should go back over the material until the other one finishes.) Then one of you (called the "recaller") helps correct, amplify, and memorize the summarized material.

After this is done, you both read the next two pages and the process is repeated with the two of you switching roles (i.e., the *recaller* on the previous summary becomes the *listener* on the next one, and vice versa. *Roles should be switched for each summary.*

This process is repeated until the entire chapter or unit has been completely studied. Your goal is to help each other maximize the learning of the material.

Details on the Technique

Study two pages using your normal methods (feel free to take notes). The one who finishes first should review the two pages until the other person is finished. Then do the following:

1. The recaller puts the material out of sight while the listener keeps the passage available.

2. The recaller summarizes out loud what has been read as completely as possible *without looking at notes or the passage.* Do the summary as rapidly as you can. Try to include all the important ideas and facts. Use note paper to draw or chart information while making the summary. The more you can represent the ideas visually to your partner the better. Put the whole summary in your own words, not the author's. (If necessary, the listener should interrupt the recaller to make important corrections.)

3. *After* the recaller has completed the summary, the listener/facilitator should do the following while looking at the passage.

   a. To improve your and your partner's understanding, correct your partner's summary by discussing any important information left out and indicating ideas or facts that were summarized incorrectly. Use *drawings* and *images* (mental pictures) whenever possible.

   b. Help both of you remember the material better by coming up with *clever* ways to amplify and memorize the important ideas or facts. One way is to relate the information to earlier material in the chapter and to other things you know. You also can use *drawings* and *mental pictures* to aid memory.

4. The recaller should help the listener correct, amplify, and memorize the summary.

5. If you complete the chapter early, go back over it using the same approach.

This entire process should be *active* and *intense*. Debates and arguments should be resolved as quickly as possible. It is very important to keep the process moving along and still do good summaries. Don't get sidetracked by trivia and irrelevancies. Remember, you should switch recaller and listener roles for each summary. (Flip a coin to determine who should be the first recaller.)

After you and your partner have completed studying for the day, it is important for you to discuss what strategies and skills you have learned from each other and how you can *improve* your cooperative interaction in the future.

Reprinted with permission from Larson, C. O., & Dansereau, D. F. (1986, March). Cooperative learning in dyads. *Journal of Reading, 29(6),* 516–520.

In general, same-sex college students work with partners to read, summarize, understand, quiz, and help each other learn. Findings indicate that taking turns at various roles (summarizer versus elaborator) and the successful quizzing of partners about what they read improves achievement in a number of ways (Dansereau, 1987; Larson and Dansereau, 1986). Recent work has extended the dyadic model to learning from lectures as well as print (O'Donnell and Dansereau, 1992, 1993).

Although the teams appear informal in their construction, they are stable throughout a period of study and fates are interconnected (i.e., positive interdependence). Studies using similar approaches (Fantuzzo, Riggio, Conelly, & Dimoff, 1989; King, 1990) have shown similar findings, providing strong evidence of the breadth of the usefulness of Dansereau's models.

In my judgment, there is no reason to suspect that these strategies would not be equally effective with high school students, a year or two younger than the subjects in all of these many experiments.

Kagan's Structural Approach

In his book *Cooperative Learning Resources for Teachers* (1992) and in an *Educational Leadership* article (1989), Spencer Kagan details a series of in-class strategies that are content-free ways to organize instruction involving student-to-student interaction and cooperation. (Table 1.3 offers a summary of selected structures.) Kagan's theory suggests that different classroom instructional outcomes require different interaction structures to be successful, that is, brainstorming is different from the development of listening skills and should therefore require a different set of activities for the students. Some of these are extremely brief and easy to do in class and some are incredibly complex (i.e., Co-op Co-op). Both his Numbered Heads Together and Think–Pair–Share (borrowed from Frank Lyman, 1987) are effective modifications and adaptations of the research base developed by the other researchers and work well in class. They are especially powerful when they are built as part of an overall stable team approach that expects students to work effectively and tolerate each other.

Cohen's Complex Instruction

A Stanford sociologist, Elizabeth Cohen, has been conducting classroom research for a decade, trying to solve the problem of status issues within heterogeneously built teams. She suggests that heterogeneity by itself may exacerbate status problems in teamwork unless students are given direct instruction about the complexity of modern life and how individuals are not just their "reading scores" (which she sees as the chief peer and teacher indicator of school "smartness"; Cohen, 1994, p. 125). Her answer is to engage students in complex projects that require a vast array of abilities and talents, too broad and too diverse to be held by any one student working alone. Her point is very well taken: She uses examples from the real world to force students to understand the interdependence of the modern world (especially in careers) and

TABLE 1.3 Overview of Selected Structure

Structure	Brief Description	Functions: Academic & Social
Team Building		
Round-robin	Each student in turn shares something with his or her teammates.	Expressing ideas and opinions, creation of stories. *Equal participation, getting acquainted with teammates.*
Class Building		
Corners	Each student moves to a corner of the room representing a teacher-determined alternative. Students discuss within corners, then listen to and paraphrase ideas from other corners.	Seeing alternative hypotheses, values, problem-solving approaches. *Knowing and respecting different points of view, meeting classmates.*
Communications Building		
Match Mine	Students attempt to match the arrangement of objects on a grid of another student using oral communication only.	Vocabulary development. *Communication skills, role-taking ability.*
Mastery		
Numbered Heads Together	The teacher asks a question, students consult to make sure everyone knows the answer, then one student is called on to answer.	Review, checking for knowledge, comprehension. *Tutoring.*
Color-Coded Co-op Cards	Students memorize facts using a flash card game. The game is structured so that there is a maximum probability of success at each step, moving from short-term to long-term memory. Scoring is based on improvement.	Memorizing facts. *Helping, praising.*
Pairs Check	Students works in pairs within groups of four. Within pairs students alternate—one solves a problem while the other coaches. After every two problems the pair checks to see if they have the same answers as the other pair.	Practicing skills. *Helping, praising.*

TABLE 1.3, *continued*

		Concept Development
Three-Step Interview	Students interview each other in pairs, first one way, then the other. Students each share with the group information they learned in the interview.	Sharing personal information such as hypotheses, reactions to a poem, conclusions from a unit. *Participation, listening.*
Think–Pair–Share	Students think to themselves on a topic provided by the teacher; they pair up with another student to discuss it; they then share their thoughts with the class.	Generating and revising hypotheses, inductive reasoning, application. *Participation, involvement.*
Team Word-Webbing	Students write simultaneously on a piece of paper, drawing main concepts, supporting elements, and bridges representing the relation of ideas in a concept.	Analysis of concepts into components, understanding multiple relations among ideas, differentiating concepts. Role-taking.
	Multifunctional	
Roundtable	Each student in turn writes one answer as a paper and a pencil are passed around the group. With Simultaneous Roundtable more than one pencil and paper are used at once.	Assessing prior knowledge, practicing skills, recalling information, creating cooperative art. *Team building, participation by all.*
Inside–Outside Circle	Students stand in pairs in two concentric circles. The inside circle faces out; the outside circle faces in. Students use flash cards or respond to teacher questions as they rotate to each new partner.	Checking for understanding, review, processing, helping. *Tutoring, sharing, meeting classmates.*
Partners	Students work in pairs to create or master content. They consult with partners from other teams. They then share their products or understanding with the other partner pair in their team.	Mastery and presentation of new material, concept development. *Presentation and communication skills.*
Jigsaw	Each student on the team becomes an "expert" on one topic by working with members from other teams assigned the corresponding expert topic. Upon returning to their teams, each one in turn teaches the group; and students are all assessed on all aspects of the topic.	Acquisition and presentation of new material, review, informed debate. *Interdependence, status equalization.*
Co-op Co-op	Students work in groups to produce a particular group product to share with the whole class; each student makes a particular contribution to the group.	Learning and sharing complex material, often with multiple sources; evaluation; application; analysis; synthesis. *Conflict resolution, presentation skills.*

Reprinted with permission from Kagan, S. (1989, December). The structural approach to cooperative learning. *Educational Leadership, 47,* 14.

FIGURE 1.1   The Multiple-Ability Treatment for Complex Instruction

A Multiple-Abilities Treatment has the following features:

1. The teacher clearly describes different kinds of intellectual abilities.
2. The teacher convinces students that the task they are about to do requires many different intellectual abilities.
3. The teacher convinces students that no one will have all the necessary intellectual abilities, but everyone will have some of the necessary abilities. ("None of us have all these abilities. Each of us has some of these abilities." Cohen, 1994, p. 122.)

she stresses that the ability to recognize and foster strengths in others will predict future life success. Her work, while not directly tied to Gardner's multiple intelligences (MI) (1983, 1993, 1995) theory, is reinforced by MI's growing acceptance.

In a Cohen lesson, students are given directions built along the lines of the Multiple-Abilities Treatment shown in Figure 1.1. This approach, of course, focuses student efforts on projects and activities, long term and complicated as well as short term and simple, and predicts that the payoffs for both learning and status equalization require a long-term teacher commitment. Finally, while every team theorist supports heterogeneous groupings to maximize the potential for challenge and for interpersonal skill, Cohen expects more difficulty than the other researchers. Her work is therefore doubly important for those of us feeling especially challenged by status tensions in our classrooms. By openly stating the complexities inherent in jobs and careers and moving standards of value away from traditional markers of school excellence (reading and math scores), she hopes to fully prepare students for the outside world awaiting them after schooling is over.

One question that arises when teachers are first exposed to Cohen is simple: What are some projects that I can do with my class? Table 1.4 provides a list of 90 classroom projects (from very simple to very complex) given to me by Gail Sullivan and Georgia Peach of the Skaneatles, New York, schools. It has been a useful resource for me and my colleagues as we set out to plan our own classes; it gives practitioners a huge set of options as they face their own mix of students.

APPLYING THE MODELS

While all the theorists would prefer to see the model implemented exactly as it had been outlined in their works, teachers generally make slight modifications as they conduct their classes. For each of the following brief classroom descriptions, try to determine which of the eight models is serving as the *basis* of the teacher's instruction and

TABLE 1.4   Ninety Activities for K–12 Students

ads (for magazines, newspapers, Yellow Pages)	essays	product descriptions
allegories	fables	puppet shows
announcements	game rules	puzzles
autobiographies	graffiti	questionnaires
awards	good news–bad news	questions
bedtime stories	grocery lists	quizzes
billboards	headlines	quotations
book jackets	how-to-do-it speeches	real estate notices
book reviews	impromptu speeches	recipes
brochures	interviews	remedies
bulletins	job applications	reports
bumper stickers	journals	requests
campaign speeches	laboratory notes	requisitions
captions	letters	resumes
cartoons	lists	reviews
certificates	lyrics	sales pitches
character sketches	magazines	schedules
comic strips	menus	self-descriptions
contracts	mysteries	sequels
conversations	myths	serialized stories
critiques	newscasts	slogans
definitions	newspapers	speeches
diaries	obituaries	TV commercials
directions	observational notes	telegrams
directories	pamphlets	travel folders
dramas	parodies	tributes
editorials	persuasive letters	vignettes
epitaphs	plays	want ads
encyclopedia entries	poems	wanted posters
	posters	wills
	propaganda sheets	

feel free to jot down any suggestions that you might have as to how she or he could implement the strategy more effectively. Here are the eight models once again:

STAD	Students–Teams–Achievement–Divisions (Slavin)
TGT	Teams–Games–Tournaments (Slavin)
JIG	Jigsaw (Aronson)
LT	Learning Together (Johnson & Johnson)
GI	Group Investigation (Sharan)
DD	Dansereau's Dyads (Dansereau)
KS	Kagan's Structures (Kagan)
CI	Complex Instruction (Cohen)

_____ 1. In his fourth-grade class, Adams often has the students work briefly with each other, depending on what task is at hand. Today, they are practicing spelling words: Adams reads the word, waits 10 seconds while they are written individually, then provides 10 seconds for partners to check each other's work.

_____ 2. Today, the eleventh graders are in the library conducting research. One group, Seth, David, Lola, and Gail, is investigating the country of Zimbabwe, and have divided up their project into various components. Come Tuesday, they will combine all of their research and present the findings of their study.

_____ 3. The ninth graders are studying poems by Shakespeare. Each team member has one poem to analyze; he or she will then teach it to the others in the group and tomorrow all four will be tested on all four poems.

_____ 4. The third-grade teams are spread about Asklar's room, making their maps of the school. Each team has either four or five members, each with a different colored pencil. The final form of the map must utilize every one of the colors and each student may use his or her own color. All children will receive the same grade on the team map.

_____ 5. Today, the seventh graders are sitting at tables of five; these fives have been formed by taking one member of each team and squaring each off in an equal-ability competition based on the math problems that the groups have been practicing. At one table, Jonathan has been the best three straight times, earning his team a total of 12 points for his efforts. If they win, his team will get their names on the board and a memo sent home. Although he is a D student, Jonathan likes this activity because he usually earns more points for his team than do his other teammates.

_____ 6. Today, Jonathan's team is practicing some more math problems. They all work on the same items for a while, then split and work on ones best suited for their past achievements. Jonathan feels that he is almost ready for the next test and hopes to improve on his pretest score of 25. If he does, he will bring points into his team as he usually does.

_____ 7. The five groups of three fifth graders sit and listen as teacher Danielle Walker announces: "In the real world, we must work together because no *one* person can do all the things that a team must do. You will be working this week on the making of a videotape of Yom Kippur. Imagine the CBC making a tape. . . . They need all kinds of skills: creativity, writing, the ability to do scenery, artistic ability. I hope that as you plan, carry out and make your tape, you have enough talents in your team to succeed. I will pass out a sheet describing the final form. Get going."

_____ 8. In the second grade, the students are sitting in pairs with their science readers open. Margie and Sam are reading to each other, one sentence at a time. After the reading, they take turns explaining what they just heard and how it fits into the whole topic. The room is full of energy and it seems that Sam is easily distracted: He appears to prefer to read, not listen. The technique goes quickly however and when he tries, it is quickly his turn again.

Answer Key

Recall that I mentioned that teachers "modify" theories as they implement them. Some of these examples are slightly different than they would have appeared had the original author used them yet we can identify the core of the models. In any case, each represents a successful attempt at using a specific model:

<u>KS</u>   1. This teacher is trying to use Kagan's structures on a regular pattern in the language arts course. Here, Think–Pair–Share is utilized to try to improve a rote memory activity like spelling.

<u>GI</u>   2. This research-based activity flows from Sharan's Group Investigation model. The team is studying a whole (Zimbabwe) by studying pieces and combining them. This model has the smallest amount of whole class work and also involves a great deal of individual work. Note, however, that members of a team are absolutely free to help their teammates complete the project.

<u>JIG</u>   3. The Shakespeare activity also studies a whole by breaking it up, but here the synthesis is not a report of the whole or even an investigation of the whole team. Here, each person studies a chunk and then teaches it to teammates; the eventual test covers all four components of the subject and is taken individually. This class fits the Jigsaw model.

<u>LT</u>   4. This map-building exercise is the type of active learning advocated by the Johnsons' Learning Together model. Here all members take responsibility and credit for the final product but must contribute to be able to do so.

<u>TGT</u>   5. These two descriptions flow from Slavin's works. The TGT involves
<u>STAD</u>   6. actual face-to-face competition between equals who have prepared together. In item 5, Jonathan is competing at the slowest learners' table and is earning points for his team. In item 6, he is competing against his own previous score (i.e., against himself) again earning points for his team. This is an essential part of STAD. Also note that STAD allows for students on the same team to study differing levels of complexity in their subjects.

<u>CI</u>   7. In this item, we see teacher Danielle Walker trying to inspire her troops to do a very complex and difficult activity. She is stressing the different intellectual and physical capacities needed for the team to succeed on the videotape and is calling for them to pull together their various talents. She is doing a good job starting a Multiple-Abilities/Complex Instruction project, from Cohen. Much of the next few days will find the students working in their teams during the whole class.

<u>DD</u>   8. Here is a case in which Dansereau's Dyads have been utilized not in college but in the second grade. The students are reading, elaborating, and summarizing, helping each other understand the material being explored. They are working actively and interdependently.

TOWARD SYNTHESIS: A CONCEPTUALIZED MODEL

I have chosen to close our discussion of the various models by attempting to provide a synthesis of their strengths and their important characteristics, a procedure that should prove helpful to most teachers.

In working extensively with teachers who have been implementing the various models, it has become clear that they frequently modify or adapt certain components in an effort to best meet their students' needs and their classroom realities. At times, this undermines the attempt of the models' designer but more frequently it has enhanced the effectiveness of the implementation. Through this research, I found myself in the position to synthesize what might be called the *essential characteristics* for teamwork to succeed. Drawing from the models described here and from the research presented in the next chapter, a synthesis has emerged. The resulting model (Vermette's model, if you will) suggests that there are four components that have to be dealt with adequately for a teacher to succeed with team learning. Three of these components are called structures, and they are the precursors to actual teamwork: These structures must be in place before success can be realized. As shown in Figure 1.2, the three structures are (1) a sound grouping policy, (2) an effective grading policy, and (3) a well-defined governance policy. These structures, the foci of the middle chapters of the book (3, 4, and 5, respectively), set the stage for the effective implementation of well-designed team activities (tasks and projects, as described in Chapter 6).

Thus, in my view, teachers can choose to follow any of the eight effective models described in this chapter, or they can synthesize their own approach utilizing the model demonstrated in Figure 1.2.

A RATIONALE FOR STUDENTS WORKING IN TEAMS

A basic underlying and unspoken assumption runs throughout the pages of this book. Essentially, there is an assumption that the use of student teams is a good thing and should be done by teachers. However, to this point I have offered no substantiation for the viability and/or value of teaming students. This section presents an attempt to dissuade the skeptic and to bolster the confidence of the advocate. Let us begin with a brief exercise.

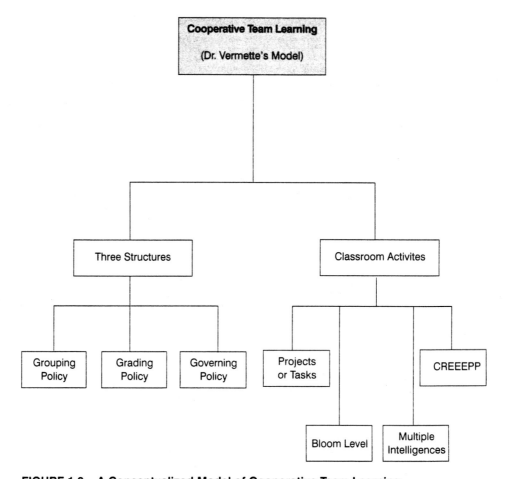

FIGURE 1.2   A Conceptualized Model of Cooperative Team Learning

The following list presents a series of possible outcomes for education in K–12 classrooms. They may be differentially desired by you as an individual or by your group (i.e., faculty, class, or department). To clarify their relative importance, take a few minutes, reflect on them and then rank order their value by assigning a 1 to the *most desirable* outcome and an 8 to the *least desirable* outcome, then rank the others accordingly.

1. Students show increased tolerance, helping behaviors, and friendship with members of other races and ethnicities or the other gender.

2. Students increase their understanding and tolerance of individuals with disabilities.

3. Students show an increase in their self-esteem.

4. Students show an increase in their achievement of content (at both upper and lower Bloom levels).

5. Students improve their problem-solving abilities and demonstrate improved cognitive reasoning strategies.

6. Students show increased comprehension, recall, and transfer of complex materials.

7. Students demonstrate a significant comfort level with computer technology.

8. Students show improved reading comprehension, spelling, and language expression.

Answer Key

As you no doubt have discovered by now, frequently there are no right answers (only better ones) especially on a task that uses *rank ordering*. Your ratings are your ratings, period! However, there are several things you should know about the list that you just evaluated. Most importantly *ALL* eight of these outcomes have been found to be the results of research studies involving the well-structured usage of team learning structures. Please reflect back on the eight items as you read and reread these brief comments about the research on cooperative learning:

Comprehensiveness: Well over 300 studies on cooperative learning techniques have been conducted and therefore it is one of the most thoroughly researched instructional innovations of all time. The results are incredibly positive, despite various methodological variations and conditions that have been utilized (see Johnson and Johnson, 1989; Slavin, 1995). Each of the eight statements has been the focus of inquiry and each has been substantiated by a quantitative study. Although the next chapter will provide details about some of these studies, it suffices to say here that each of the eight outcomes listed earlier is within the reach of well-implemented cooperative learning classrooms.

Although there is no magic bullet for teaching and there is no one right way to do things, the thoughtful use of teams may be your preferred avenue of choice regardless of your ordering.

Breadth: The findings cited as statements above were the result of a variety of specific cooperative learning methods that met the basic criteria of teams as established here. Some studies, as you will see, indicate that improper implementation of the method results in failure. The use of teams must be done thoughtfully, carefully, and with purpose in mind. (Recall the six classrooms that you classified earlier in this chapter: No successes were expected from the three using improper implementation.).

Depth: The findings presented as statements were drawn from research done with students of varying ages (first grade to college) and in all subject areas. Cooperative learning, done well, is not just for social studies or language arts classes; it can be effectively used everywhere in the curriculum and at every grade level.

In summary, to answer the question that served as this section's heading, students should work in teams because they (1) stand to learn more, (2) will think more critically, (3) will become more tolerant and understanding about human diversity, (4) will like school more, and (5) will feel better about themselves.

Those are some pretty good reasons to keep reading this book.

CHAPTER 1 SUMMARY

This chapter explored the meaning of the concept *cooperative team learning* as it has been used and analyzed during the past 20 years. The chapter also sought to develop a rationale for its continued use.

I defined cooperative learning in this way: "A cooperative classroom team is a relatively permanent, heterogeneously mixed, small group of students who have been assembled to complete an activity, produce a series of projects or products, and/or who have been asked to individually master a body of knowledge. The spirit within the team has to be one of positive interdependence, that is, a feeling that success for any one is tied directly to the successes of others. Moreover, these groups have to have been assigned by the teacher and they have to include regular direct face-to-face interaction in the classroom setting." Whereas a synthesized view of the instructional strategy is provided in this definition, it has been operationally defined in other distinct and varied ways. The eight most famous and useful models were described.

Robert Slavin has designed TGT and STAD, two team-based competitive forms that seek to provide students with peer motivation. Eliot Aronson has created Jigsaw, a system in which work is parceled out to team members who produce summaries and who teach their components to teammates. Shlomo Sharan generated Group Investigation, a strategy that has teams subdivide a large project into smaller components for research; these parts are then synthesized into a whole. Roger and David Johnson invented Learning Together, a system in which team members use pure cooperation to generate products of their learning. Donald Dansereau's many research teams at TCU have honed a two-person system in which the Dyads read, discuss, analyze, quiz, and probe each other until satisfactory levels of learning are reached. Spencer Kagan designed the Structural Approach, which seeks to match specific desired outcomes with an appropriate learning structure. For Kagan, some activities require two persons to share time, others four students working for a long period. These structures are formed by the interaction of the activity's demands and the students' reality. Finally, Elizabeth Cohen, who is extremely concerned with the prospect of losing low-status students within team learning, designed Complex Instruction, a project-based system that demands a great number of skills and a great deal of time. Projects are completed by teams of students who have different strengths and weaknesses. An appreciation for many talents is seen as a major goal of this model.

The chapter described these models and provided an opportunity for the reader to compare them and apply them to classroom situations. Although each stands alone as an effective system, I attempted to pull them together and isolate the common factors necessary for an effective implementation. The resulting model was presented in the chapter: It calls for the teacher to develop *three necessary structures* for the teamed class and suggests a need for *effective classroom teaching strategies*. Teachers must have a sound grouping plan, a carefully articulated grading policy, and a systematic plan for governance if cooperative learning is to succeed. With the structures in place, a concern for quality activities is the final piece of my model. (Explanations of these components form the foci of Chapters 3, 4, and 5.)

Finally, the question of rationale was raised: Why do cooperative learning? A simplified answer—"because it works"—was offered and then defended by the demonstration of team learning effectiveness in reaching eight desirable educational outcomes. According to the research presented in the next chapter, team learning increases tolerance and understanding across gender, race, and disability; improves self-esteem; increases achievement and problem-solving abilities; improves comprehension, writing, and the ability to transfer knowledge and skills; and increases student comfort with computers. These tendencies provide a worthy rationale for its use.

REFLECTION QUESTIONS

1. Using the material provided in the chapter, try to decide which of the eight model(s) might be appropriate in pursuing the following outcomes:

   a. Challenge students to accept a broad, diverse, and ill-structured problem and to solve it as a team.

   b. Increase students' ability to compete in a teamed situation.

   c. Increase the chances of students' recognizing diverse talents in their teammates.

   d. Maximize the participation of every individual in the group.

   e. Provide a more emotionally secure environment for students to engage in active thinking and/or experimentation.

2. Each of the models presents itself as a "package," offering the teacher a series of suggestions. Here are some challenges to several of the systems for which a teacher needs to plan a contingency. Try your hand at these:

   a. Teacher Roberts is using the Johnsons' approach and faces the dilemma of one member of the group signing the paper but contributing no work.

   b. Teacher Washington is using Slavin's TGT approach and has the same team (the "crows") finishing last in every teamed competition—and rapidly losing any desire to participate in the activities.

   c. Teacher Goldfarb is using Sharan's GI approach and is finding that students do not seem to know how to begin their investigations.

d. Teacher Franklin is using Cohen's Complex Instruction and is finding that the students are often impatient and try to do it as individuals, not as teams.

e. During the final segment of her Jigsaw session, Teacher Rappold is finding that her students will not pay attention to their teammates' presentation to them. (When she made them take a test on the work last time, they had horrible marks and got angry at each other.)

f. Teacher Duran finds it very confusing to match accurately the Kagan Structure and his own classroom activity. Sometimes students who like Think–Pair–Share will begin to do that activity when another has been called for, adding to the confusion.

3. Briefly describe a cooperative activity to facilitate these instructional demands:

a. Fifth graders are asked to master 25 new spelling words.

b. First graders are asked to decorate the classroom for Thanksgiving.

c. Twelfth graders are asked to identify the flaws in each of two dozen TV commercials.

d. Seventh graders are being asked to show their understanding of life in the American colonies.

e. Third graders are reading a story and have been asked to explain its plot.

f. Tenth graders have been asked to analyze the Russian Revolution, identifying causes, effects, and consequences.

4. Look again at Vermette's definition (or description) of a classroom team. Briefly speculate as to what could go "wrong" with a group activity if the following components were ignored:

a. Group size reaches eight or nine.

b. The group is too "alike" (i.e., homogeneous).

c. Individuals seek to compete with teammates, *not* cooperate.

d. Students are assigned to different groups each day.

t w o

A REVIEW OF RESEARCH ON
COOPERATIVE LEARNING

A brief caveat to the reader as she or he begins this chapter: This chapter is not for the squeamish. Although college teacher types spend their days talking about what the research says, K–12 teachers seldom do. This difference in perspective, what Leming (1992) calls the "two cultures" of education, often gets in the way of bringing the two groups together. Let me make a stereotypical assumption: Teachers want advice about how to use the team learning technique, whereas college instructors want to know how the research supports or refutes that advice. Let me also say, true to the spirit of heterogeneity, that both are legitimate positions and they can be reconciled to the benefit of both parties.

Here is the plan: I am not going to review meticulously the same sets of studies that have served as foci for Slavin (1995) or the Johnsons (1989). I am not going to enter their debate over "best evidence" and "meta-analysis" nor am I going to debate their propositions about what counts as evidence. Furthermore, I am not going to take the readers' time to review qualitative case studies of successful cooperative learning implementations such as those by Logan (1986), Smith (1987), and Crabill (1988), nor will I provide nonresearch anecdotal testimonials. What am I going to do is provide a brief review of numerous acceptable quantitative research studies that shed light on and support the instructional procedure of team learning and also highlight particularly important aspects for teachers.

This chapter is not a true review of the literature in the sense of a meta-analysis, nor is it a compilation of stories about people who have used learning teams effectively. Instead, this chapter seeks to expose both college-level and K–12 teachers to some basic data about the history of cooperative learning research in an attempt to shed light on its popularity and to provide advice to practitioners hoping to implement it well.

The first part of this chapter asks you to recall the eight outcomes of team learning that you rank ordered at the end of the previous chapter.

1. Students show increased tolerance, helping behavior, and friendship with members of other races/ethnicities or the other gender.
2. Students increase their understanding and tolerance of individuals with disabilities.
3. Students show an increase in their self-esteem.
4. Students show an increase in their achievement of content.
5. Students improve their problem-solving abilities and demonstrate improved cognitive reasoning strategies.
6. Students show increased comprehension, recall, and transfer of complex materials.
7. Students demonstrate a significant comfort level with computer technology.
8. Students show improved reading comprehension, spelling, and language expression.

These eight outcomes are actual findings from acceptable quantitative studies that serve as prototypes of implementation. The studies reviewed in this chapter provide evidence to substantiate my claims of success for the technique and provide information about how success has been achieved. For each finding, at least three studies have been annotated here, providing at least some diversity and breadth to the strength of the finding.

The last part of this chapter provides a slightly different service to the readers. Numerous studies have provided insights about the cooperative learning process, yet they do not necessarily deal directly with the eight outcomes discussed next. For example, you will be exposed to Ross's (1988) study, which suggests that STAD (Students–Teams–Achievement–Divisions) does not work and his fascinating explanation of why not.

One final note before the reader begins: This chapter requires far less active participation from the reader than does most of the rest of the text. I have chosen a straightforward expository approach. However, I wish to draw your attention to the end-of-chapter activities. These activities will help readers contemplate what they've read about the research reviews presented. In fact, readers may wish to look over the activities *before* continuing.

In truth, research studies provide the best "proof" that cooperative team learning works and they should be examined frequently by all teachers in K–12 schools. Familiarity with the studies and confidence in their results should help equip teachers with both positive attitudes and effective techniques. I hope the reviews presented help the reader realize this intention.

RESEARCH ON THE OUTCOMES OF COOPERATIVE LEARNING

Increased Racial and Gender Tolerance and Friendship

DeVries, D. L., Slavin, R. E., & Edwards, K. J. (1978). Biracial learning teams and race relations in the classroom: Four field experiments using Teams-Games-Tournaments. *Journal of Educational Psychology, 70,* **356–362.**

In a series of finely tuned experiments in Florida, 558 students in grades 7 through 12 were taught via TGT (Teams–Games–Tournaments) or a traditional model for an extended period of time. Teachers were unaware that the purpose of the study was to assess friendships across race. Under various teamed conditions, students consistently increased their number of cross-race friendships. The authors contend that if a lack of friendships and a lack of helping behaviors exist across racial lines, it is a result of miscommunication or limited contact between races, and the use of the TGT strategy may be appropriate.

One of the earliest and most consistently held findings about cooperative learning is its impact on relationships between teammates. Contemporary American society seems to be as divided racially now as it was during the 1960s Civil Rights days and attempts to create a smoother multicultural milieu quickly lose ground. It is interesting to me that this study—the first of a convincing series—has been largely forgotten or ignored by many of those who call for educational interventions favoring tolerance.

The sample of 558 students is large enough to carry great credibility with many researchers and the controls, including the varied durations, also support its believability. Keeping the teachers unaware about the purpose also negated a possible Hawthorne effect, increasing its credibility.

Blaney, N. T., Stephan, C., Rosenfield, D., Aronson, E., & Sikes, J. (1977). Interdependence in the classroom: A field study. *Journal of Educational Psychology, 69*(2), **121–128.**

A year before DeVries et al. examined TGT, Aronson's group had put Jigsaw to the test. Using 304 fifth-grade students in Texas, experimental classes using Jigsaw were set up and compared to traditional classes. Teachers of the experimental classes were trained in special workshops and then transformed from transmitters to facilitators: Control teachers, selected for their competency by the experimental teachers, taught as they always had. Experimental classes broke students into four- to six-member teams, varied for diversity. For 6 weeks, students met three times a week for 45 minutes, with students in Jigsaw doing most of the teaching; control students faced regular instruction during that time. Results showed a great increase in liking and friendliness toward those who had not been liked before *and* did not show this increase to be at the expense of previous friendships (i.e., students broadened their range of relationships). Moreover, the authors contend that the entire school experience was competitive *except* for this small component and therefore the results are even more impressive than they would be if the students were familiar with cooperative structures.

This famous study exposed Jigsaw to the world and had a huge impact. Except for the selection of the control teachers by the experimental group, the methodology is impeccable. Professionals seeking to develop intergroup relationships ought to take note.

Johnson, D. W., & Johnson, R. T. (1981). Effects of cooperative and individualistic learning experiences on interethnic interaction. *Journal of Educational Psychology, 73,* 444–449.

In one of my favorite studies of all times, the Johnsons simply took 51 inner-city fourth graders and divided them into stratified groups (i.e., they matched for gender, ability, ethnicity). Half were taught cooperatively and half individualistically. Instruction took place for 45 minutes a day for 16 school days and measures were gathered on 10 outcomes. Interaction, helping, liking, and free-time interactions all increased across race and gender (and ability) in the cooperative setting.

Johnson, R. T., Johnson, D. W., Scott, L. E., & Ramolae, B. A. (1985). Effects of single-sex and mixed-sex cooperative interaction on science achievement and attitudes and cross-handicap and cross-sex relationships. *Journal of Research in Science Teaching, 2,* 207–220.

In this study, 154 fifth and sixth graders were involved in structured science lessons for 45 minutes a day for 21 days to allow the investigators a chance to assess the power of various instructional strategies. In the cooperative condition, students helped each other learn, shared ideas and materials, and were instructed to check each other's learning. Tested individually, these subjects received a bonus built on the total achievement of group members. (There were both mixed-sex and same-sex groups.) The control subjects were given packets of materials that they worked on independently; they were tested that way as well. Attitude and achievement measures were measured at the end of the instructional treatment. Observations were made to determine that the procedures were being followed as designed.

Several results are worth noting: Students with disabilities in the cooperative teams were not ignored; instead, they were included and became an integral part of a positive affective experience for members without disabilities.

Although overall achievement between the various conditions was the same (i.e., no advantage was found in the two teamed conditions), children with disabilities in the teamed situation did achieve more than children with disabilities who worked alone.

The students in the teamed conditions had far more positive attitudes toward the other gender than was found in the individualistic condition. Working together improves attitudes toward the content and toward each other *if* they are mixed-sex groups (single-sex groups stayed the same), suggesting that attitudes clearly do not worsen when teachers put boys and girls together. The study also supported previous work (Cooper, Johnson, Johnson, & Wilderson, 1980) which showed that it is more difficult to generate cross-sex friendships than cross-race or cross-disability friendships. The findings also dovetailed nicely with a contemporary study (Warring, Johnson, Maruyama, & Johnson, 1985) which showed that after working together in mixed-sex fourth- and sixth-grade teams, boys and girls significantly increased their friendships and contacts both outside of the team and outside of the school.

In the debate over gender equity, there is evidence that well-structured and well-implemented cooperative learning structures can produce more excellence *and* more equity (Scott, 1985). In 1984 Lockheed and Harris found that typical fifth-grade teachers provided almost no cross-gender contact and cross-gender attitudes were correspondingly awful. Reports by Sadker and Sadker (1994) suggest that traditionally run modern classrooms are little better today, but cooperative teamwork does offer a potential respite from that dismal track record.

Increased Understanding of Children with Disabilities

Johnson, R. T., Johnson, D. W., DeWeerdt, N., Lyons, N., & Zaidman, B. (1983). Integrating severely adaptively handicapped seventh-grade students into constructive relationships with nonhandicapped peers in science class. *American Journal of Mental Deficiency, 87,* 611–618.

To a large degree, the lengthy title of this study tells the story: Compared to individualistic class structures, cooperative four-person seventh-grade teams, each containing one individual with severe disabilities, were more likely to produce attitudes that were positive and helpful toward students with disabilities.

Several noteworthy components mark this study. First, there is lengthy treatment of the logic behind propositions that oppose this finding; in other words, careful support is offered for the hypotheses *not* supported by the results. Doubters of cooperative learning get a fair hearing in the introduction and have their opposition challenged by the findings.

Second, as usual, the Johnsons carefully trained the teachers used in the study. They were all versed in both team and individual treatments and were rotated during the study so that no teacher bias was involved.

Third, the team carefully defined what is meant by the term *handicapped* (the term of choice in 1983). Of the 48 suburban students used, 9 were categorized as "severely handicapped" and had low IQs (8 were below 80) and 1 was autistic.

Finally, the dependent measures (i.e., the results) did include achievement on which there was *no* difference between the two treatments. Despite the appearance of being a negative, this result is actually not too bad from my perspective: It says that teachers can get a host of positive affective outcomes (being together during free time, feelings that disabled persons actually belong in the class, and inclusion of disabled persons in actual classroom team discussions) without losing any achievement outcomes for *either* disabled or nondisabled students. This complex sentence should be duly noted by any school attempting to promote inclusion plans or, for that matter, seeking to eliminate a tracked system of curriculum. Failures of inclusion and detracking are often the result of teachers *not* having tools available to maximize the gains. The study here shows that the traditional individualistic condition did actually result in much greater failure than did the cooperative teamed condition. All this occurred in a science class no less—a fact that should be noted by advocates of separation, tracking, and traditional instruction.

Johnson, R. T., & Johnson, D. W. (1981). Building friendships between handicapped and non-handicapped students: Effects of cooperative and individualistic instruction. *American Educational Research Journal, 18,* 415–423.

Two years before their team explored a similar question with seventh graders, the Johnsons' conducted this study with 40 suburban third graders in mathematics. Five males and three females were seen as having learning disabilities (two years behind classmates) and/or behavior impairments. They had been referred to special education *and* had been rejected by classmates (based on sociometric data). Groups stratified by sex, ability, disability, and peer status were built and two treatments structured: individualistic and cooperative (containing one member with a disability). Students were taught math lessons for 25 minutes for 16 days, each lesson having a teacher presentation portion and a student practice session.

Several findings are noteworthy. Communication was much better between children with disabilities and those without in the cooperative condition. Four times as many comments were made by children without disabilities to those with disabilities and 94% of the comments were positive or neutral. Thus, the nagging or picking on children with disabilities that many teachers feared would occur in such a condition did *not* happen! Second, students did gather and share free time outside of the structured activities when they were teamed, evidence that the positive effect does transfer beyond the classroom. The Johnsons also stressed that the teachers who feared that the students with disabilities would use team time as a forum for "acting out" should note that this did *not* happen.

Finally, the resulting friendships that developed under teamed conditions should be noted carefully: Many of us are seeking to move toward a "learning community" in our schools, a community that includes regular and special students (Udvari-Solner & Thousand, 1995). This study provides evidence that it can be done and offers one way to do it.

Slavin, R. E., Madden, N. A., and Leavey, M. (1984). Effects of cooperative learning and individualized instruction on mainstreamed students. *Exceptional Children, 50,* 434–442.

While it is obvious that much of the research on this outcome has been conducted by the Johnsons' teams, other researchers have also been effective, as evidenced by this study from the other big name in cooperative learning, Robert Slavin. This study, conducted with 117 intermediate (third- to fifth-grade) suburban students, focused on the effects of three conditions—team-assisted individualization (TAI), individualized instruction (II), and the traditional control approach—on mainstreamed students in mathematics classes. Unlike treatments that moved all groups through the same content, these treatments sought to vary the material for the ability and previous achievements of the students.

TAI is a five-step process that creates mixed-ability groups that collaboratively study their own materials. Teammates are used as checkers, helpers, encouragers, clarifiers, explainers, and evaluators. Teams receive scores and recognition based on the average achievement of teammates. With individualized instruction, there was no team recognition and individuals actually worked without team help. (Note that the six "roles" identified for TAI are functions, not formal roles as specified in some studies. In II, only teachers could help.)

Interestingly, both TAI and II improved achievement over the traditional control approach, but did not differ from each other. Moreover, both TAI and II improved attitudes toward math, social acceptance of students with disabilities, and teacher ratings of the behavior of students with disabilities. This finding suggests that both approaches are useful for schools moving toward inclusion. The explanation for the positive effects of TAI revolves around the spirit of interdependence formed and the actual help provided. Explanations for the findings on individualization include the perceptional changes about students that occur during individualization and one interesting side note from the authors: During the individualized study time, students often wandered around to share, help, and talk with neighboring classmates, creating a TAI analog on their own!

While potentially contaminating the purity of this study, I wish to note that the findings here do not damage the claims of cooperative theorists who say that their alternative is worthwhile. At the very least, this study shows that collaborative teams working together help students learn math and learn to be friends with peers who have disabilities.

Increased Self-Esteem

Johnson, D. W., & Johnson, R. T. (1985). Classroom conflict: Controversy versus debate in learning groups. *American Educational Research Journal, 22,* 237–256.

This study is probably the most important of the hundreds that have been conducted over the years. It was well constructed, complex yet believable, and examined vitally important topics. Seventy-two sixth graders were divided into three groups: One utilized cooperative debate, one used individual study, and one used cooperative controversy, a system that created four-person teams and provided materials pro and con for an issue (hunting versus conservation). The instructional pattern included 2 days of study, presentation, synthesis, and review. The controversy group followed a similar pattern but concentrated on winning the debate (not reaching synthesis and understanding) at the end of the four days. Instruction was continued for 55 minutes a day for 11 days and was marked by the continuous addition of new information provided by the teacher. The individualized group simply studied all the materials.

Measures were drawn that showed the following results: The cooperative controversy group showed the greatest amount of oral interaction between parties, the most active search for organization and ideas, the most reevaluation of a position, and the *highest* self-esteem. This last point is crucial; the study's authors suggest that the form of the students' interaction may have given the participants a sense of confidence, a sense of importance, and a sense of control (my words) that led to higher levels of self-esteem, as well as other positive affective effects.

This study suggests that students can learn to disagree agreeably and that conflict, a natural behavior, can be turned into a positive experience. One traditional form of school academic conflict, debate, was not as powerful a technique as was the cooperative controversy condition, an important note for teachers of courses that regularly deal with conflict such as English (literature) and social studies.

Johnson, R. T., Johnson, D. W., & Rynders, J. (1981). Effect of cooperative, competitive and individualistic experiences on self-esteem of handicapped and non-handicapped students. *Journal of Psychology, 108,* 31–34.

In a short, clean study, the researchers stratified 30 middle school students into groups for 8 weeks for a physical education activity (bowling). Nine of these students had severe disabilities. Measures of self-esteem were drawn from the Minnesota School Affect Assessment instrument and were administered orally and individually. (Subjects responded to statements such as "I feel that I am doing a good job in learning to bowl.")

Results favored the self-esteem achievements of the students in the cooperative (teamed) section; scores were also higher for the students without disabilities than for those with disabilities, indicating a general rise in self-esteem by the treatment but *not* an equalization effect.

Johnson, R. T., & Johnson, D. W. (1983). Effects of cooperative, competitive, and individualistic learning experiences on social development. *Exceptional Children, 49,* 323–329.

In another of their many studies, the Johnsons created three groups for 15 days of 60-minute instruction on two topics: the wolf and the use of coal. The subjects were 59 fourth graders from an urban district and the study used six trained teachers. The treatments were cooperative (teamed), competitive (each day's rankings were posted), and individualistic (alone). Measures of self-esteem were taken for three aspects of that variable: general, school, and peer. Each scale had eight items, exemplified by these examples: "I am satisfied to be just what I am," "I am proud of my schoolwork," and "I have many friends." Dependent measures revealed that all three scales were higher following cooperative study than they were after both of the other two approaches. In discussing this finding, the authors suggest that cooperative teamed work allows students to see themselves as worthwhile and important. Previous data had suggested that students were better able to take another's perspective (empathy) when working cooperatively, and this was true for both the disabled and nondisabled students in this study.

Slavin, R. E., & Karweit, N. L. (1981). Cognitive and affective outcomes of an intensive student team learning experience. *Journal of Experimental Education, 50,* 29–35.

Positive findings for self-esteem measures are a frequent result of cooperative learning studies; as has been noted, a great deal of the Johnsons' work revealed this pattern. Moreover, the Blaney et al. (1977) study discussed earlier showed that an alternative form of teaming, Jigsaw, also led to these positive effects. The Slavin and Karweit study reviewed here utilized TGT STAD, *and* Jigsaw combined—and found the familiar positive self-esteem effects. Apparently, working together in many teamed formats is a positive experience for youngsters.

In this rather large study, 456 fourth and fifth graders in rural Maryland were assigned to a control (traditional) condition or an experimental (cooperative) one. The latter group had their school days marked by the daily use of different teamed formats (Jigsaw, STAD, and TGT). After a semester, measures were taken that revealed a positive effect for the cooperative treatment(s) on liking for school, language, and reading achievement, and self-esteem as determined by the Coppersmith, the most widely accepted measure of esteem.

This major study was marked by some interesting comments from the authors. They speculated that the self-esteem finding was important and was possibly produced by these factors: (1) Working in teams is pleasant and results in human friendships and good feelings, (2) teamed students are simply more likely to succeed in schoolwork and therefore feel better about themselves, and (3) because they like teamwork, they like school more and thus feel better about themselves and the experience. These explanations are most cogent for me and are the likely explanation behind this common finding.

Increased Achievement

Nichols, J. D., & Miller, R. B. (1994). Cooperative learning and student motivation. *Contemporary Educational Psychology, 19,* 167–178.

Extending Slavin et al.'s TAI technique to high school algebra learning, the authors divided 62 students into two conditions: cooperative learning (TAI) and traditional lecture method at the start of the school year. After pretesting, the two groups received different instruction until the midterm (December) and then were switched so that both groups experienced both teaching structures.

Two clear results appeared: Student achievement was much higher under the teamed conditions and the students liked the team approach better (even complaining when they were switched out of that approach!). Moreover, the study assessed motivation and discovered support for Slavin's theory that a combination of group reward (recognition) and individual accountability (each individual is tested) produces positive learning effects.

An important design function in this study was the pretest/post-test approach (and the use of ANCOVA) to measure the change within individuals over the course of one- and two-semester stretches. Intrapersonal changes favored the cooperative group.

Secondly, a potential bias should be reported here: In the cooperative condition, TAI allowed students the option to retest if they wished, an option *not* open to those in the traditional section. The researchers controlled for this by running the data a second time, eliminating those few students who had retested: the results were the same, indicating that the positive effects were not solely caused by the retest, but were related to the overall, long-term use of the teamed approach.

Mesch, D., Johnson, D. W., & Johnson, R. (1987). Impact of positive interdependence and academic group contingencies on achievement. *Journal of Social Psychology, 128,* 345–352.

In a study that lasted 24 weeks, the research team used two groups of 10th-grade suburban social studies classes (54 students, including 4 with academic disabilities), one using individualized approaches and one using cooperative learning. In both cases, homework was assigned 4 days a week and quizzes were given on Fridays; after 6 weeks of similar schooling, baseline measures were taken and the comparisons begun. The experimental group used positive goal interdependence (all students had to help others and sign off that they had done so) and, later, academic group contingencies (bonuses arranged on individual growth and team achievement).

The cooperative team scored much higher on the teacher-made tests of content achievement (80% to 73.5%) and the synthesized use of the two contingencies helped the most. Moreover, the heterogeneous nature of the groups, including the students with academic disabilities, did not hamper these gains; the study provides strong evidence for heterogeneous groupings in the typical high school.

Sharan, S., Ackerman, Z., & Hertz-Lazarowitz, R. (1980). Academic achievement of elementary school children in small-group versus whole-class instruction. *Journal of Experimental Education, 48,* 125–129.

To assess the value of a specific approach to cooperative learning and its effects on higher order learning for 217 children in the second through sixth grades, Sharan et al. designed this study. Comparing traditional presentation and large group discussion to a system in which the pupils planned their own lessons, divided the labor, conducted research, and discussed with each other, the study found an advantage on higher order test items for the group approach. Topics and duration of instruction were as follows: second grade—the clinic (9 hours); third grade—fire (9 hours); fourth grade—transportation (12 hours); fifth grade—Palestine (12 hours); and sixth grade—Kibbutz (12 hours).

Although the positive effects were not uniformly strong across all the grades overall, the Israeli children did profit academically from their small group interactions. The research team cited the existence of spontaneous drawings on the tests of teamed youngsters as evidence of their sparked creativity (25%, while it never occurred under the traditional format). Moreover, a test of word fluency favored the group format over the traditional, indicating its positive effects on writing ability.

Increased Problem-Solving Abilities

Johnson, D. W., Skon, L., & Johnson, R. T. (1980). Effects of cooperative, competitive and individualistic conditions on children's problem-solving performance. *American Educational Research Journal, 17,* 83–93.

Forty-five first graders were matched by gender and ability and put into various groups of cooperative, competitive, and individualistic classroom structures. This study sought to examine the learning of complex problem-solving types of challenges in order to draw comparisons with older studies of mechanical skills. Cooperative groups of size 3 were told to "work as a group, help each other, ensure that everyone was involved, and share materials." Competitive groups were built so that the groups were homogeneous in ability and they then competed for prizes (first-, second-, and third-place awards). Three tasks were assigned: (1) word recall, (2) spatial reasoning (identifying ambiguous triangles), and (3) math story problems.

The cooperative group showed the highest achievement and the best reasoning strategies. The authors took special note of the effects of the strategy on high-ability youngsters: They seemed to have benefited the most from the "discuss-what-I-do-not-understand" procedure. They also conclude that the competitive and individualistic conditions were not significantly different, reinforcing the idea that the group work encouraged learners *and* provided thoughtful interaction opportunities for children this young.

Johnson, R. T., Johnson, D. W., & Stanne, M. B. (1985). Effects of cooperative, competitive and individualistic goal structures on computer-assisted instruction. *Journal of Educational Psychology, 77,* 668–677.

This study, conducted with 71 middle-class, Midwestern American suburban eighth-grade boys and girls, sought to examine attitudes, achievements, and abilities resulting from differentiated types of computer study. Three formats were chosen for a computer simulation on navigation: The students were required to study, problem-solve, and make decisions after being given preliminary data and, later, more data from their previous decisions. (Clearly, this was an interactive assignment and forced the use of higher level thinking.)

Fully trained teachers worked in each of the three formats. The cooperative condition created stratified (balanced) four-member teams that worked together, changed roles each of the 10 days, and made joint decisions. The competitive mode also used groups of four, but in this condition they were asked to strive to be the best; students were ranked in proficiency and had their ranks portrayed publicly. In the individualistic condition, students were assigned to a group of four, but were enjoined to do their own work and turn in the results of their personal decisions and the consequences. They were asked not to share or exchange ideas and they were privately given daily feedback about their efforts.

Note that each of the very different conditions (cooperative, competitive, and individualistic) made use of grouped students: They differed in how they interacted *after* the grouping and *during* the series of activities. After 10 days of this project, it was clear that the students working in cooperative groups had learned more, recalled more, and did much better at problem-solving tasks than did the students in the other two conditions. Moreover, the fact that this study used computers is critically important; the results also showed the females were much more comfortable with the machines (had better "attitudes scores") in the cooperative mode as well.

Because cooperative boys also had higher achievement and better problem-solving skills, this study supports the notion that learning to use the computer and learning to be a good problem-solver can both be advanced by using cooperative groups of students. (Research in later decades suggests that these girls may also have been helped by their having been assigned important and specific roles within the problem-solving groups. This structuring technique may have lessened the chances that the group could have solved the problems *without* female input, a not unfamiliar—and damaging—occurrence.)

Skon, L., Johnson, D. W., & Johnson, R. T. (1981). Cooperative peer interaction versus individual competition and individualistic efforts: Effects on the acquisition of cognitive reasoning strategies. *Journal of Educational Psychology, 73,* 83–92.

This article was added to this review for the simple reason that it, like the study reported earlier, focused on the development of reasoning strategies of *first graders* under conditions of cooperation, competition, and individuality. To my mind, a relatively small portion of the cooperative learning research has been done on young children because of the difficulty using paper-and-pencil tests to assess the dependent variable (either learning or attitude). This difficulty was overcome here by the use of trained interviewers who sat and individually interviewed the 86 first graders after the interventions were applied.

Also of interest is the fact that in the cooperative and competitive conditions, half the students were in mixed-ability groups and half were in same-ability groups. They used this study to look at early identification of ability grouping discussions on the reasoning strategies of first graders. The result: Cooperative interaction promoted the highest levels of achievement and developed superior reasoning strategies. Furthermore, the results were the same regardless of the ability mix of the group: Heterogeneous groupings produced just as positive a result as did homogeneous teams! Back in 1981 this study gave us the first reason to believe that heterogeneous groupings coupled with cooperative learning produced the most desired cognitive effects.

Finally, I wish to use this annotation to operationalize cooperative interaction as the Johnsons saw it then—and see it now. Students in the cooperative condition were asked to do the following:

1. Work together as a group.
2. Complete one set of papers as a group.
3. Share materials and ideas.
4. Help each other.

Furthermore, feedback and teacher praise were contingent on the collective performance of group members on *individual* tests. Thus, individual accountability resulted in team success and everyone felt that she or he had to achieve.

The Johnsons have always used somewhat complicated and elaborate research designs so as to give more credence to their findings. In this one, they used three different types of learning tasks to assess reasoning: the memorization and categorization of 12 nouns, the use of metaphors and explanations, and 10 math story problems. Thus, students were assessed on a variety of content areas, making the positive results for cooperative learning all the more meaningful.

Increased Comprehension, Recall, and Transfer

Humphreys, B., Johnson, R. T., & Johnson, D. W. (1982). Effects of cooperative, competitive and individualistic learning on students' achievement in science class. *Journal of Research in Science Teaching, 19*, 351–356.

In a study that lasted for 6 weeks at the end of a school year, 44 Midwestern suburban average-ability ninth graders were taught *three* science units (heat, sound and light, nuclear energy) under one of three conditions: cooperatively (in teams stratified by gender), competitively, and individualistically. Interestingly, various limiting conditions were placed on each treatment. For example, the cooperative team took individual tests but received the average of their team's grades; in the competitive condition, a wall chart displayed rankings and achievement and a norm-referenced test assessed learning; in the individual condition, help could only be solicited from the teacher.

Instruction for each 2-week unit (9 hours) focused on lab activities and ended with a unit test, which was lengthy and objective. Attitude measures were also gathered. Finally, 1 week after the units all ended, students took a retention test to assess the longer term effects of the various treatment. In all aspects, members of the cooperative team scored higher; they liked their classes better, they learned more, and they remembered more for a longer amount of time. This evidence suggests that studying as a team promotes a more stable and valuable recall ability than does competition or individual study.

Of some note, the authors also measured attendance during the units, one of only two studies that I have seen that did so. Like the other (Moskowitz, Malvin,

Shaeffer, & Schaps, 1983), attendance under the cooperative condition saw fewer absences than did the other two conditions, a fact that may be worth noting for many of us concerned about getting our students to classes. (The authors note 23, 34, and 33 as the actual numbers of absences for the team, the competitive, and the individual conditions, respectively. The differences are not monumental, but they are important and significant.)

Yager, S., Johnson, D. W., & Johnson, R. T. (1985). Oral discussion, group-to-individual transfer and achievement in cooperative learning groups. *Journal of Educational Psychology, 77,* 60–66.

Once again, a Johnsons-based research team compared three learning treatments for youngsters (75 middle-class Midwestern second graders), but this time the study contrasted individual learning with two versions of cooperative teams, which differed on the use of specific role assignments and the use of highly structured oral discussion mandates. Thus, one group simply invented their own problem-solving and discussion patterns and the other followed what later researchers (i.e., O'Donnell and Dansereau, 1992) called *scripts*. Of secondary interest, this study was designed such that effects on different abilities could be examined. Instruction was presented for 36 minutes daily for 18 days. Three 12-minute segments were adhered to: (1) teacher explanation, (2) oral discussion, and (3) large-class discussion. In the structured condition, learners were asked to restate and summarize, ask probing questions, and evaluate ideas. These roles were rotated daily. The learning of the topic (maps) was assessed in three ways: daily achievement, unit achievement (70 test items), and retention (in the form of a 50-item test given 18 days after the units ended).

The results strongly supported the cooperative and structured discussion approach, and these results ran across all three student ability levels (high, medium, low) providing evidence favoring the use of heterogeneous groups.

A paraphrase of Vygotsky might sound like this: "What a child can do as part of a group today will be something that she or he can do alone tomorrow." This study certainly provides supportive evidence for that statement.

McDonald, B. A., Larson, C. O., Dansereau, D. F., & Spurlin, J. E. (1985). Cooperative dyads: Impact on text learning and transfer. *Contemporary Educational Psychology, 10,* 369–377.

This study, one from the stock of Don Dansereau's Texas Christian University team's research, utilized college students in two experiments to compare various team conditions. I have included it here to extend the review to "older" students and to offer a clear elaboration on the Yager et al. study discussed earlier. Here, students in a laboratory setting were trained in one of three conditions: individual (30), systematic strategy pairs (30), or unsystematic pairs (27) (the figures were drawn from the second experiment reported). In the first session, subjects "learned" the material from a 2000-word passage "The Root." In session 2, two passages were used; one used the trained system and the other did not. The third session involved an essay test. By varying the conditions in session 2, that is, by sliding from a teamed approach to the individual, the effects on transfer from group work to individual study strategies could be assessed.

The results favored the structured strategy, as did Yager's for second graders. By shifting from recaller to listener in the team portion and then working on the essay alone, subjects seem to have mastered the learning strategy and then applied it when faced with individualized challenges. Thus, more support was provided for Vygotsky's transfer ideas.

Many teachers distrust pure laboratory research and studies done with college-level students. However, this study is one of many conducted by the team and is representative of their fine work. Its findings are consistent with many others and should be noted as such. The transfer from an effective team study strategy to an individual study skill appears to occur regularly for those who work in groups and thus provides teachers with a way to model and develop study skills in their students.

Increased Comfort with Computer Technology

Johnson, R. T., Johnson, D. W., & Stanne, M. B. (1986). Comparison of computer-assisted cooperative, competitive and individualistic learning. *American Educational Research Journal, 23,* 382–392.

In three different rooms, 25 or so eighth graders of both genders "hung out" near six computers. For 45 minutes during each of 10 consecutive school days, they worked on a computer simulation called "Geography Search" that taught them about the computer and about geography. In one group, the students worked by themselves, kept to themselves, and took turns (individualistic). In a second, they worked as four-person teams, shared ideas, helped each other, and gathered team points, but were tested individually. Moreover, this teamed group, called the cooperative group, rotated assigned roles: captain, navigator, meteorologist, and quartermaster and thus rotated assigned functions (or scripts). In the third room, groups of four were created that competed with each other at the terminal: daily rankings of first, second, third, and fourth best were made public, and members of the group were asked to share terminal time.

This image describes the essence of this study's structure. The authors assumed that computers in schools would be shared by groups of students and they wished to examine the effects of various strategies used by those groups. The result: The cooperative setting produced the most daily achievement, better problem-solving skills, and more task-related student interaction, and also increased the status of females, who were thought to be less preferred teammates. Five dependent outcomes were taken and measured as follows: (1) *achievement*—a 16-item test, with various Bloom levels represented; (2) *daily achievement*—worksheet items correctly completed; (3) *problem-solving*—amount of daily bonuses accrued ("gold"); (4) *task-related interaction*—statements counted per minute; and (5) *acceptance of females*—nomination instrument requiring the listing of desired work partners.

Two key findings complement this cooperative computer study. One, females profited greatly, both in achievement and in the enhanced perceptions by others, no small matter in this time and age. Secondly, this study shows a most interesting finding: As the students gathered around the computer in the competitive modality, there was more off-task behavior as measured by "social " statements made (as opposed to "task" statements). This is evidence that the cooperative learning approach does help keep students on task, focused, and, in this case, more comfortable with technology than does traditional competitive teaching.

Johnson, D. W., Johnson, R. T., Stanne, M. B., & Garibaldi, A. (1990). Impact of group processing on achievement in cooperative groups. *The Journal of Social Psychology, 130,* 507–516.

In an interesting investigation into the learning of computers, 48 African-American high school seniors/college freshmen were divided into four heterogeneous teams for a 4-week summer project (Project Excel at Xavier University). The four treatments were as follows: (1) Cooperative learning plus no processing; student teams were encouraged to work together and were rewarded on the basis of the progress of all three members. (2) Cooperative learning plus teacher-led processing; students did the same work as group 1 *and* were instructed to summarize ideas, encourage each other, and check for agreement. They also engaged in a daily 5-minute feedback session on how well they were doing as a group. (3) Cooperative learning plus teacher-*and* student-led processing; students did everything as indicated in group 2 *plus* they had a daily 5-minute feedback/discussion session led by students. This session focused on the effectiveness of the group's functioning as a team. (4) Individual students shared the terminal but did *not* share with each other; they were instructed to work alone.

Students in the three cooperative conditions outscored the students in the individual group on both problem solving and achievement measured here by the accumulation of points, *not* by a single administration of a test. Moreover, the group with the two levels of group processing achieved the most, indicating that cooperative learning helps students learn with computers especially if the group is allowed to assess itself regularly. The authors suggest that this result might be traceable to the concept that the feedback in the processing sessions increased the effectiveness of the work by supplying models of metacognition (thinking), reducing self-doubt, reinforcing existing behaviors, and/or increasing individual efficacy. They do not specify which of these factors was the most important. Perhaps all of these desirable behaviors are related to the use of cooperative teams that do analysis of their own work.

Chernick, R. S. (1990). Effects of interdependent, coactive and individualized working conditions on pupils' educational computer program performance. *Journal of Educational Psychology, 82,* 691–695.

Eighty third and fourth graders in suburban New York City were exposed to computer instruction in one of three formats: (1) Individual students worked in isolation on their tasks, each with his or her own computer; (2) interdependent teams used one microcomputer; and (3) coactive subjects worked alone, but next to and in full view of students doing the same activity. For each of three 30-minute sessions, rewards were handed out differentially. Recognition was made of the "best" student in the individual and coactive conditions, simulating the competitive classroom. The teamed group was offered a group reward based on the average of the achievement of team members.

Measures were taken to assess achievement on high- and low-complexity problems. The interdependent team outperformed the others on the low-complexity problems, but no differences were found for high-complexity problems. Note that the strategies used by interdependent teams were effective, but did not completely transfer to the individually done post-test; these included division of labor (a form of Jigsaw), pooling of resources, cross-checking errors, and cued recall.

Finally, Chernick makes a strong case for the shared use of computers in the classroom. He notes that while neither the interdependent nor the coactive approaches *hurt* learning on high-complexity issues, they had other positive effects. Their use provides greater access to computers, offers models to follow, encourages social facilitation, and, in general, is conducive to providing what is today thought of as a learning community. By conservatively saying that their use "is not detrimental" (Chernick, 1990, p. 695), he is suggesting that we use groups to teach with and about technology.

Improved Reading, Spelling, and Language Expression

Stevens, R. J., Madden, N. A., Slavin, R. E., & Farnish, A. M. (1987). Cooperative integrated reading and composition: Two field experiments. *Reading Research Quarterly, 22,* **433–454.**

In two studies, a total of 911 third and fourth graders in suburban Maryland studied the language arts under one of two ways. The traditional approach utilized standard practices, including worksheets, a published spelling program, whole-class writing, and, in some cases, ability grouping. The experimental treatment, called Cooperative Integrated Reading and Comprehension (CIRC) was a complicated construction that utilized heterogeneous teams, direct instruction, and cooperative team practice sessions. This condition's design was consistent with the theory that all schoolwork was connected and that language arts activities overlapped and supported each other and called for a fully integrated approach. To further articulate this system, note that in reading, students worked with peer partners on decoding, prediction, and explanation activities. For writing, teachers used direct instruction to first "teach" the ideas and then group activities were used as support and practice (a la Slavin's other strategies, TGT and STAD).

The two interventions lasted 12 weeks and 24 weeks, respectively. At the end, achievement was measured by a subscale of the California Achievement Test (form D). Writing was assessed using a reliable analytic scoring approach. The results showed a clear advantage for the CIRC students on reading comprehension, language mechanics, language expression, and spelling.

The authors make a point that this study supports the ideas that all language arts activities are connected as a unified curriculum and that the integration of the best aspects (my words) of two instructional theories can produce the best results. In this case, direct instruction and cooperative learning were thoughtfully combined and produced the greatest amount of achievement, including improvement on students ability to express themselves in writing.

Katstra, J., Tollefson, N., & Gilbert, E. (1987). The effects of peer evaluation on attitude toward writing and writing fluency of ninth grade students. *Journal of Educational Research, 80,* 168–172.

In contrast to the Stevens et al. review just discussed, this study was chosen because it focused on *attitudes* toward writing and language arts activities instead of achievement, reflecting the author's perspective that attitude is a key to writing and that achievement effects may take longer to accrue than the 1-week length of this study. (In fact, achievement, defined as writing fluency as measured by word count, showed no differences between the peer treatment and the other, suggesting that the system used here did *not* "damage" writing skills in the short run.)

All 187 ninth graders in the classes of three teachers were the subjects of the study. All students were "sensitized" through journal writing and the study of a unit designed to help develop empathy. At that point, attitude measures were taken, the first a researcher-made 15-item questionnaire and the second, a 40-item scale called the Emig-King Writing Attitude Scale. Over the course of the next few days, there was large group presentation, independent writing, and teacher feedback. In the peer evaluation treatment, students responded to each other's work in a "respectful" and "positive way" and encouraged partners to rewrite or improve aspects of the writing. The study does not tell us much more about specific behaviors of the peers because they were not following scripts, that is, detailed behaviors: Students were instructed not to use any "put-downs" (standard ground rules for cooperative groups) and the groups were built of heterogeneous ability-matched partners.

The results showed a clear advantage to the attitudes of the students in the peered format. Students indicated that they liked writing and reading other's writing and they sensed an improvement in their ability. Girls developed these attitudes to a greater degree than boys, offering more evidence of girls' responding particularly well to cooperative learning. In effect, the less hostile environment sought by many educators appears to be a cooperative one.

Louth, R., McAllister, C. E., & McAllister, H. A. (1990). The effects of collaborative writing techniques on freshman writing and attitudes. *Journal of Experimental Education, 61,* 215–224.

In contrast to the other reviews offered on this final outcome, the Louth et al. study is offered because it (1) utilized college freshman, a group that is simply 3 months past high school but that is often see as vastly different than K–12 youngsters; (2) used a design that required 8 weeks of instruction (not 6 days or 24 weeks); and (3) used three treatments instead of two. Other college writing studies could have been used (O'Donnell, Dansereau, Hall, & Rocklin, 1985), but this one best suits our purposes here.

One hundred thirty-six freshman served as subjects. They completed a pre-test writing sample and, after 8 weeks of study, a post-test sample that was scored and compared to measure change. Attitude measures were also taken to assess that change as well.

The three treatment conditions are interesting: the control group, independent writing that followed a standard, and a personal approach. The two collaborative approaches were as follows: Interactive writing includes such activities as brainstorming and peer evaluation, ones that involve students in each other's work but which results in a single person being responsible for his or her own piece. Group writing results in a single piece for the group, one produced by the combined efforts of all team members.

The results are slightly complicated, but interesting. Because the pretest achievement scores were highest for the independent group, there were *no* significant differences found across the three treatments on the post-test assessment of writing ability. However, secondary analyses revealed that growth within the three groups occurred *only in the two teamed structures*. Once again, students showed significant improvement in their own writing in the two cooperative conditions but not in the independent one. This is a major finding for those of us seeking to help older writers improve their abilities.

Secondly, a clear advantage in terms of attitude changes accrued to those working collaboratively, just like the one that was found with younger students. They felt better about themselves, liked writing more, and showed a greater likelihood of taking more writing courses in the future.

In closing, these authors suggest several ideas generated by their study. One, they found no evidence of "social loafing" on the parts of students; working collaboratively does not hurt learners by inducing coasting. Second, they suspected that teaching students how to interact as partners was important. While the authors did not specify roles (as did the Johnsons) or use scripts (as did Dansereau), they did show students how to learn from one another. They are absolutely convinced that this was an important aspect of the successful trial.

SPECIAL CONSIDERATIONS

In the previous section, I provided annotations for studies that supported the eight general outcomes for cooperative learning. The studies reviewed included a wide variety of subject areas and covered the gamut of subjects in terms of the K–12 population. The studies offered here provide the reader insights into a few other pieces of research that either do not directly fit into one of the eight outcome categories or that had an interesting and meaningful finding. They are reported here both to broaden the research review for the reader and to offer a few key insights into the functioning of cooperative learning. In some particular way, these studies tapped into important information for practitioners.

Gender Concerns

Webb, N. M. (1984). Sex differences in interaction and achievement in cooperative small groups. *Journal of Educational Psychology, 76*(1), 33–44.

Until the time of this study, little was known about the processes going on inside of cooperative groups. The studies by the Johnsons, Slavin, and Sharan had shown that teams worked, but no one was sure what students actually did during group work: who talked, to whom did they talk, etc. One major question unaddressed at this time regarded mixed-gender groups and this is exactly what Webb explored. She has become an absolute leader in this line of research and her studies are very important to practitioners and researchers alike.

Seventy-seven middle school subjects in mathematics classes were given a 40-item reasoning test for determining math ability and for setting a baseline. Study groups were developed that had varying ratios of males/females: five groups had two boys and two girls; six groups had one female and two boys; six groups had one boy and several females; and three groups had all boys. During a 2-week unit on exponents and scientific notation, the teams studied together. They were instructed to work together, *not* to divide the work, and to ask for help if needed. The sessions were audiotaped and transcribed. At the end of the unit, a final achievement test was administered individually to measure learning.

The results are interesting and extensive: (1) Although they were equal in ability, the males learned more than the females. (2) Females were more responsive to requests for help from others than were boys; this was true whether the seeker was male or female, a finding untrue for boys. They typically responded only to other boys. (3) Ability did not matter as much as gender while help was sought; lower ability males often got questioned more than high ability females. (4) In *equal-gender* groups (two and two) achievement was normalized, as was interaction. This finding suggests that female achievement and interaction patterns are based on numerical equality within the group. In three-boy/one-girl groups, the single girl was often ignored both when help was given and when help was sought. In three-girl/one-boy groups, the single boy was the focus of the girls' attention and most of their effort.

This is a key study and one that speaks volumes to those of us who believe that team learning will lead to both excellence and equity in the classroom: Teachers need to monitor carefully what happens within the base groups as they operate. Teaming is not enough; there must also be an equal exchange and acceptance of roles, a quality that must be sought and taught by the teacher.

Racial Interactions

Slavin, R. E., & Oickle, E. (1981). Effects of cooperative learning on student achievement and race relations: Treatment by race interactions. *Sociology of Education, 54,* 174–180.

Like the Johnson and Johnson study (1985) showing the value of cooperative controversy and the Webb (1984) study presented earlier, I consider this study to be among the absolutely critical ones for practitioners. In this study, Slavin and Oickle continued their investigation into what happens when teams are used (in this case STAD) in comparison to individual study and they looked at the English achievement of 230 middle schoolers over 12 weeks.

Two major findings resulted. The students in the teams learned more, yet this effect was "disproportionately due to outstanding gains by black students" (p. 174); there were also more cross-race friendships made, but this was due to "whites gaining black friends" (p. 174). Interestingly, this study demonstrates the powerful impact of cooperative teams on the achievement of traditionally unsuccessful students. It also suggests that teams provide a context for whites to overcome the stereotypes and biases that may well exist in larger proportion for them than for blacks. Moreover, these effects were found without the counterpart groups incurring a loss; in other words, black achievement gains did *not* come at the expense of white learning; white friendships did not "cost" black friendships; thus, school is not a zero sum game, where every gain by group X is a loss by group Y, a belief commonly held by many conservative thinkers. Apparently, cooperative learning may be disproportionately beneficial to some groups on some tasks, but it does not damage other groups' gains in the process.

Webb (1984) has shown that males and females gain the most in teams that are gender balanced; Slavin and Oickle show that nobody loses cross-gender relationships or English achievement with teamwork.

Use with Concept Mapping

> **Okebukola, P. A. (1992). Concept mapping with a cooperative learning flavor.** *The American Biology Teacher, 54*(4), 218–221.

Okebukola has conducted a series of studies on cooperative learning in high school biology in Nigeria. I chose this rather recent one for the purpose of showing that cooperative learning can be used in conjunction with other instructional strategies (see also Mevarech & Susak, 1993; Kourilsky & Wittrock, 1992; Stevens, Slavin, & Farnish, 1991) *and* because it examined the effects of teaming on students who differ in their preferences for learning styles and in their attitudes toward the use of teams. Of course, its inclusion also broadened this review's geographic base to Africa as well.

In this study, Okebukola explored teamwork and concept mapping, a technique based on Ausubel's (1968) work regarding prior knowledge and Novak's (1990) practical explanations.

One hundred forty-seven 11th graders in two schools were tested for their learning preference. In one school, 49 students then studied topics (including photosynthesis, digestion, excretion, osmoregulation, and mineral nutrition) in traditional whole-class style; they served as the control group. Three other treatments were created, each using 15 minutes (of six 80-minute classes), for teamed concept mapping exercises. Of these, one was composed of students who preferred cooperative learning and one was composed of those who did not prefer cooperative work. The third group was composed of those who preferred working alone and were allowed to do so.

The 80-item post-test measure revealed that working in one's preferred mode did *not* produce the best results, that is, the highest achievement. All three teamed groups scored higher than did the traditional class. Second, the *ranking* of achievement gain followed this pattern: prefer team, work in teams, 1; prefer alone, work in teams, 2; prefer work alone, work alone, 3. Thus, this study reveals that students can learn when they use a valuable technique (or in this case, integrated techniques) *even* if they prefer not to do so.

This finding is no minor item. Many teachers fear that "forcing" students to do teamwork will hurt them or damage them. When Okebukola did this to his students, they profited from the use of the instructional strategy. Moreover, there is reason to think that perhaps with enough successful practice using cooperative learning, those who preferred to work alone may also change their minds about their preference.

Effect of Team Failure on the Individual

Chambers, B., & Abrami, P. C. (1991). The relationships between student team learning outcomes and achievement, causal attributions and affect. *Journal of Educational Psychology, 83*(1), 140–146.

A Canadian study conducted in Montréal, this research examined the differences between team success and team failure and did not contrast teams with a control group. The subjects were 190 second through sixth graders studying mathematics for 5 weeks. Independent variables included prior achievement (high versus low), individual TGT score (success or failure), and team outcome (success or failure). At the conclusion of the treatments, a 30-item exam was given and measures of student attribution and satisfaction were taken.

Results showed that successful teams felt better about themselves, felt deserving of reward, were comparatively more likely to attribute success to ability and luck and effort, and were happier about the outcome. These results in real classrooms substantiated Ames's (1981) lab study, which had caused many teachers to worry about the effects of failure of teamwork on individuals. Like Ames, these researchers found the highest rated cause of either outcome to be effort, a finding that I am pleased with. Team success moderates the effects of individual performance in school just as it does in the sports world. The ballplayer's comment, "We won today . . . we did a good job . . . my contribution was part of the team's success" parlays his or her effort into the larger goal and has its analog in the cooperative classroom.

Like Ames (1981) these authors have a fear about the effects of failure on the low achiever, perhaps making it like a "double whammy"; they also worry about learned helplessness, a condition that may cause some teams' successful low achievers to discount their contributions. They suggest that these latter two points are unresolved issues at this time.

This study suggests that team failure outcomes (although relatively rare in noncompetitive settings where there are enough successes for everyone) may produce great stresses for low achievers. Certain groups of traditionally low achievers in school have been helped a great deal by cooperative learning, yet they may be at the greatest risk if they should fail in that setting.

Strategic Talking and the Use of Guidelines

> Melothe, M. S., and Deering, P. D. (1994). Task talk and task awareness under different cooperative learning conditions. *American Educational Research Journal, 31*(1), 138–165.

Like the previous review, this study compared two cooperative treatments in an attempt to establish patterns within these conditions. In this study, fifth graders worked together for 2 weeks under two conditions. Recognizing the importance of particular types of interaction within the groups (Webb & Farivar, 1994; O'Donnell et al., 1987; Palinscar, Brown, & Martin, 1987), one condition (the metacognitive) provided *think sheets* that forced learners to reflect and analyze their learnings. This was called the *strategic condition* and sought to improve the metacognitive activity of the subjects. The other condition, the *reward condition,* also provided think sheets for use during study-together time, but these did not probe metacognitive ideas at all. Essentially, the reward condition simply offered a stimulus that was supposed to increase effort and motivate learners to mastery and interaction.

The 206 students and their classes engaged in text-based activities on metamorphosis and in cooperative discussions (with think sheets); the interactions were observed and transcribed and, later, several students were interviewed.

The strategic condition produced more explanations, more task-related questions, and more academic content about the topic. This finding suggests that teachers should attempt to empower group members to engage in discussions that tap deeply analytical questions. These items should prompt deep processing of information, concepts, and meanings and not just rely on the promise of rewards to promote effective interaction. The authors worry that an overreliance on the strategic think sheets may result, but my interpretation is that given practice, students will learn to utilize their own effective questioning strategies. Social psychology has urged us to use rewards to produce effective interdependence within teammates, and now cognitive psychology has helped us see the value of asking questions such as these (1) When do you use that [content] elsewhere? (2) What did the group do that helped you think about this [content]? (3) How do you use this [content] when answering similar questions? (4) What information did you have or need that helped you learn this [content]?

Coercing the students to think about their thinking and to think about others' thinking may be a great asset to the effectiveness of the already better than traditional strategy of cooperative learning.

"Unlearning" Misconceptions

The final annotation that I wish to provide the reader is a very brief and yet interesting study about dealing with the science misconceptions of seventh graders. It is a *failure study* and by that I mean that it is one of a small pile of studies that have been published in which cooperative learning has *failed* to produce a positive response and, as a matter of fact, has produced significantly lower outcomes. (This result, by the way, is very different from a finding of *no difference*. Recall that reports of "no difference" findings were discussed earlier.)

It has been my contention that these studies are very interesting because they produce a dissonance or disequilibrium within the researchers and most of the readers of this book. Certainly, the followers of cooperative learning theory are troubled by these findings and need to think about what they may imply. In the following paragraphs, I describe one such study and make reference to several noteworthy others. I also hope to use this piece to balance the other selections in this chapter. Overall, there is no doubt that the research supports team learning in the proportions presented here, yet it is not a perfect system.

Snyder, T., and Sullivan, H. (1995). Cooperative and individual learning and student misconceptions in science. *Contemporary Educational Psychology, 20,* 230–235.

In this study, 385 seventh graders studied photosynthesis for 6 days in either a cooperative or an individual practice arrangement and half of those two groups were offered either an incentive (a $1 snack certificate for reaching the criterion) or were given nothing. The cooperative group was ability stratified and made to work face to face; one teammate's notebook was randomly scored each day. The individualized treatment saw students work alone during practice. It is not clear how much time during the 6 days the students actually worked together and that may be one factor that helped produce the results: The alone group scored higher on the test, although the cooperative group preferred the cooperative structure (except, notably, high-ability boys!).

The authors try to explain their surprise by noting that perhaps the teachers did not implement the technique properly, a factor related to a failure finding for a Jigsaw process in 1983 by Moskowitz et al. (Although Moskowitz's second failure study in 1985 suggested that Jigsaw is just not very powerful for academic achievement because it does not force students to work together.) While this may not have been the case for Snyder and Sullivan, they do make note of student comments ("get to work . . . you should be listening. . . . " p. 235) that indicate that the students were not practicing the necessary learning behaviors needed to make teams successful. The structure may have looked acceptable, but the student-to-student interactions were not happening; teachers cannot use team learning as a black box, that is, teachers cannot just "throw 'em together and let 'em learn." The student-to-student interactions are needed for the lesson to be effective and that is why teachers must carefully and thoughtfully plan their activities and their interventions.

Another plausible explanation for this failure is that the groups simply reinforced the misconceptions being studied; that is, the content was so hard that they simply stayed stupid together. I personally doubt this explanation; Kourilsky and Wittrock found the opposite result in favor of teams for economics concepts (1992) and, in general, team elaborations and analyses are better than those of individuals (provided they actually do the activities).

Furthermore, a Canadian researcher, Ross, has produced the final two failure studies that I want to mention. In 1988, he found that whole-class direct instruction outperformed Slavin's STAD on the development of problem-solving abilities in fourth graders. Although it appears to me that the STAD technique was an unsuitable choice to produce problem-solving skills, Ross felt that it had warranted a trial. Ross speculated that the necessary helping behaviors had not occurred as planned within the teamwork sessions. Because of the structure STAD provided, the teamed treatment did not have as much thought-provoking "time on task" as did the whole-class students. This same thing may have happened in the Snyder and Sullivan study just discussed. Again, it is clear that the teacher must help provide the structure necessary for success.

Finally, the last failure study was not really a failure but it does shed light on this last batch of reports. Ross and Cousins (1994) looked at 9th and 10th graders learning to do correlational problems under STAD conditions and studied their helping behavior as compared to their verbal intentions to help. The result was interesting: The students had talked at length about giving help in their plans, but they could not carry this out in practice. Perhaps, the words *did not* carry them out would be more appropriate. Knowing what to do and actually implementing those practices are two separate functions, as the Johnsons have known all along. That is why they teach cooperative skills and effective behaviors and other advocates use scripts, think sheets, and different roles.

It is quite possible that the study by Ross and Cousins answers the "why" behind the small set of failure studies: The students did not implement the activities correctly and just being together in groups was not enough to produce the desired outcomes. The large set of studies that have realized significant findings favoring teams without serious training may be ever so impressive because of this fact. With careful and proper training of students, future students may show teamwork to be more powerful than its history has shown it to be until now.

CHAPTER 2 SUMMARY

This chapter provided brief annotations for 38 specific cooperative learning research studies drawn from the available literature. The studies are representative of the large research base that has given theorists so much confidence in the affective and cognitive success of cooperative learning. Covering the years since 1977 and using the common forms of cooperative learning (including Jigsaw, STAD, TGT, the Johnsons' Learning Together, dyadic instruction, and group investigation) the reviews show the positive impact of the instructional strategy and its utility at every level of schooling from kindergarten to the first year of college.

Several interesting studies were included because they offer practitioners some specific insights into the setting up of their teamed activities. Among these were the following:

1. Noreen Webb's work (1984) evidences concern for middle school girls who get placed into groups unbalanced by gender. She suggests that teachers either use two-boy/two-girl groups or four-girl groups if the teacher wishes to keep the girls from being "lost" in the interaction.

2. P. A. Okebukola (1992) found that high school students who combined cooperative learning with another instructional strategy learned more than those who worked alone—even for students who *professed a preference* to work alone.

3. A recent study, by Chambers and Abrami (1991), discovered that students who fail under teamed conditions may be at a tremendous disadvantage compared to those who fail working alone. However, the *number of failure students is also drastically reduced* by teamed learning, so that this may not present a really important factor in a teacher's work. (This will hold true unless the teacher uses competitive teamed strategies, thus assuring some losers; under such conditions, the weak student may be under even more duress for having caused the team's failure.)

Overall, the research says that cooperative learning tends to produce more desirable outcomes on motivational, self-esteem, and achievement measures when compared to traditional instructional strategies and competitive or individualistic ones. This generalization is supported by studies across 13 years of schooling and is true for students of both genders, all ethnicities, and across various disabilities. Cooperative learning provides a healthy, cognitively challenging and supportive environment for all students and will succeed if several conditions are met:

1. Students should be taught why they are being asked to work together.

2. They should be shown how they are expected to interact with each other.

3. The groups should analyze (or process) their own effectiveness.

Finally, I should add that content for these many studies was drawn from the entire K–12 curriculum, which reveals that teams work well in science and social studies and English and . . . bowling! Moreover, they also are very effective in teaching students with and about computers, a point that is critically important for the many districts that are now upgrading or reconceptualizing their technology component.

The fact that students learn a lot and learn to like and respect each other when working in teams is certainly a strong argument for teachers learning to implement cooperative techniques. The fact that the plethora of available research studies comes down so heavily on the positive side of the cooperative learning ledger provides further support for the power and the promise of teamed learning structures.

REFLECTION QUESTIONS

Because of the nature of the research review, the questions posed here have a different texture and tone than those after the other chapters. I hope that some of the readers find this tactic helpful and productive.

1. The research review began with a caveat based on the tendency for many of us to dislike thinking about research. Many of us do not trust numbers and statistics and feel that they are often used to distort and obfuscate ideas. My review played down numbers intentionally, although, unintentionally, I may have also played down other components that bothered you or made you a little wary about my reports. Take several of my analyses, read them carefully, and write down five questions about the way the study was set up that my annotation did not answer. Some sample questions include:

   a. Did the researcher observe the teamwork going on as it was planned?

   b. How big was the difference in achievement favoring the teamed group?

   c. The study went on for X weeks. What did they do with subjects who had high levels of absenteeism? etc.

   After generating those questions, ask yourself this: "Does not having the answers to these questions seriously damage the credibility of the study and/or Vermette's interpretation of the study?" If your answer to either part of this question is "yes," you may want to take a look at the actual study; part of the rationale for picking them is their availability. If the answer is "no," you ought to accept the findings without further ado.

   Please note that I do trust the researchers to present their work accurately and have attempted to interpret their work for you as well as I can. I also encourage you to take a look for yourselves and to delve into new research following the pattern that I have used here.

2. *An Explanation Quiz:* To get readers to think deeply about a subject (or to look critically into it), one could simply challenge them to explain its truth. For example, if I asked a child why the moon shines, she or he would probably generate some accurate and inaccurate explanations, but she or he would probably do some actual critical thinking and later be able to recall the factual statement about the moon shining. Moreover, I would suggest that the child would likely also be far more open to examining the right answer when provided. This approach is somewhat different than asking a "true/false plus explanation" type question; this one gives you the true answer up front.

   In the following list, I offer you the findings from several more interesting and important pieces of cooperative learning research. For each, generate some plausible supporting explanations and tell them to another person. It would be helpful to reflect on your explanations as well.

T   (a)   After being trained in reciprocal teaching procedures for a paired learning activity, tutors' efforts helped increase the achievement of those tutored that had engaged in scaffolded learning activities (Palinscar, Brown, & Martin, 1987).

T   (b)   The way in which partners assess each other depends greatly on the outcome of the paired activity: Failure depressed perceptions of the partner significantly (Harris & Covington, 1993).

T   (c)   Individuals come to group work with differential statuses. To increase the effectiveness and the achievement of members, interventions must be included that improve the status of those low-status members (McAuliffe & Dembo, 1994).

T   (d)   Latino and African-American seventh-grade math students learned more in cooperative groupings after they had been taught communication skills *and* academic helping skills (Webb & Farivar, 1994).

T   (e)   Successful cooperative learning strategies can be learned by teachers engaging in long-term in-service programs; moreover, the students of these teachers tend to realize gains in reading achievement (Talmage, Pascarella, & Ford, 1984).

T   (f)   Students in cooperative learning situations are on task more than those working competitively or by themselves (Lazarowitz, Hertz, Baird, & Bowlden, 1988).

T   (g)   Low achievers in tracked high schools learn more geography using the STAD team structure than they do under traditional instructional strategies (Allen & Van Sickle, 1984).

T   (h)   Cooperative learning strategies contain differential levels of competition and these result in achievement differences for various groups: Mexican-Americans, African-Americans, and females all prospered *more* under the less competitive STAD technique than they did under the more competitive TGT (Widaman & Kagan, 1987).

T   (i)   By teaching about multiple abilities and by publicly identifying the positive abilities of low-status members of a cooperative learning group, teachers can increase their interactions and their learning without damaging the participation rates and learnings of high achievers (Cohen & Lotan, 1995).

T   (j)   By restructuring via cooperative learning, mainstreaming, peer coaching, and parental involvement, elementary school teachers raised student achievement in reading, language, and math, saw a great improvement in the accomplishments of students with disabilities, improved cross-student attitudes, and raised the achievement levels of "gifted and talented" (top 10%) students (Stevens & Slavin, 1995a, 1995b).

T   (k)   After cooperative group discussion, the thinking of male and female college students became *more* similar in terms of their understanding of sexual harassment than when they simply read about it individually (Erickson, Vermette, Cheshire, & Sheeran, 1996).

T   (l)   In *unstructured* and *loosely* organized mixed-sex cooperative teams, boys begin to like working with girls but the girls' preference for single-sex teams does not change (Lockheed, 1986).

T   (m)   Fifth- and sixth-grade immigrants to Toronto made more cross-ethnic friendships and learned more when working in Jigsaw (Ziegler, 1981) than when they were not teamed with other ethnicities.

T   (n)   College students in large classes ($n > 250$) learn more and are more likely to attend in classes where they do teamed activities than in ones where they passively take notes (Grabowski, Birdwell, Snetsinger, Lui, Hong, & Harkness, 1995).

T   (o)   College students taking a music course to become elementary teachers learn more and like music more when their grades are contingent on teammates' achievements than if they work for themselves alone (Hwong, Caswell, Johnson, & Johnson, 1992).

T   (p)   Students of diverse ethnicities learn to be tolerant and helpful toward each other when they work in stable teams for a long period of time (Wiegel, Wiser, & Cook, 1975).

3. The chart and analysis question: The 32 studies presented in the first section of the chapter have not undergone any aggregate analysis, that is, they have not been combined to examine a general pattern. There are existing approaches to do this and several have been conducted on various aspects of cooperative learning (Johnson & Johnson, 1989; Sharan, 1980; Slavin, 1986a, 1991; Qin, Johnson, & Johnson, 1995). Moreover, an informal survey approach called vote counting simply takes all the studies and counts: X favor the treatment and Y do not favor (and Z show no difference). That was not done here, either. I have simply tried to sort through hundreds of studies and select those that are most representative of the overall pattern and those I judged most valuable to you.

Now, you may be interested in doing an *internal* examination of the studies I have presented. If so, here is an interesting and informational charting system that may help you decipher patterns related to this batch of studies:

author (year)	Coop form(s)	students/grade/subject	length	journal

Here is a sample entry:

Johnson & Johnson (1985)	LT	72(urban)/6th/science	11 wks.	AERJ

Finding
Increase in self-esteem, liking of school, and interaction with others forming cooperative condition.

Please note that if you do this exercise for all 32 studies, you may find the following results:

a. Cooperative learning takes many forms, and different forms are somewhat related to different specific results. Each of the forms tends to produce better results than do traditional forms of school instruction.

b. Cooperative learning groups seem to function effectively in all grades from first to college and in all subject areas (from bowling to high school science).

c. Studies on the use of team learning have a record running from the 1970s to the present day and have been published in a wide range of established, credible journals.

d. Studies showing the effectiveness of team methods have been done in numerous countries, in different types of school settings (urban, rural, suburban), and for different durations of time. Apparently, the methods tend to be effective everywhere (certainly in North America) and do not "wear out" if implemented for more than a couple of weeks. (*Note:* This last point suggests that the research discovered gains are not attributable to the fact that this is a novel—and therefore exciting—new approach).

e. Cooperative learning works.

P A R T

t w o

THE THREE STRUCTURES OF TEAM BUILDING

GROUP BUILDING FOR SUCCESS

Much can be learned by studying the operations of a real classroom; this is especially true with regard to the group-building processes used by a teacher. Take several minutes to study Figure 3.1. As you do so, use a clean sheet of paper to jot down any insights, ideas, or theories that come to mind about the groupings of students, seating arrangements, or the teacher's habits. Moreover, ask yourself these questions: What strikes you as odd or unusual? What patterns come to mind as you try to figure out what is happening? What information is missing that would help you make sense of the picture? What data does not seem to make sense?

As you may have figured out, this illustration shows the seating arrangements and names of 30 students in a 40-minute class. It also shows the monitoring (and traffic) pattern used by the teacher, Fran Jones, during the 40 minutes of group work. What you do not know is that Jones is a student teacher and the setting is an inner-city third-period seventh-grade English class. This is Jones's first use of cooperative groups and the veteran associate teacher has chosen to leave the room. Jones's lesson did not go well; in truth, it was a failure.

Here is a sampling of the questions that other readers have generated and that you may have developed yourself:

1. Why did Jones spend so much time at the desk?
2. Why did Jones ignore three groups and spend only 3 to 5 minutes at the other stations?

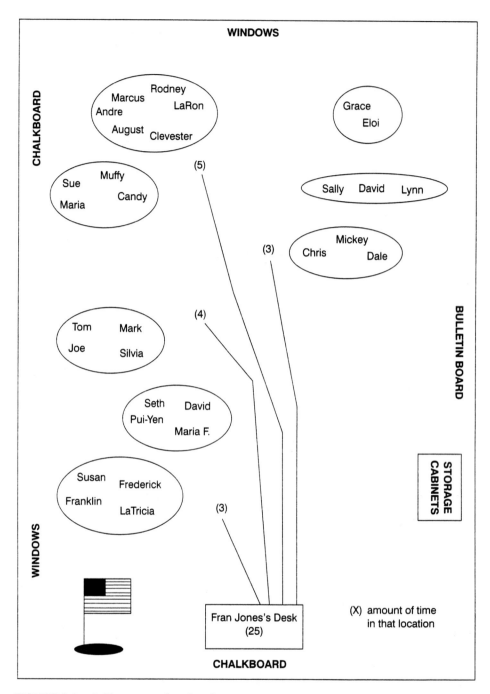

FIGURE 3.1   A Classroom Seating Arrangement

3. How did the students get assigned to teams?

4. What activity were they were doing?

5. What was done to increase the positive interdependence of the teammates?

6. What were students told about working together?

All six of these questions are great analytical probes in that they seek to uncover the structures set in place to make the lesson work. Moreover, they demonstrate the ability of the questioner to empathize with Jones. The process of asking the question may have led the reader to prepare tentative responses from Jones's point of view. (Peer collaborating and peer observation take advantage of the tendency of a person to conjure up hypothetical answers to real questions.)

Recall that the lesson failed. Several plausible explanations can be offered for such results. Look again carefully at the makeup of these teams, noting that Mickey, Lynn, Pui-Yen, and Dale are female and that Marcus, Rodney, Andre, LaRon, August, and Clevester are the six black males in the room. Moreover, note the different sizes of the groups. A pattern seems to be arising, one that suggests that Jones has let the students choose their own groups, an absolute sure-fire design for failure (Vermette, 1994b).

While there is no clear evidence in this specific case, common undesirable trends do arise when students of any age pick their own groups:

1. Students will stratify their groups by gender.;

2. The alienated, outcasts, and loners will be left alone or will group themselves as a "loser" group.

3. Friends will build play groups, not work groups.

4. Ethnic, racial, and social classes will stratify the classroom.

5. High achievers will seek to work with those they perceive to be like themselves.

6. The making of new acquaintances will become a rare event.

7. Students will not experience the true diversity that they will face in the outside world.

8. Differences of opinion and challenges to one's perceptions will become rare, thus curtailing critical thinking opportunities.

9. The increasing appreciation for diversity of talents and skills will not be a common event.

10. Stereotypes will be reinforced.

Reading through this list of consequences troubles me greatly; they are precisely the outcomes that I do *not* wish to see occur in my classroom. I want students to receive challenges to their opinions; I appreciate diversity and learn every time I work with someone different from myself—as should the students; and, finally, I think that it is important for me to interact effectively with people unlike myself in terms of gender, ethnicity, and social class and wish the same for my students.

Given these beliefs, and the research findings already cited about diversity, three general propositions surface about group building: (1) The teacher should build and periodically rotate membership in the teams, (2) a blending of diversity and similarity should govern the construction (a "mixed balance"), and (3) the teacher should use both private decision-making and public announcements to construct teams.

Let us examine each proposition carefully and then provide some examples so you can practice with implementing each one.

THREE PROPOSITIONS FOR TEAM CONSTRUCTION

The Teacher Builds the Teams

Left to their own devices, students will not build the most effective teams. Even if some students self-select into effective groups, others will not; moreover, some students will be left out all together and, most certainly, respect for individual strengths will be ignored. Cohen (1994) has postulated that youngsters see each other's value as students contained solely in their reading scores and many students will find themselves out in the cold or in teams of kids that high-achieving students did not want to work with. Others will find no one "wants" to work with them.

Aside from the clear negative stratifications that would occur, another undesirable outcome awaits teachers who let the students pick their teammates, namely, the reinforcement of the idea that the world is set up to convenience students and will continue to allow them a choice regarding associates. In the rest of the world, choice is limited. Aside from friendships (which are not the goal of student teams), very few relationships in the modern world are clearly chosen. Some examples provide thoughtful examination:

1. Although we may pick our spouses, the in-laws, friends of the family, and neighbors come along without choice.

2. To a certain degree, we may "choose" our job (in most cases, the first one that comes along!) but we definitely do *not* pick our co-workers, our partners, our bosses, and/or our clients/customers.

3. We can pick our school, but not our classmates or our teachers.

4. We can even pick our organizations (Little League, parish, PTA) but we cannot choose the members of those organizations.

Thus, in the *real* world, relationships are often foisted on individuals, and the ability to cope effectively in these situations is a central one to success. Students should be made aware of this cultural reality and learn to accept teacher-structured teams as an analog of the outside world and as an opportunity to develop positive attitudes and social skills.

Diversity and Similarity

In addition to the previous points, students should be made aware of the positives associated with working with diverse populations. First, different people have different strengths and these will be modeled for all individuals during teamwork. One learns from associates. Also, others will be in a position to appreciate the skills and knowledge that the individual brings to the mix. In many cases, more peers will like and respect the individual. For example, while Katie, age 9, is learning to understand, appreciate, and model Jackie's abilities, she is also being appreciated for her own abilities. Life becomes a two-way street and a wider circle of positive experiences is inevitable under a teamed system.

Private and Public Considerations

The third proposition concerns the factors used by the teacher when building the teams. Although more detail is offered shortly, suffice to say here that certain rationales for compositions should not be made public. For example, we might cringe to hear a teacher suggest that students were put together to beef up the weakness of one particular student or that a group needed a particular student because he represents the "white perspective" or the "Hindu viewpoint" on an issue.

I like to think that I have never made a bad group. In fact, I often like to say "Some people say that God doesn't make trash . . . well, I've never made a bad group . . . your team has a great blend of strengths and skills that you will discover and uncover in due time." This is intended to challenge the students to see each other in a positive light and to avoid the negativism that can arise out of a perception of tokenism or a *balance of weaknesses.*

So, please note that the teacher needs to explain the teaming policy, not just construct the group. Both of these are central to group building: Without good teams and a good rationale, the cooperative team may begin to unravel.

TEAM SIZES

Like many of the areas of decision making within the cooperative learning community, the decision about group size has revolved around the results of formal research studies such as those reported in Chapter 2 and the practice of teachers who have used teams in their classes on a regular basis. Clearly, there is agreement on several topics within this debate, as discussed in the following paragraphs.

Avoid Teams of Five or More

Groups larger than four present problems that otherwise would not exist and that endanger the functioning of the team. For one thing, it is much easier for a reluctant student (or a lazy one) to hide or play a reduced role in groups of five or larger. Moreover, it is difficult to account for everyone's opinion or input during class work and it is much more difficult to orchestrate outside responsibilities as well. Although research found (Blaney, Aronson, Rosenfield, Stephan, & Sikes, 1977) that Jigsaw was successful with a group of six, recall that Jigsaw relies heavily on independent work and does not utilize the group discussion and problem-solving activities that are favored here.

Harken back to those great college classes called *seminars* that you or an associate took. Seminars were often billed as small classes that would provide lots of discussion, an opportunity to really get to know the instructor, and a chance to exchange ideas with fellow students. Very rarely were they as small as 5 students; in fact, they were usually 12 to 15 with only a few students participating; many of the students merely watched and listened, or were just ignored.

Any team larger than five students would only work under extraordinary conditions and I would never advise a teacher to place more than four in a regular classroom situation.

Teams of Two

Pairs of students work well in teams—as you can imagine, it is very difficult to drop out of a pair! Moreover, paired learning carries with it the benefit of high interdependence because many activities require student 1 to learn about, teach, or investigate student 2. There is nothing more motivating than being needed; therefore, a team of this size has great potential.

Furthermore, a great deal of college research has been done with pairs (King, 1990; O'Donnell & Dansereau, 1993) and has shown the system to be a success.

However, several potential flaws can arise when using pairs. For one, the issue of absenteeism requires the teacher to mix and match certain cross-team partners on a regular basis or have some students work alone on some days. A sense of continuity is easily lost.

Second, research has only been done in same-sex pairs. If imitated at the K–12 levels, a potentially effective gender experience will have been lost. Cross-gender interactions in teams can be a tremendously positive experience and limiting teams to same-sex pairs cannot promote this possibility.

Furthermore, while pairs can make the students more active, they can also limit the number of insights available for discussion and can cut into the potential skill and knowledge base of the problem solvers. Four students can simply generate more ideas than can two. Four students also have broader skill and experiential bases than do two students. Moreover, such pairings might be interpreted as pushing the limits of intimacies such that certain students might be intimidated by being part of a pair.

In summary, well-monitored pairs can provide tremendous sharing and learning experiences. They may also limit the possibilities within a team and create uncomfortable scenarios for some students.

Ideal Team Sizes

By definition, it looks like teams will often be made up of three or four students! The research base has most frequently used these sizes and it has shown a great deal of success for cooperative teams. With three or four students, the teacher could reasonably expect a balance of interests and personalities, a mix of strengths and talents, a broader range of Gardner's intelligences, a divergence of philosophical perspectives, differing levels of perseverance, and a good chance at sparking some creativity.

For the most part, teachers prefer using teams of four more often than anything else. It allows a full mix of ideas, sufficient opportunities for sharing, plenty of diversity, and room for consensus to be found on different items among the different membership. Teachers report that groups of four often end up discussing things in a familiar pair and pair format, with ultimate resolution crossing the pairs and engaging the entire team. Four is also small enough to keep track of everyone's individual contribution over several days' worth of activities and it allows more room for mixing of genders, ethnicities, religions, social classes, and learning styles. Furthermore, most of the research reported in Chapter 2 that dealt with integrating children with disabilities into mainstream heterogeneous teams used groups of four; such a structure allowed these children to participate fully and become accepted by teammates. The research also saw the stereotypes of nondisabled students diminish quickly.

In summary, advantages can be found in groupings of two, three, or four students. Few, if any, advantages accrue to teams larger than four at any grade level. The choice of the group size may then hinge on the personalities of the four students, the purposes of the exercises and activities, and the desire of the teacher to maximize the opportunities for diversity at that time.

An example may help the reader see an application. On the first day of a Niagara University course that I teach, I wanted the 40 students to meet someone else to lower the feelings of anxiety that exist on the first day. It was my intention to get a feeling for the academic abilities of the students. I also hoped to introduce them to the expectations of working cross-culturally and collaboratively across gender. I also sought to have them appreciate the unique skills of their fellow students and learn that the bell curve is broken in my class.

A simple solution was generated. After a brief introduction and an explanation of the purposes of the task, students were assigned to cross-gender pairings. The students then conducted a cross-cultural interview of the partner, focusing on his or her name. The interviews took 20 to 25 minutes (I observe each pairing extensively) and were followed by an introduction session in which pairs were combined to create mixed foursomes. (At this point the few same-sex pairs that were required because of unbalanced numbers gained access to at least one member of the other gender.) Oral introductions were made and the groups of four also cooperatively evaluated the exercise in terms of its accomplishment of the stated objectives.

This exercise is a safe, important, meaningful, active, and interesting opening foray into a study of getting along (in this case, the cultural meanings of a name). It is a tremendous help in getting the course started and in getting students to appreciate and enjoy working with an assigned diverse assortment of other students.

Practice Session 1: How Should These Students Be Grouped?

Having provided an overview to the critically important team composition problem, it is time to let you try your hand at constructing some groups. I have provided you with brief descriptions of twelve 10th graders from an inner-city school. They provide a diverse lot so many factors can be built into the teaming. On a separate sheet of paper, construct either three or four teams, thus holding to the most common and effective team sizes of three or four. Also note that you should be building the teams as I have suggested. Please keep track of the rationale used for the construction and consider what positive things you could say publicly about the teams as they go to work.

Maurice (age 17): The third illegitimate son of a local drug pusher, Maurice has been in trouble in school for years. An IQ measured at 90 and a great truancy problem have resulted in a boy who hates school, is angry at authority, and has poor skills. He has no stated future aspirations, except to date Heather.

Susie (age 15): Susie ranks 15 in her class of 194 and plans to be an orthopedic surgeon. She is a nice, clean-cut, attractive girl. Very verbal, she also is class president. She scored 100 in the Course I Mathematics Regents Examination last year.

Honey (age 16): The youngest of six children, her grades have been a solid 78. She has plans to become a social worker or a beautician. She does not spell well or write fluently, but has a good memory. She is a dedicated Jehovah's Witness. She hangs out with Denise.

Mookie (age 15): A self-proclaimed "good athlete," Mookie is a sharp dresser, snappy "jive" talker, and all-around cool guy. Extremely verbal and aggressive, Mookie "comes onto" girls quite a bit; they generally dislike him *and* laugh at his jokes. He once got a 90 in eighth-grade art class.

Michael Walter (age 16): A shy and rather effeminate young man, he is frequently laughed at by most of his fellow students. He cries easily and yet is quietly attaining an 88 average, and is respected as the school authority on jazz. His oldest brother was murdered in a botched robbery attempt 2 years ago.

Belinda (age 15): A hardened, unpleasant, and tough young girl, she found this school to be the first from which she has not been expelled. Socially promoted from district to district (and state to state), she is withdrawn, bitter, and pitiable. A large, hulking figure, she is also a lousy dresser.

Jose Carlos (age 16): The eldest son of two local college professors, JC is a rather unmotivated underachiever (with a 72 average). With his rock-group-of-the-day

T-shirt adorning his back, his sly (almost slick) approach is either seen as cool or a complete turnoff. He almost always chews a toothpick and wears a baseball hat.

Heather (age 15): White, pretty, well made up, and slim, Heather is a solid 78 average, never-in-trouble kid with a very small vocabulary. Noted around school only as a "cool babe who knows rap," her teachers are aware of her ambition to someday become a model, or just someone who hangs out. Last made honor roll in the first quarter of seventh grade.

Chris (age 16): Chris is a plain, quiet, and ordinary youngster in every way. Chris is not athletic, having been cut from both the soccer team and from drama; once Chris wrote a poem for the fourth-grade newsletter. Chris has a pet dog named Chipper and wears Chipper T-shirts.

Nilish Wong (age 16): Nilish's father was a Chinese nationalist and mother a Native American. Orphaned at age 13, he lives with a foster family and has a houseful of "siblings." A brilliant loner, he has become a follower of an obscure religious sect and dresses in traditional clothing often. His goals are to become a holy man and a scientist; he carries a 93.2 average. He once had a story published by the *New Yorker*!

LaDay (age 17): LaDay is a 6 foot, 7 inches, 235-pound all-star athlete. His IQ was once measured at 130 but his former school district put him in Option I and called him "retarded." He wants to be a pro athlete and go to a major college (and major in education). He also has a tendency to become violent when frustrated, although he has no police record.

Denise (age 15): A pert, vivacious, and pleasant girl, Denise carries an 81 average toward her college major, pre-law. An immaculate dresser, she is everyone's "favorite kid." She likes cats, but is allergic to them.

Some Possible Combinations

I asked three relatively new secondary teachers to also build the groups and share with us their rationales for the composition. To provide some comparisons, I did not hold them to the three- or four-person team limit, nor did I ask what they would say publicly. We do have their thoughts about teaming and their private rationales. As you read their responses, compare their thoughts with yours.

Rose Mastroianni, a foreign language teacher, created these groupings:

1. Denise, Honey, Mookie, Belinda, Heather
2. Susie, Nilish Wong, Michael Walter, Maurice
3. Jose Carlos, Chris, LaDay.

Group 1 In a group of five, Rose placed Denise, Honey, Mookie, Belinda, and Heather. Her rationale is as follows: Denise seems to be a person who speaks her mind and would not be easily manipulated or influenced, suggesting that she could handle a "cool guy" like Mookie. Since Honey wants to be a social worker she will have the opportunity to experience three very different and opinionated young men and women. Since Honey does not spell well or write fluently, needed instruction can be best conducted in small groups when it involves slow-paced learning. For example, activities designed to promote social awareness and acceptance would help her greatly in this setting.

Instructing students in appropriate interpersonal and small-group skills is important. Students cannot merely be placed together and told to cooperate. Mookie needs instruction in ensuring that he participates actively in groups and that he treats everyone with respect. He will eventually learn to do the assigned tasks and work cooperatively and the teacher should focus on that aspect of his performance.

Since Honey and Denise are friends, they are already comfortable with each other and therefore the atmosphere in their group will be less tense than otherwise. Perhaps if Belinda sees how much fun these two can have with school she might be motivated to learn and she will want to become a part of school. The teacher should monitor the group to ensure that Belinda is not excluded.

If Heather recognizes that she is interdependent with other members of her group she will realize that she can make a difference. She will perhaps be influenced by the achievers in her group and bring her academic achievement up to the level she once had and have higher expectations for career opportunities.

Group 2   Rose's second group included Susie, Nilish Wong, Michael Walter, and Maurice. Susie's nature might enjoy being involved in the Slavin program of Team-Games-Tournament. It would be a productive activity for her and perhaps the curriculum will seem more interesting to her. Also, both she and Nilish Wong would be comfortable in the Learning Together program, taking advantage of heterogeneity.

This team would be a good place for Michael Walter to begin to experience cooperative learning especially if he has not done so previously. By making it clear that it is acceptable for students not only to talk but to contribute directly through sharing ideas, he would build up his self-confidence and learn to trust those he works with. He does not have to take part in the extracurricular activities that Susie and Nilish enjoy, but just being around them will possibly motivate him.

Rose would put Maurice in with these three students because they are mature and dedicated students from whom Maurice can learn a great deal. Also, she felt he and Nilish might be able to relate to one another because both their home situations cannot be classified as "normal." They both basically had to learn how to survive independently.

Group 3   Rose put Jose Carlos, Chris, and LaDay together in an incentive structure program. (This is also called a *reward structure* or a *goal structure* program and refers to methods used for motivating students to perform the task. Students are rewarded or not rewarded based on whether they meet specified performance criteria, regardless of how the rest of the class performs.) In Chris's case the rewards should be properly implemented and not taken away from him because he cannot succeed in a task. (*Author's note:* Rose interpreted Chris to be male and built her groupings with that in mind.) If students give their all they should be rewarded for the effort. If someone is able to reach Jose Carlos and motivate him to learn, he may change his attitude toward school and being around Chris might help. LaDay has college aspirations so he might be a good influence on both Jose Carlos and Chris.

The next teacher, Brian Carlson, a biology teacher, created these groupings:

1. Susie, Maurice, LaDay
2. Nilish, Belinda, Honey
3. Denise, Jose Carlos, Mookie
4. Heather, Chris, Michael Walter.

In an attempt to recognize the ownership inherent in this process, Brian's rationales are presented in his own voice:

In accordance with advice from Good and Brophy (1994) and Slavin (1986), I have attempted to construct the groups with either one high achiever and two low achievers or, as in the case of group 4, three average achievers. Good and Brophy suggest that these two combinations will work the best to promote interaction between group members. I have also attempted to create as much diversity (heterogeneity) in each group as possible while keeping in mind the individual needs of the low achievers (Clarke, Wideman, & Eadie, 1990). Research indicates that high achievers will perform well no matter what situation they are in (Bennett & Cass, 1988; Mulryan, 1989). This being the case, and with an eye to giving each group the benefit of a high achiever's perspective and input, I began by simply splitting the three obvious high achievers, Denise, Nilish, and Susie, into three separate groups.

My next priority was to try to place the lowest achievers into situations that may be most beneficial to them. With Maurice I put LaDay because he is an intelligent underachiever who has some direction and may be able to relate to Maurice or at least have a positive influence on the others by modeling career goals. In group 2, I put Belinda, who really needs help, and Honey, a person with a generous nature. I am hoping that Honey, who is a Jehovah's Witness and has aspirations of being a social worker, will be able to somehow work with Belinda and with Nilish and be able to draw the best out of Belinda, bringing her into group interactions. This is asking a lot and I would plan to keep a close eye on this group.

In group 2, I assigned Mookie and Jose Carlos, two "stylin'" guys. Working with Denise, this should prove to be the best working and highest achieving group. No one would appear to be in danger of being shut out, and neither Mookie or Jose Carlos is academically snobbish enough to prevent group interaction because they only want to listen to their own ideas. Denise may also have a good influence on the underachieving Jose Carlos.

Finally, group 4 is made up of three average achievers perhaps with the exception of Chris. (*Author's note:* Brian does not seem to use Chris's gender as a criterion for placement.) I am hoping that Michael Walter and Chris may find some commonalties and that Chris will rise to the level of the group. It might be good for both of their egos to be in the same group with one of the more popular girls in the class. This group will also bear close observation to make sure it functions well.

Adjustments may have to be made to all these groups after a period of time especially if there are any unforeseen pairings that are destructive, although it is best to catch these before the groups are made up. (*Note:* Separating members of a nonfunctioning group should only be done as a last resort because the message it sends to the rest of the class is not good. If it needs to be done, it should probably be hidden within a general shifting of groups.)

Julie Grando is a science and biology teacher. She chose these groupings:

1. Mookie, Michael Walter, Nilish Wong, Belinda
2. Honey, Chris, Heather, Jose Carlos
3. LaDay, Susie, Denise, Maurice.

As with Brian, Julie's rationales are presented in her own voice:

What a diverse bunch of kids! I have arranged the students in pairs and then into base groups. In a science class the pairs would serve as lab partners. With such a diverse bunch of kids they would all benefit from working with each other at one point during the course. I have listed one possible combination that I would work with for perhaps the first two units. The pairs and the groups would in all likelihood be changed with two exceptions. If either Maurice or Belinda is responding to their partners then I would not change their pairings. These kids carry so much dislike of school with them into the classroom that if there is a positive reaction I would not want to risk ruining it ("if it ain't broke, I won't fix it").

Base Pair 1: Mookie and Michael Walter. Mookie, who is oozing with "manness" (though generally not too successful in the girl department) might serve as an interesting role model to the effeminate Michael. If Michael only picks up on some of Mookie's "cool guy" mannerisms as desired, then perhaps he would improve his social standing. Mookie can learn a few study habits from Michael as well as some sensitivity.

Base Pair 2: Nilish Wong and Belinda. I hope this one works! I am giving Nilish an opportunity to decide if he really wants to be a holy man. Most holy men are associated with healing. Belinda needs lots of healing. Although he is a loner, he seems to have found a way to cope with the difficulties in this life, whereas Belinda has not. I am also hoping that they both realize that there are other people who face life's problems. I hope (and hope is the key to this pairing) Nilish will pull Belinda out of her negative world and give her a few study tips so she can experience some success in school.

Base Pair 3: Heather and Chris. These appear to be two ordinary kids. Chris appears to be more comfortable with language than Heather. Hopefully it will rub off on her. Being more social, Heather will probably help Chris along with some of his social skills. (*Author's note:* Julie assumes Chris to be male.)

Base Pair 4: LaDay and Susie are the high IQ pair of the class. However, LaDay needs to be motivated to reach his potential, which hopefully Susie can help with.

Susie needs someone who is her intellectual equal but also presents a challenge. I think LaDay fits the bill.

Base Pair 5: Denise and Maurice. I know Maurice wants to be with Heather, but I thought that by pairing those two there would not be much school work done though attendance might increase. However, what would happen if Heather gave him the rub-off? He might leave school again. So, Denise, who can survive even if her partner does not show up to class (very likely in this case), and Maurice become partners. Maurice would give Denise a wonderful opportunity to study the effects of the law on an individual. Denise also seems to be an easy person to get along with and has good study skills, which would be to Maurice's benefit.

Base Pair 6: Honey and Jose Carlos. Jose Carlos needs a role model concerning working to your full potential. Though Honey is not brilliant she must apply herself in some way to achieve a 78 average. Jose Carlos may be Honey's first case as a social worker.

Groups can be used to review test materials in group presentations or for "big labs" (those that are more complex or those with less available equipment). The following larger teams are formed by joining base pairs.

Group 1   Base pairs 1 and 2 consisting of Mookie, Michael Walter, Nilish, and Belinda. I doubt Belinda would cause as severe a distraction in Mookie's schoolwork as another girl would. Nilish is the intellectual of the group and Mookie is the social leader. Michael Walter, though not quite as intelligent as Nilish, is at the same level; hopefully the two would be able to relate at that level.

Group 2   Base pairs 3 and 6 consisting of Honey, Chris, Heather, and Jose Carlos. The first three are good kids, and Jose Carlos is just a little misdirected. They are academically at the same level but Honey and Heather will probably add the additional motivation necessary for the group to function well.

Group 3   Base pairs 4 and 5 consisting of LaDay, Susie, Denise, and Maurice. Maurice is the only one out of his intellectual depth in this group. However, he needs all the positive role models that he can find. These kids will be responsible for helping him understand his work so as to decrease his frustration. He will in all likelihood not be a leader in this group but he will be kept on task. My only concern is that the other kids will catch on quickly and leave him behind. I might try to prepare Maurice before the lab so he feels that he is on equal footing with the others when he walks into the class and "wows them" with his knowledge. [Elizabeth Cohen (1994) has suggested that strategy; it would bring him up to a more "equal" footing with the others.]

Author's Comments

In reviewing the preceding examples of group building, it is instructive to note that each of the three teachers teamed differently and had different explanations for their groups. All three groupings were well defended and well supported. (You may want to write each teacher's "public pronouncement" about the teams. Note that perceived weaknesses did surface during the decision-making process but these should not be promoted publicly at any time.)

Note the plurality of considerations used to match teammates: Low ability means that Honey needs potential helpers and Belinda is perceived as needing a positive role model (Rose); high achievers do not need to work together to maintain quality so Denise, Nilish Wong, and Susie should be separated (Brian); and Nilish Wong can use opportunities to practice his moral and religious convictions and can be of great personal help to Belinda (Julie). The three teachers provide as diverse a set of reasons as I can imagine.

Moreover, please look carefully at your own treatment of Chris. Chris appears to be a plain, ordinary, and easily overlooked youngster, especially in this class of strong personalities. Rose wants him to associate with two boys who may motivate him, Julie sees Heather as a good model of social skills for him, and Brian sees Chris, regardless of gender, benefiting from direct contact with a popular girl. Thus expectations and the placing of Chris may have changed with perceived gender.

Now, the gender neutrality of Chris's description was not a trick or an attempt to frustrate. It was designed to force awareness of some of the factors that actually go into the group-building process. Gender, a key variable in anyone's personality and to their individuality, obviously matters and yet it may *not* dominate all other factors (i.e., for Brian, it did not matter at all).

Gender is just one of many factors that go into the art, not the science, of team compositions. As you can see, the teachers we have listened to actually used personality and its motivating possibilities as the key decision-making factor. My own experiences verify this trend. Teachers who build teams often do it by sensing who will have a positive impact on someone else and who will work well together. This is the "stuff" of art and not science, although in the next section I offer some suggestions about the process.

CONSIDERING CERTAIN CHARACTERISTICS

As the teacher sits down to look over her class roster, many teaming variables come to mind. Some are clearly more important than others, a fact demonstrated by our guest teachers' comments. As a warm-up exercise, look at the following list of factors and then judge them by their relative importance: H = high, M = medium, L = low.

_____ 1. academic ability/achievement

_____ 2. social class

_____ 3. race/ethnicity

_____ 4. handedness

_____ 5. religion

_____ 6. gender

_____ 7. personality

      _____ 8. previous success at team learning

      _____ 9. learning style

      _____ 10. aspirations

      _____ 11. perseverance

      _____ 12. birth order

Interestingly, the various mixing of these variables has not been the focus of exhaustive empirical research, yet they have been used as real factors by various teachers in their practice.

Perhaps item 8, previous success at team learning, supersedes the others, because if someone has had success previously, she or he will know how to do teams, want it to succeed, and have both positive expectations and the necessary social skills. However, assume that the teacher has never seen students work in groups or pairs before. Assume also that the teacher wants the first experience to be very positive so the pressure is on to create "great teams." What should be made of the other factors? Let us deal with them in groups based on similarity of importance.

Academic Ability, Perseverance, and Aspirations

Much of the research reviewed in Chapter 2 utilized teams constructed around the single variable of academic ability/achievement. The key operative suggestion was to balance achievements across teams, as was done by Brian. The models suggested by Slavin, Teams–Games–Tournaments (TGT) and Students–Teams–Achievement–Divisions (STAD), require intrateam study for interteam competition and a balance of achievement is therefore required (he literally calls for an equal average in each group). The Johnsons have discovered a great positive benefit for low achievers who worked in mixed groups, and the research cited by Slavin (1991) states unequivocally that high achievers are not hurt by heterogeneous ability grouping.

This last statement needs to be emphasized. Mixing high- and low-ability students with average-ability students does *not* damage the learning of the high achievers. Most opposition to cooperative learning has come from people fearing the "dumbing down" of the bright and/or the "abuse" of the gifted as teachers or peer tutors. The research, however, says that, when done well, cooperative learning has a great positive impact on the learning and conceptual development of bright kids.

Ironically, low achievers also show great gains in teams that are heterogeneous mixes of ability. These students profit from access to and interaction with the top students. It would be a mistake to group the slowest students together.

It is interesting to note that my own research suggests that teachers who use cooperative learning a great deal strive to temper ability with other traits such as aspirations and perseverance. It is as if they are not as concerned with the level of intelligence a student has, but how hard she or he will work to use it. Often, they see a hard-working, B-average student with high aspirations as the potential intellectual leader of a newly formed team and will balance these youngsters across teams. Every group needs someone to push them, to remind them of their task and to motivate them. Sometimes this type of leadership comes from the brightest students, but often it does not.

Social Class, Handedness, Religion, and Race/Ethnicity

Imagine for a minute a teacher announcing new groupings: "Marge, they need a girl over there. You're it." "Anthony, Vito, Tony . . . you guys will need a Polish kid . . . Stan, you go with those guys." Or "Wanda, Graeme, Phillip, . . . Jesse, you're from lower town, you work with those preppies." Finally, "Guido, a Catholic, Roosevelt, a Baptist, and Gloria, a Lutheran . . . you'd better work with Haim, he's Jewish." *UGH!*

In each of these cases, the student faces the serious problem articulated in the work of Miller and Harrington (1992). In every one, the students are being set up to see the last team member as a token representative of a particular group and not as an individual. This is an important issue if the student is also seen as a member of an outgroup, one with lower power or social standing. Minority status carries a negative connotation and it makes acceptance and inclusion in the team problematic.

Obviously, there is nothing wrong with being Jewish, or left-handed, or in a low-income bracket or Hispanic, but being perceived as having no value other than as a representative of the group places the student at a disadvantage. Thus, statistical replication of demographic realities cannot be the only factor used by the teacher as he or she builds groups.

Going back to the earlier example of Jones's room, we recall that all six African-American boys segregated themselves when allowed to build their own team. If the teacher separates all of them and instead divides them evenly across six groups, it would suggest that they are being asked to play a role in each team, a role that is not personal or individual but stereotypical.

The answer to this challenge is to build balanced and mixed teams, but *not* to use category membership as the only criterion, especially as the only public one. For example, Haim might feel a lot better about being in his group if the teacher had said this instead: "In group three, we have Guido, Roosevelt, Gloria, and Haim . . . a good mix of perspectives and opinions and a whole team of hard workers. That group should have very loud and effective discussions."

Many of you reading this are asking "Why does the teacher have to say anything at all about the team? Whatever is said may also be damaging. . . . " The answer is very controversial and important: If the teacher does not speak to the qualities of the specific group, he or she *must* speak to the qualities embedded in every team in a general sense. Students are very curious about the grouping process and need to know something about how decisions were made. Listen again, as the teacher does things slightly differently here: "Every team is loaded with a mix of opinions and with strengths. Each has been blended to maximize all kinds of things and you will discover the strengths of your partners in a short time. Guido, you're with Roosevelt, Gloria, and Haim. Max, you're with. . . . " Done this way, positives are accentuated and a call has been made to look for individual strengths, a more desirable practice to many readers.

If, however, nothing is said at all and Miller and Harrington are right, students will perceive certain kids as tokens for their teams. It will simply be assumed that they were assigned that way and it will have damaging consequences. ("Oh, so Haim is gonna be our team's non-Christian.") Thus, this otherwise neutral-sounding pronouncement may also produce problematic overtones: "OK, get in the teams that I've assigned. Guido, Roosevelt, Gloria, and Haim."

The ideal group is made up of a blend of race, religion, interests, abilities, social class, gender, and handedness and sees itself not as a group of token representatives but as a team of diverse individuals. Someday, diversity will be seen as strength by everybody and the fear of negative tokenism will disappear.

In closing, let us look at the issue of handedness for a moment. Some readers will think that the inclusion of handedness in this category is ludicrous, yet I find it instructive. There is some support for the belief that being left-handed makes a huge difference in schooling, especially for young males. In effect, being left-handed is sometimes seen as a huge detriment to success. Therefore, having a lefty on the team may be undesired or the focus of many jokes. Interestingly, a presentation at an Association of Teacher Educators conference years ago saw presenters advise teachers to group all the lefties together for their own mutual support and understanding. Once again, we face the dilemma of segregating the individuals of a single trait, thus denying them access to others, or mixing them with a fear of prejudice or tokenism.

The answer here is simple and provides an analog to the other factors discussed: Mix students according to many traits, not just the one that may be perceived as negative. Shawn, a lefty, is also a Baptist, a Democrat, a liberal, a good guy, a hard-working B student, a baseball player, a good storyteller, a saxophonist, a Grateful Dead fan, etc. He is more than just a left-hander and actually is more than the sum total of all his category memberships. He is an individual and should be perceived that way; the perception of his placement in a group should reinforce that view.

Gender

The third somewhat important factor is that of gender and it is too simplistic to just say "mix" on this variable. Two distinct sources of data suggest that the ratio of males and females in a group may not involve *only* the issue of tokenism described earlier but may also involve distinct cultural roles as well.

The first source is represented by the long line of well-constructed studies conducted by Noreen Webb of the University of California at Los Angeles. As discussed in Chapter 2, Webb has been interested in the actual internal workings of cooperative learning groups and has done great work in middle school math classrooms. Her findings can be summarized by these two generalizations:

1. Girls in female-majority groups spend their time making sure that the boy of the group learns the material, is attended to, and enjoys himself. In short, he is catered to extensively.

2. Boys in male-majority groups spend their time ignoring the girl(s), letting her exist in a quasi-isolated state.

Both of these findings suggest that girls are automatically at risk in cooperative learning groups, a theme trumpeted by the Sadkers in their 1994 work, *Failing at Fairness*. While Webb's findings may be largely attributable to the nature of middle adolescence and/or mathematics content, they do exist and should be noted. At the very least, there is evidence that boys will ignore girls when they have other males around, and that females will disproportionately attend to a male when he is found in the minority. Teachers should be aware of these possibilities in their own work and may simply want to ensure that groups either (1) do not have a solitary female or (2) consist of all females. Ironically, the Sadkers seem to prefer the latter structure, citing as evidence data on the effectiveness of all-girl schools.

The second source of data is from Deborah Tannen's two major works (1990, 1994) on communication patterns among Western females and males. In short, Tannen postulates that men use talk to solve problems, build hierarchies, and maintain power, whereas women tend to use it for absolutely different ends, including the building of communities, forging connections, developing rapport with equalitarian standards, and simply for venting. Since these adult patterns exist, they must have formative analogs among youth and teachers should watch for these patterns in the behavior of their students.

The real issue of examining and monitoring interteam communication is one of the foci of Chapter 5, so more will be said then. Suffice to say here that a two-male and two-female team typically (*not* stereotypically) may be a true cross-cultural group. Assuming that different expectations and roles have been in effect in their lives, the students in such a team probably have individuals aboard who are (1) sensitive to others' opinions, (2) open to meeting new people, (3) interested in solving or completing the task at hand, and (4) willing and happy to serve in a leadership capacity. All four qualities would help make a team productive. If Tannen is right, a teacher has a high probability of getting at least three of those four desirable qualities in a team by simply building it along the lines of a 50–50 gender split (which, of course, satisfies Webb's key concern). Those four qualities, along with intelligence, perseverance, willingness to encourage others, and the ability to stay on track, contribute greatly to a team's success, and the balance provided by half male/half female teams makes them likely to be found.

Quite simply, by balancing genders in a group, we might anticipate these results:

1. The girls are less likely to be ignored.

2. The boys are less likely to always be the leader.

3. Both genders will have a chance to examine different communication styles at close range.

4. A mix of positive qualities is more likely to occur than would develop in single-sex teams.

5. There is a greater chance that more complex and effective cross-gender relationships will develop and these will prove to be more equalitarian than past cross-gender patterns have been.

In fact, the final result listed is not just a hypothesis or wishful thinking; it is the finding of several research studies during the past 15 years (Warring, Johnson, Maruyama, & Johnson, 1985; Johnson, Johnson, Scott, & Ramolae, 1985).

Although cross-gender relationships have been seen as more difficult to build than cross-race relationships (Cooper, Johnson, Johnson, & Wilderson, 1980), these two studies provide evidence that they do occur. Compared to the abysmal existing cross-gender interactions in regular modern classrooms, getting the sexes to work together and treat each other with dignity would be a great advance.

Disabilities

The various studies reviewed in Chapter 2 (Johnson, Johnson, DeWeerdt, Lyons, & Zaidman, 1983; Johnson, R. T., & Johnson, D. W., 1981; Slavin, Madden, & Leavey, 1984) indicate that fully including students with disabilities benefits them and benefits the attitudes of nondisabled students. Thus, the "mix" and "blend" advice given earlier holds true here as well.

Birth Order and Learning Style

Among the many attempts at defining differences in style or personality, two topics have made it into common discussions and yet hold low importance for team building. Birth order (position among one's siblings in the life of the family) seems to have some predictive ability for variables such as perseverance, responsibility, and drive. However, I never seek this information about students and do not use it for decision making because I have better evidence for the same variables. In other words, on this variable I can predict perseverance better from observation than from a data bank.

Second, many attempts at defining learning style have left us with quite a bit of confusion. A review by Ellis and Fouts (1993) suggests that all we really need to know is that students are different in their abilities and they need to work from their strengths and build on their weaknesses. There is no research to suggest proper structuring or balancing of various styles. Even a major advocate of this approach, Rita Dunn, suggests that students need exposure to styles with which they are unfamiliar and need reinforcement from others who have the same style (Dunn & Griggs, 1988).

My advice on learning styles is to let random chance take over. This advice extends to a concern for Gardner's multiple intelligences (MI), which he does *not* see as examples of learning styles, but as potentialities inherent in each individual. There is currently no research to suggest the proper balancing of these within a team either; perhaps this research gap will be closed in the future. The more effective approach to the current use of MI theory (and perhaps learning styles) is in the design of tasks and classroom activities, a focus of a later chapter. (Chapter 6 also provides an overview and an analysis of MI theory.)

To summarize, ignore birth order and learning style until such a time when more research or field practice indicates that they are viable variables with which to construct teams.

Personality

As used by teachers, the term *personality* refers to the personal qualities that each child brings to the class *and* the likelihood that two or more students may work well together. Look briefly at the teams set up by Rose, Brian, and Julie. Each takes into account a subjective hunch that students may well be effective partners because of who they are and how they interact (i.e., Brian thinks Maurice may react positively to LaDay, and Julie suspects Jose Carlos will benefit from the model provided by Heather).

Personality traits are very important to real teachers in the field and are used to produce a thoughtful expectation of interaction. My advice is to trust your intuition and observations, but be careful to observe the results and take notice of any negative recurring patterns. For example, you may end up with one team of individuals with lousy personalities or the most liked students may all be in one group. If you spread the students with lousy personalities and those who are most liked into different groups, you will probably like *all* of the groups a little bit more than before!

Ken Smith's Fifth Grade

This latest point about the many personality factors used by teachers to construct teams is best illustrated by a story about Ken Smith and his classroom. Ken had used cooperative learning often and had realized some success with it, but he was not convinced that it was that beneficial for all the students; clearly, some students were not responding or participating. Here are some of my comments from an observation of his class in 1991. As you read, try to explain the reasons for one group's failure.

> I immediately noticed several striking contrasts. In the near corner, adjacent to Ken's desk is a silent, solemn-looking group of four boys. None has his book open and only one, Jeff, has paper and pen available. Across the room, three noisy groups are talking, gesturing, and arguing (I think). Farthest away, the Honey Bears are loudly discussing their imaginary trip to Mexico, replete with plans and detailed costs. All four girls are fighting for the floor, happily offering ideas, saying "good" all the time, overlapping and connecting various ideas. Nearby, Guns and Roses, a group of two boys and two girls, is quietly and yet forcefully analyzing the flaws in their plans. Nearer to me, the Giants (two girls and two boys) are laughing and kidding each other about the types of food they will need on their trip. (One boy keeps saying "Kaopectate," which makes them all laugh.) Finally, the Dead Crows, the first group, really seem dead. The other groups work and function well; why not these guys?

In truth, Smith had been very successful except that he did not trust the cooperative structure to work with "bad apples" as he called the four boys who formed the Dead Crows. He had assembled that group first, using the criterion of grouping "the four boys that cause trouble and don't work well with others." Smith's expectations doomed the group and did not let the positive effects of cooperative learning kick in. His self-fulfilling prophecy held true.

Interestingly, Ken thought that he had done the best thing, fearing that these youngsters would ruin all the groups if integrated. It was no surprise for me to discover later that three of the boys were from the low-income housing project near the edge of town and the fourth was the son of a local criminal. Ironically, one boy, Omar, was actually from Mexico and had a lot to offer; but his valuable life experiences and knowledge were lost on a group that had no pro-school attitudes. School was a dismal experience for these boys and being put in a hopeless group did nothing to make their lives better.

This story of internal tracking has one other aspect that relates to the whole issue of grouping. Having built the groups, Ken almost immediately avoided this one that needed the most help. My notes show that he approached this team once in 30 minutes to warn them that "this grade counts." He did not help them, he did not explain to them the rationale for their work, and he did not give them advice. He built his loser team and let it fail.

Although a travesty of cooperative learning, it is interesting to note that Ken's other groups profited handsomely from the experience. In fact, many teachers tell me that they are willing to "sacrifice" those "kids who don't want to work for the good of the others" and would build similar teams themselves. My response has always been for them to try it correctly at least once and balance the teams to give everybody a chance. Those four boys could become better students and there was a good chance that separating them would have motivated them. Second, recall that distributing these youngsters around the various groups will not hurt the high achievement being enjoyed by the others. Moreover it may prevent the likelihood that in a short time, with nothing else to lose, the "loser group" will stand to disrupt the other functioning teams. As strange as it may seem, having isolated one dysfunctional group of students does not make it go away. Often they find themselves with their needs unmet and they become jealous of those who enjoy class, so the only way left to gain power is by disrupting the others. Include them in a balanced group instead of banishing them to the fringe.

STUDENT DESIRES

Several teachers I work with are very concerned that we do not often take into account what the students feel they want or need from others in the group. They suggest that it is odd for people like me to tell students everything and then claim that I am making them into decision-making adults.

This concern of my associates may well be a concern for many of you. To help those for whom this is a major issue, I offer some of the results of small surveys that I have conducted with students of various ages and at different grades in Canada and the United States. Essentially, I have asked them "What do you want in a teammate?" Before you read representative responses, make your *predictions* of the results:

_____   1. to be with existing friends

_____   2. to avoid members of "undesirable" groups

_____   3. to be with someone fun

_____   4. to be with somebody who will do the work

_____   5. to feel included in the group

_____   6. to be with people who do their share

_____   7. to be with people who will not place blame unfairly

_____   8. to be with popular kids

It is informative and interesting to listen to youngsters talk about what they feel that they like and/or need *from* their team. Embedded in the following comments are clear suggestions about how students see their teammates and what they require for success. In the following statements, make note of the key comments made by each child:

Jason (age 5): "I liked to work with fun kids like [name]. For a girl, she was OK. I like to work and do stuff."

Damien (age 7): "I like it if we have fun so I want to be with others who are going to be easy and fun. I like to work and laugh . . . and I like to be with fun guys."

Joanna (age 10): "I usually don't like to work in teams because they give me kids who don't work and then I get to do all the work and if we don't get a good grade, I get blamed. I like to have fun and do my work, but I don't want to do all the work . . . and be picked on if we don't get enough points."

Loretta (age 11): "I don't like to be with boys who make crude jokes or who are mean . . . and act mean. I like to work with other people because we share the work and we can help each other . . . but you got to feel safe. If they do their part and act nice, it is great."

Darrel (age 12): "I don't like groups . . . the other kids are always picking on me, making me try to do my work. Once, I didn't feel like it and they got mad and they said it was my fault. Most of the time I just do my part and . . . (in response to a question). Well, one group I liked was when we did some science stuff and we each built a part of a model. It was fun and the other kids didn't mind me making jokes and acting myself."

Manual (age 13): "I like to work with people who are a lot like me . . . not too tight and not too loose. Mostly, I like to work with people who will help make the class time go fast and also who will do their share. I also never like to work with guys like [name] who pick on me or call me names . . . they're like racist and stuff."

Rosella (age 14): "Last year the teacher always built our groups. I really liked them all . . . nobody was too judgmental (or uppity) except [name] and she did her work. Once though, I didn't do a good job on my part of the report and [name] said that it cost us an A. Mr. [name] gave us all the same grade, a B+, I thought it was odd but I didn't like them being mad at me. Overall, though, they weren't too bad. I was surprised that most of the kids liked to work with new guys."

Crynthiana (age 15): "I don't really like school too much so I like it when the teacher lets us work in teams. If I get to pick, I'll work with Damartha and Jarriel . . . but we always just kind of glide. When I worked with some other guys last week . . . yes . . . the teacher assigned the teams that day . . . it wasn't as much fun . . . but we did get our work done. It was OK too; I got to work with some people I never knew before and they were OK. I was really surprised that they treated me nice . . . and were serious about getting the work done."

Cornelius (age 16): "Most of the kids did OK in groups. Some were a little gung-ho, but hey, that was OK because those guys always made sure that we got the work done. I done my share . . . and I showed up for our team sessions in Social. We kind of made the class go easy, talking, sharing and. . . . The teacher always checked to see how we were doing . . . and didn't allow us to rag on each other. I liked it."

Scott (age 18): "I'm planning for college so I want to work with other kids who are serious about their work. I also don't want to get real uptight so I like it when I get to work with easy-going guys . . . or girls; I don't mind working with girls. It is very much like at work . . . we just do our work, relax and actually learn."

Tanisha (age 21): "In college, we just work with whomever is assigned. I prefer to work with people like me because I don't feel as much on display as when I get put with strangers for the first time. After a group has been together a little while, though, it is OK to work with new guys. The big thing then is that people do their share and not just wait for others to carry the load."

The various needs of team members are summarized in the following subsections.

Enjoyment

At every age, students want to enjoy their time in groups. One great advantage of cooperative learning is that this possibility actually exists for everybody—few students actually have fun working alone in class (and most of them don't really like to actually work alone when others are in groups; those that say they prefer to work alone either have no choice and are *excluded from others* or they prefer to use working time to goof off!).

Thus the teacher would be wise to expect students to have a certain amount of enjoyment included in their group time; indeed, Glasser (1986) calls the need for *fun* a human satisfier that cannot be met in solitary efforts.

Inclusion

The second need expressed by students appears to be their desire to feel *included* without feeling like a token. Recall that Miller and Harrington (1992) stressed this point too; in these students' words, they appear to prefer working with "friends" who clearly see them as individuals with personalities and egos. Care should be taken to make sure that new pairings include strategies to build acceptance and personal interactions that help students to see each other as valuable and important individuals.

Fellow Workers

Another need that comes through students' comments is the desire to have teammates who will do their share of the work. In peer tutoring structures (like Slavin's TGT or STAD) the need is the willingness to accept help or to give help; these models, of course, accentuate the interdependent reward structure so that all individuals gain. Students do not want to get "stuck" with teammates who will not help or will not accept help when it is expected.

In group problem-solving types of strategies (like those of the Johnsons or Sharan's Group Investigation technique), this need for "hard workers" who do their share is even more important. Here, individuals often have to "carry others," which is deeply resented. People hate to feel that they have been taken advantage of and will resist this possibility being imposed on them.

Teachers must take care to motivate every member of the various teams, and they must monitor closely those groups that don't match the desired expectation (see Chapter 8).

No Unfair Blame

Finally, in several cases students mentioned that they did not want to be *blamed* for team failures. Several researchers (Harris & Covington, 1993; Miller & Harrington, 1992) have made a strong point about the damage that an unfair attribution of failure can do to an individual. When groups fail, a realistic assessment of why that happened must be made, usually with the teacher's help. Realistic assessment of effort and ability can lead to future plans to improve performance.

Interestingly, the fact that this concern was offered by several of our small sample may be attributable to a number of factors. One that the reader may wish to acknowledge is the possibility that in noncompetitive team structures, failure is a rare bird. Most teams experience success and never have to get around to blaming anyone for failure. Moreover, when failures do occur it is more often caused by nonparticipation (laziness, discipline, or absenteeism) than by lack of ability. Thus, attribution of blame is often self-evident and the team is not hurt as much as the individual is. In other words, *unfair* blame is rare! Overall, individual students accepting responsibility for their own efforts in relation to others is another of the great advantages of cooperative learning.

Thus, students have identified four key needs for their membership in a group:

1. They need to be able to enjoy themselves.
2. They need to feel included and accepted as a person.

3. They need teammates who will do their share.

4. They need to know that they will not be unduly blamed if a failure occurs.

Teachers would be wise to follow monitoring procedures to ensure that these needs are being met (see Chapter 5). All the suggestions about team composition offered in this chapter have been made with these concerns in mind.

Practice Session 2: Joe Sanders's Sixth Grade

Having been exposed to many ideas about group construction, public announcements, and students' needs, now is a good time for you to analyze an example.

The classroom setting is Joe Sanders's sixth-grade class. It is Monday at 8:00 a.m. and Joe is about to use cooperative learning for the first time. Last week he watched as his student teacher, Maggie Jefferson, built teams and used them very successfully in a unit on animals. Now that she has finished her tour of duty, Joe is willing to try it for himself this week. He has decided to use it in spelling, although he knows that it is a very traditional topic and one that requires simple rote memory skills. Listen carefully to his words and try to identify the positive and negative aspects of his planning:

Class . . . quiet down . . . good morning . . . thank you for looking so awake today. We are going to do spelling first today (groans fill the air), but we are going to do it in a different way (a stillness fills the room). Just like Ms. Jefferson did last week, I am going to use teams . . . but I am going to use pairs. No, don't get with the guys you worked with last week. . . . Janie . . . Tom, turn around. OK! I'd like each of you to find a partner who . . . hold it . . . stay put for a second, a partner who is different than you in some key way. You have one minute to rearrange the room.

As chaos fills the room, Joe tries to do a visual roll check, but cannot because of all the student movement. He then goes to the desk and picks up the spelling book.

OK . . . wait a minute . . . nobody . . . Jorge doesn't have a partner (laughter arises from the back quarter) . . . Tony, how is it that you and your brother, Vito, are working together? And there is not one boy/girl pairing (a muffled sound escapes from various seats) . . . and both of my black boys managed to find each other. We are going to try it again. I want you to get a chance to work with a new partner . . . you know that you may find new friends that way . . . and somebody different . . . diversity is a strength, you know. And I really don't want . . . well, we need one threesome because there are twenty-one of us . . . but Jackie's not here . . . OK . . . an even number is here, so let's get ten pairs. Wait . . . there are ten girls and ten boys, let's make each partnership a gender mix. Ready, go . . .

Unlike the noisy first experience, this time his request is met by almost total paralysis. Few students move, and only Juanita gets up and looks around. Joe's interpretation is that they are all watching to see who goes where . . . and are worried about the social implications. He then finishes:

Wait a minute . . . this is easy . . . you guys are all talented and fun to be around. I'll assign . . . Juanita, stay there with Joe. Tony work with Marsha, Vito with Glenda. Senish work with Davida, Monroe with Hilda, Harriet with Marcus, Doug and JoAnne, Helen and Chris, Jason with Annie and Penny would you please go all the way over to sit with Simon. The first words you are going to spell are your partner's name and his or her parents' names. I'll give you three minutes to get going. I'm going to come around and observe that you treat each other nicely . . . and stay on task.

Answer Key

Let us see how many of your comments match up with mine. Interestingly, Joe has chosen spelling for the subject for experimentation. I would have chosen a more complex discipline, one in which the task would have forced the students to get to know, listen to, appreciate, and understand their partner a little more (i.e., an interview or the writing of a dialogue). However, he does start with spelling of the partner (and family) name, a very personal and meaningful task. Poor subject, but a good choice within the topic.

Second, Joe had not anticipated that the students would remember who they worked with last week! I think that he badly underestimated the power of their previous work and he never expected to have to undo or redo that experience.

Third, Joe is not organized enough to make effective pairings and to articulate his rationale. He ends up with brothers together, racial segregation, and an isolated individual—all of these are ineffective and may leave a bad impression on the youngsters. His cry to work "with someone different" may well force students to look at an isolated social characteristic such as race, ethnicity, disability, or gender and possibly promote stereotyping. Sociologists including Miller and Harrington expect that this reaction will happen and that it will damage egos.

Finally, Joe recognizes late in the game that a gender mix would be ideal and actually he is somewhat effective at setting it up as he "wings it." Note that the students actually obey when he seems to know what he is doing. What is weak here is the fact that he does not offer any rationale for the gender mix and his first attempt was met by the stone silence similar to that of the middle school dance floor: boys to one side, girls on the other (and maybe a few girls moving). Thus, he missed an opportunity to explain why working in these particular teams would be useful, interesting, helpful, informative, easier, and/or valuable.

Practice Session 3: Pairing Fourth Graders

While it is safe to work on hypotheticals or models, it is also instructive to do so. Let us try again.

Described below are six fourth graders in an inner-city school. They are a microcosm of the class and your job is to read each description carefully and then construct three two-student pairs as if you were setting up pairs for a week of work in language arts. On a separate sheet of paper, record your pairings and briefly jot down your private rationale for the pairings and prepare your public announcement.

Juanita Ramirez: Juanita Ramirez is a petite, cute, and always immaculately dressed young lady. She is bubbly, eternally happy, and optimistic. ("Don't be sad, the rain will end later . . . and it's good for the flowers!") She will play with all artifacts in the room, and try all activities. She reads well and tries to do her best in school. Supported by two hard-working parents who are active in the PTA, she says that "Jesus is her favorite person" and "sky blue" is her color. Last year, she received four B's, two A's, and a C in physical education. Her artificial arm is of little notice in school settings.

Kyle O'Flaherty: One of five boys in a single-mother household, Kyle is aggressive and funny. Always last with his class work and first with a joke or a smart remark, he is loved by the other boys. He is a good athlete and the first in class to get to the door at the end of the school day. Kyle is at a solid 50th percentile in everything academic. While he appears to be a "tough" kid, nothing seems to bother him very much, including his father leaving home last year.

Annadrea Washington: A sullen and quiet girl, Annadrea is the product of a split, biracial couple. Annadrea shows little initiative and sometimes keeps to herself during break. Her reading is below average and so is her math score. Annadrea enjoys art and has completed several projects including one with a song that she wrote. At midterm, she had C's in all subjects and had missed nine days of school.

Kafir Ahmed Assiz: KA, as he is called, is a curious and analytical little boy. A high achiever from a family of professionals, KA always wants to be number one in his class! His hobbies, computers and chess, usually involve older kids, including his brother, and are often practiced at lunch. A devoted Muslim, KA has expressed unhappiness with Western religions and holidays and he seems to be uncomfortable in small groups. He does enjoy many forms of music and plays the violin decently.

Carmston Anthony: A big boy for his years, Carmston is a pleasant, hard-working, and industrious youngster. Seemingly everyone's friend, he seldom shows anger or disappointment and always does his work on time. A bit awkward and clumsy (befitting his left-handed stereotype), he laughs at his own mistakes and consoles others about theirs. He enjoys card games and recently has done magic tricks in class. His B's and C+'s reflect his attitude and his abilities. An only child, he appears to be close to his working-class parents, who want him to go to college.

Paula Stancek: Since her latest operation, Paula has become a little introverted and withdrawn. An average student in all areas except reading (A+), she had wanted to become a doctor. After all these months in hospitals, it is now the last occupation on her mind! Paula is the only child in her class who regularly listens to a Walk-Man, perhaps imitating her five older siblings. Her mother, an active

PTA parent, is very worried about her attitude and about the other kids' making fun of her limp and lisp. She often feigns illness to miss part of the school day.

Answer Key

For the record, I would build three boy/girl matches and place Carmston with Paula; from a personality standpoint, she might profit from his positive attitude and his confidence. He will not be deterred by her difficulties and will empathize well with her problems.

Next, I think that Annadrea and Kyle will help each other. Again his light touch will help her and he may be fascinated by her artistic abilities. Their academic abilities—his average and hers—will force them to both work to complete their tasks, a healthy situation.

Finally, Juanita will be a positive influence on KA; he needs safe exposure to others and a chance to be secure in himself. She will profit from his professional background and his intellectual pursuits and she will enjoy lightening up his personality.

You may have noted in this example that religion, disability, and race were not a part of my decision making. My focus was on gender, ability, and personality, and I showed a small concern for social class. Publicly, I would tell the kids the following:

> I have made some boy/girl pairings for this week. It will be fun to work with somebody of the opposite sex; you may have more in common than you think. If not, you know that it's good to work with people who have different strengths. Each pair has many positive characteristics and is stronger than you working alone. Go to work.

OPTIONS TO TEACHER-ASSIGNED TEAMS

Random Sort

One of the most inviting alternatives to teacher-imposed teams is that of pure random sort. Imagine a teacher of 24 seventh graders facing her class. In her hand is a stack of three-by-five cards with a student name on each card. She shuffles them thoroughly, has a student in the front row cut the cards, shuffles them again, has another volunteer cut them again, and then deals them in six groups of four. Voila! The pure random sort! While this system seems infinitely fair and therefore powerful, it does have flaws. A close examination of this approach is warranted.

The practice of random assignment to student teams is predicated on some very interesting propositions that I have discovered through the years:

1. Life is a series of chance events, and random teaming provides students with an opportunity to experience that truth.

2. Chance is also "fair." Being assigned to a specific team by luck is equally valid to all members of the class and they can see that there is no favoritism and "all are equal."

3. American xenophobia is so great and our fear of heterogeneous mix is so deep that we must control and plan everything; a pure heterogeneity—resulting from random chance—is a great way to open the system and live out the dream of equality that we preach.

Now these arguments are stirring and certainly challenging, but the random sort can create some problems. "Seth" and "Ahmad," representing traditional Middle Eastern enmity, are analogs for all the kids in modern America who really do hate each other. They could end up being paired; they could also end up in trouble. In some places, they might also hurt each other. I would want to have a veto power (at minimum) over groupings and that veto destroys pure random chance. Once violated, the maxims of random chance are no longer valid and the teacher has begun to move toward the position I prefer, teacher construction of the teams.

Homogeneity that does not foster desired curricular ends could result, depending on the class makeup. Only rarely would the two or three highest achieving students end up in the same four-person team in a random sort, but it would occur far more often than under a teacher-constructed system. Likewise, teams of disproportionately weak students would occur more often than should be allowed. Finally, the diversity of strengths so useful to cognitive growth would frequently be lost under a random sort system. In effect random grouping ensures randomness, *not* any sort of balance of thoughtful integration of personalities that teachers trust so much.

When the teacher constructs the teams, he or she can suggest to students that strengths have been built into the system (an example is given later). Identification of every student's special gifts or talents can be made and publicized. When diversity results from random choice, weaknesses will be the first thing perceived: Instead of "Here is a group that has reading skill, artistic skill, perseverance, and creativity in abundance . . . David, Johnny, Jonni, Gloria," we would hear, "The next group is . . . let's see . . . Gloria . . . Jonni, Johnny, and David" and hope that there are no loud groans of disappointment. The former model suggests that the teacher has *seen* and has *built* on the strengths of kids, whereas the second approach literally hopes to see if any are perceived.

Thus, when the teacher carefully announces the teams and does not imply a sense of tokenism ("Well, group one needs a white kid's perspective . . . so I gave them Julius" or "We have got three Polish students, we will need an Irish balancer . . . so you get Mickey. . . . "), then the team will carry the prospects of positive expectations.

Finally, it is instructive to hear what teachers say about some of the combinations that could be produced by random sort, pairings or matches that *never* would have occurred by teacher choice. Each of these statements, offered by a veteran teacher, illustrates a potential problem that comes into play if control over teaming is surrendered. Listen to their rationales as they once again use personal considerations or personality issues to build their teams.

> I try my best to keep Ramon away from Francesco and Roberto. There is a great deal of drug and gang activity around the school and I have reason to think that they are rivals. Ironically, I had their brothers a few years ago, and they worked well together. But times

change, kids change. I'm keeping them apart . . . and working with other kids for the time being. (9th grade)

I could never put Mark with Tony. Their families hate each other and actually there was a murder attempt at one time. They must be separated. (8th grade)

Max is a Nazi racist . . . it'll be a long time before I could put him with any of my African-American kids. Actually, Skyler would be good for him eventually . . . he is a Black Power advocate . . . but it would be too volatile right now. (12th grade)

The kids are funny. They play well together, but Roger is in a touchy, exploratory phase . . . I'm going to keep him away from the girls for a while. He'll do OK in all-male groups. (5th grade)

Marlene is having trouble dealing with the crime. She is going to be better off for the short run in an all-girls teams. I don't like to do it, and eventually she'll have to work with boys again . . . but not now. (10th grade)

I like to mix the kids up all the time, but David is so good with Matt . . . and this inclusion business is hard enough. I'm keeping them together and will probably move them as a duo for a long time. (2nd grade)

Seth's parents and Ahmad's parents have rivalries that go back to the Mid-East for 30 years. They absolutely are at war with each other. I keep Seth and Ahmad apart . . . and will only bring them into one team when I have worked a miracle. (6th grade)

Apparently, Rod is a bully on the bus and "beats up" Wayne all the time. There is no way that I'll put them in a pair for reading . . . and it's *not* racial! (3rd grade)

Student-Built Teams

My opposition to student-built teams has been well developed throughout this Chapter. I have no confidence that they will benefit most of the students most of the time.

However, under certain circumstances, student-generated teams have worked well for some of my colleagues. The following subsections provide some examples of those circumstances.

Enrichment

Chapter 4 describes a series of grading policy alternatives available to teachers. One of these policies suggests that students be given a satisfactory grade for their efforts and achievements as a group. This may translate into a B on a report card. For extra credit, projects may be chosen that will allow individuals to improve their grade to a desired level. These extra projects, called enrichments, could be done in teams that students build themselves. The choice of an enrichment project here includes the choice of associate(s).

Jigsaw

This is a complicated circumstance, so pay close attention. In Jigsaw, every team has its members working on one aspect of the project. For example, Table 3.1 shows

Simpson's fifth-grade class. The teams are read across the lines (i.e., Billy is with Angie, Monica, and Loas). However, as part of the planning, students from different teams but with similar obligations work together to share information, plan the teaching, or write a test. Instead of assigning these cross-groups (which could be done by reading down the columns in the example), the teacher may let the students choose their topics and thus choose who they wish to work with on that part of the assignment. (*Note:* Unlike the enrichment example, this structure forces every child to be included in a new team. It modifies choice by mandating total inclusion.)

In the example, Billy chose to study Italian immigration, as did his best friend, Casey, and two other boys, Jerzy and Mark. Likewise, Monica arranged with her friends Lucia and Geena to study German immigration and wound up with Fedak as well; he is a new student to the class.

Again, in this case, the element of limited choice does exist, and results in all students being involved.

Alternative to Individual Assignment

One of the great benefits of regular use of cooperative learning is the expectation that a true learning community may develop in a class. In such a community, all individuals are accepted and valued; their learning complements others and is important to others. Such a community avoids all the dangers that are inherent in a bell-curved system, which pits students against each other and which, by design, seeks losers. A community of learners, in contrast, measures its successes by looking at everyone's achievement.

Given that such an affective reality does exist, assignments that are given to individuals may prompt the desire by students to work in pairs or groups. Likewise, tutoring needs may be identified and student tutors may be sought. Under certain conditions, students may be wise to select their own partners for these tasks. The conditions include the following:

1. No one may be turned away if they desire a team or a tutor. Someone truly wishing to work alone may do so, but a student who wants help must be given it.

2. All requests go to the teacher first. In that way, fewer egos are likely to be bruised and there should be fewer hard feelings. Students do not automatically "pick" their workmates but go through the teacher to have their requests approved.

TABLE 3.1 Simpson's Class: Jigsaw on U.S. Immigration

Team	Italian	Irish	German	Japanese
1	Billy	Angie	Monica	Loas
2	Casey	Mitch	Fedak	Ed
3	Jerzy	Vic	Geena	Daniella
4	Mark	Matt	Lucia	Fern

Notice that this option is built around two ideas: one, that a learning community does exist and therefore everyone is involved in the class. Also, that this option does *not* replace the regular team learning base groups that are already in place. While not exactly enrichment, this alternative comes into play when extra help is needed or when an individual assignment is thought to be done more effectively with help.

Finally, this option allows me a chance to describe to you a practice carried out by several teachers that I have studied. They do not let students pick their own teams, but give them some "say" in the matter. For instance, students are asked to make a list of the five people in class they would most like to work with (in some variations, the five least liked are sought as well). The teacher ensures students that everything will be done to accommodate their desires and that at least one person on that list will be placed on a team with him or her. In this way, the teacher keeps some control but listens to the voices of the students and shows respect for their wishes.

This technique fits perfectly with the "alternative to individual assignment" option just described. It provides a way for the teacher to make sure that nobody is excluded while ensuring students that they will be on an extra team with a person of choice.

Mix and Match Daily

One final alternative to teacher-built teams is one used by many practitioners. In its many variations, it is a daily mix approach. In other words, no permanent teams are assigned. Students in class on a particular day are simply placed with others to do the day's activities. Since students usually sit in the same place every day, this usually results in some *de facto* teams that arise from simple chair moving. Although this approach does effectively deal with the high absenteeism rates in many schools and allows students some choice over their workmates, I find several flaws with this structure:

1. Since the team disbands and reforms daily, there is no sense of continuity, permanence, or responsibility built into it. The sense of interdependence promised by cooperative learning would be all but lost. There is no research support for the use of these *ad hoc* teams.

2. On any given day, students may feel no need to work with their given teammates. Instead of trying out their social skills and developing strategies to cope, students finding themselves in awkward situations would simply wait it out—until tomorrow when they are grouped with new partners. Many of the isolated and alienated students would "lose" in such a system.

3. Such a system is limited to effectively working on no project for longer than a day or for a class period in a grade 7–12 building. Long-term gains, including tolerance and respect, would be lost. Students need to be joined in a permanent team if they are to challenge stereotypes, overcome prejudice, and develop strong positive bonds.

I have often noted that the military builds somewhat permanent squads. Sports teams have some stability, and police partnerships are usually long term—all of these build on the idea of relative permanence. Much would be lost if those organizations changed their compositions daily (or regularly); in particular, their effectiveness would be curtailed.

I do not advise the mix and match daily approach be used if the gains of cooperative learning research are truly sought.

DEALING WITH SPECIAL CASES

Having traveled throughout North America to do cooperative learning in-services, I have had a chance to work with great teachers in diverse settings and with schools that have unique characteristics. During the inevitable question-and-answer period, many topics and concepts are usually explored but there is one question that appears at virtually every single site. Its most common version goes something like this: "I'd like to do this team thing, but I don't have any idea of what to do with . . . " and then a student's name is offered, usually accompanied by knowing nods from the rest of the teachers. This query suggests several things to me, but before I provide some ideas about what to do with such a student, I would like to have the reader think about deeper meanings of the question.

Often, this question appears to be a smoke screen for a teacher who really does not want to try out the new technique. By citing some apparently insurmountable problem, the teacher has cleared himself or herself of any responsibility for innovation. When that problem is an incorrigible student, the teacher is essentially blaming the victims and "copping out."

At other times, this questions appears to be a surrender to the demands of problems presented by a particular student who can only be controlled by "traditional" models. I doubt seriously that the traditional patterns are working, so nothing will be lost by trying something new. Second, it is at best a statement of low teacher efficacy and at worst a confession of failure. In truth, there are few such terrible kids and even fewer teachers who cannot deal with difficult students.

At times, this question simply means what it says: "I have a student for whom this approach will not work . . . and so I cannot try it." I have trouble dealing with this perspective, because I have never met this youngster (or anybody like him or her) and I cannot believe that there are teachers who would change their entire strategy because one student found it unworkable. Imagine the following statements: "I cannot ever use in-class tests with my students because Paul doesn't test well under pressure," or "I cannot ever show films because Antonia is blind and seeing films would be too great an advantage for the others."

In each of the special cases that have been cited, alternatives are usually created to facilitate the working of the special student. It is rare that the whole class is denied an opportunity because of one student's circumstances. ("Class, we won't be reading this year in language arts because Mark doesn't like to read and feels it is a waste of his time!")

Thus, I am serious when I say that all students should be realistically exposed to cooperative learning and be held accountable for doing it successfully. Exposure may not be enough, however. The teachers need to have expectations that the technique will work and that it is imperative for modern society that it be made to work—the life prospects for students who cannot function in cooperative teams in school are dismal indeed. Prospects for a pluralistic democratic society that has many young- sters who *cannot* work effectively with each other are even more dismal yet.

Thus the special cases that are discussed here provide simple pieces of advice about how a teacher might facilitate the transition of a particularly difficult student into a cooperative learning environment. Each case presents a brief and unique por- trait of a situation. You should jot down your ideas about dealing with the youngster and then compare them with my suggestions.

Finally, advocates of individualized instruction and multicultural education may see these cases as adaptations of models drawn from their fields. To a large degree, that is exactly what they are. Cooperative learning is a teaching strategy that fits into the reality of diverse students and in diverse situations.

Nikisha, the New Student

Nikisha is an 11th-grade African-American girl who has recently moved in midyear from an inner-city school to a suburban district. She was an honor student in her previous school and was a student leader. Her arrival in the school has prompted comments by some white students—to a certain degree her arrival is a novelty, and to some, a problem.

From the records, the teacher is aware that Nikisha likes jazz, softball, Langston Hughes, and English class. Her SATs were 450 verbal and 575 math and she indi- cated that she wishes to become a writer. She was freshman class vice president and sophomore queen of the prom at the old school.

The new school is conservative and old fashioned. Only 3 of the 34 faculty use cooperative learning and Rudnicki is the only teacher that Nikisha has that does so. She is the first African-American in the school since 1982 and her parents, both elderly and retired, chose the district to increase her chances of getting into a fine college.

Suggestions: I do not see Nikisha's team assignment to be very problematic, except for the fact that there may be racist students among her new classmates. Because she may have a difficult time fitting into the new environment, placement in an existing team in your class is important. I would try to place her with a team that is marked by liberal and tolerant youngsters, perhaps one with a strong female lead- ership and one that will be required to *learn about her.* To a certain degree, Nikisha will be on display for a period of time because she is the only African-American in the school—having a ready-made team will help her in the transition.

I also suggest that her introduction to the class not be made into a big deal; she should be introduced and exposed to the rules and expectations and put to work.

If racist comments have reached Nikisha directly, these will have to be taken up by the teacher with the whole class. If they are simply background noise, they should be ignored in the short run and emphasis should be placed on teaching Nikisha and her teammates the class rules and procedures.

All in all, the literature is abundantly clear that the use of teams (1) helps facilitate the entry, (2) increases the acceptance, and (3) improves the achievement of minority youngsters, be they Native Americans (Little Soldier, 1989), Asians (Ziegler, 1981), Hispanics (Cohen, 1994), Mexican-Americans (Wiegel, Wiser, & Cook, 1975) or African-Americans (Slavin & Oickle, 1981).

Billy, the Bully

Billy is a large, hulking fifth grader who has learned through his short years that being a bully is the only way to gain recognition. He is big, has a mean streak, has hit his classmates, and many of them live in pure terror of him. Teachers alternately pity him, seeing him as a caricature of a gangster, or despise him, seeing him as the destroyer of all good discussions and crusher of group work. He carries a D+ average, reads well below grade level, hates sports because he lacks the perseverance to turn strength into skill, and does stupid things to maintain his reputation. For example, he publicly ate crayons to scare first graders last year, and last week was accused of kicking in the headlight of a neighbor's car because "it splashed him with water." One final note: Teachers do not believe that he learns well in any setting, including home schooling. They do not put his class into groups because the students assigned to him simply will not work with him.

Suggestions: Whenever a Billy is described to me I like to respond in two ways. First, I cannot believe that the behavior of one child should dictate what a teacher can do with his or her class. (To repeat: I cannot imagine a teacher foregoing homework because of one complaint; I cannot imagine a teacher canceling a film because one child does not like to sit in the dark.) This is the classic case of being forced into a bad decision because of one student's bad behavior. The rest of this class should not miss out on all the advantages of cooperative learning because of Billy's whims and tantrums.

Paradoxically, I both agree and disagree with mainstream cooperative learning theorists on this Billy scenario. Like the Johnsons and Sharan, I wish to have him included and left there with no hope of quitting the group. As he is placed in the team, his teammates will most likely not scream for help or run. But they will be perturbed and my guess is that all others will hold their breath when teams are announced. Be that as it may, I think that Billy should be included, preferably in a team scenario that includes some self-confident youngsters and *not* those who are very outwardly afraid of him. Also, the first assignment should be a direct one-on-one assignment, like an interview or a paired writing assignment with strong positive interdependence. The idea here is that Billy cannot be allowed to stay at the periphery of the assignment but must be involved intensely and briefly; that is, he could be the subject of the interview. Having him start with a successful task may shape him in a direction that allows him to be successful in class, and gain confidence; he can choose to let down the tough guy persona. Moreover, it also shows him that you are willing to treat him fairly and (somewhat) equally and that you do not have bad expectations for him.

On the other hand, my extensive work in the schools has shown me that there are students who *can surrender* their privilege to work as a member of a team or group. Constant disruptions, terrorizing of partners, threatening of peers, and an absolute lack of contribution means that the teacher may opt to withdraw Billy from his team. This removal is not permanent, however. Isolation from peers is often the only punishment that has any power over the lives of youngsters in our schools and it may well work as a negative reinforcer: To avoid isolation, the student must follow the interaction rules established in the classroom.

If Billy is removed, I recommend the following actions. First, the teacher must explain to Billy and his teammates exactly why this is happening and how it could have been avoided. Suggestions to Billy about improving his behavior and the consequences of his choices must be made public. Suggestions to the group as to how they might have helped Billy assimilate more effectively must also be made clear to all members.

Second, Billy must be clear about the conditions under which he may return to that team and that team only—he cannot use his bad behavior as an avenue to work with his buddies or to avoid particular students that he may not like. Moreover, Billy must be made to complete the assignment by himself, because he has sacrificed his privilege for help. While Chapter 6 details dozens of effective class activities, in this instance if the group is doing a project or taking a team test, Billy must work alone after his banishment. This is serious business and failure to work with others is a sign of failure with this youngster's education. Billy must suffer the consequences. The rest of the group, understood to be innocent victims, may work together but cannot realize any of the bonuses built into some successful team activities. (These bonuses reflect the cooperation of all involved.) In this way, they have a vested interest in Billy's "shaping up" and his eventual return to the group. Only after he has proven himself absolutely incapable of interacting satisfactorily, would I allow him to be permanently removed from the group.

Since most teams stay together for a relatively long period of time (2 weeks, a marking period, etc.) Billy's permanent removal from a group remains in effect only until the next set of teams is formed.

Alison, the Absent

I have dubbed Alison Absentia as the given name of the youngster who simply does not show up more than 15% of the time. Teachers occasionally disavow the use of cooperative learning because of students like her, but this is a mistake. It is quite possible (and perhaps the subject of forthcoming dissertations) that Alison's attendance will rise because of the use of teams in her classes, so we must at least give it a try. It is conceivable that if her absences arise from feelings of alienation, loneliness, disaffection from peers, or a sense of hopelessness about school, cooperative learning may be a positive factor in getting her to school.

Suggestions: Be that as it may, what do we do with the youngster who only shows up once a week for her lesson? I have several thoughts. The teacher could put her in a team, treat her like the others, and expect her to contribute. These ideas are as mainstream as can be but are often unheeded. She is a class member and deserves that treatment. Moreover, she should be placed in a team based on the qualities described earlier, but you should *avoid* putting her in a team with other youngsters likely to be absent. She needs interaction with students who come to school and needs to see and experience models of people who find attendance meaningful. Avoid the tendency to put the four most absent kids together because "they won't be there anyway."

Recognize that Alison misses school. Her team is not stupid, they will notice that she is frequently absent. Ask *them* what can be done about it, perhaps offering them a bonus if they can help her see to it that school is worth attending. I would *not* take away bonus opportunities for her teammates in this case. If Alison is really out more than she is in, I would simply allow the group to work with or without her there. I do not advocate the use of many group-graded projects under any conditions, but some of the readers will. In such a case, adjust the scoring so that her absence will not damage partner grades and further alienate her classmates.

Remind Alison's teammates that she is still part of the team and must be remembered that way in cases where handouts are made, tests are returned, etc. Thus, she is there as part of the team even when she is not there. Having some of her teammates take some responsibility for her might help her feel more a part of the school enterprise.

Mookie, the Clown

Mookie is the class clown, an 8-year-old who drives adults crazy and kids spastic with his antics. A crayon up the nose, a loud sound reminiscent of flatulence, a burst of laughter as the teacher is reading a sad story are all part of his repertoire. When he is older, he will either be the funniest guy in town or hated by most everyone. In the third grade, he is seen primarily as an obstacle for the teacher.

Suggestions: I reiterate the same advice that I have been giving all along: Start out dealing with him as a "regular" student, which of course he is. However, take special care with this boy's teammates. Place him with peers who want to get good grades and will work hard and, if you can find a few, those who like to laugh. Unlike many other students who are disruptive, Mookie has a gift that can be recognized by all teachers as special and valuable: He will keep things light and moving in his group and, if they can stay on task, they will love working together and he will enjoy an opportunity to entertain, learn, and stay within the rules.

Note that the regular classroom pits the teacher *against* Mookie in that every Mookie witticism is at the expense of the regular classroom process, even if the teacher herself thinks it is funny. His antics also cry out for imitation and the dreaded "free-for-all" lurks behind every remark. But things are different in the cooperative group because as long as they are working on their task, the students are urged to interact, to help, and, indeed, to keep things moving.

Mookie can learn to turn his gift into the positive force that humor often is for adults. Other teams will want Mookie, perhaps encouraging him, but his group also needs him to stay on task, keep working, and modify his displays so that they are socially appropriate. Notice these last few words: In the regular classroom, humor's place does not exist except as a challenge or threat to stability. In the cooperative team, humor can help bond a team into a coherent whole and it can make school pleasant; it also does not threaten the teacher directly, nor is it likely to come at the expense of teammates who are seated facing the comic. Mookie has a valuable asset, and in Elizabeth Cohen's world, tasks are multi-ability; the world needs diversity to run smoothly and the class clown can be a valuable asset to a team that otherwise may be uptight and anxious about its performance.

Jacinta, the Gifted Student

A great deal of controversy surrounds the placing of gifted students in heterogeneous cooperative groups. Although studies such as that by Slavin (1991) reveal that gifted students do well in these settings, advocates have argued against that placement. Somewhat reassuring is a statement by advocates for the gifted, Gallagher and Coleman (1994), who have indicated that they see many potential benefits to the gifted student in a cooperative learning setting. They also maintain, however, that teachers should not abuse these students by making them "teach" everything to the less able students, expecting them to do all the work and/or ignore them by forgetting about enrichment opportunities. I think that both of these pieces of advice are excellent.

Thus, we see Jacinta, an extremely bright 12th grader working in a physics class with a set of classmates having diverse abilities.

Suggestions: I would place her in a team using the criteria already developed, that is, with students of mixed ability (within the physics class) and whose personalities would allow her to work effectively. I would also give her many opportunities to reconceptualize the content and have her try her hand at using these reconceptualizations to teach others. Clearly these cognitive activities would profit her (Bargh & Schul, 1980) and they would be analogs to the mental activities that exist in studies of teacher planning (Benware & Deci, 1984).

Interestingly, a Niagara University research team (Vermette et al., 1993) that examined a specific seventh-grade classroom, focused often on the brightest child in the school. While she worked in the heterogeneous teams, she loved every minute. The case study uncovered several reasons for her joy:

1. She was appreciated by her teammates because she was quick, creative, and a real help to them.
2. She could take a leadership role and shape the directions used by the team on many upper-level challenges.
3. She was intellectually engaged by the many ideas that she had not conjured up personally but could understand and extend once she heard them.
4. She mastered simple memorization tasks immediately, and then found it interesting to hypothesize about her teammates' struggles and to test her theories concerning helping them!

Recalling the fears about females in base groups offered by the Sadkers and Webb's middle school studies, the extremely positive experience of this young girl is overwhelming. The possibility exists that the students who have the most to gain from heterogeneously mixed teams *are* the gifted and talented kids. Certainly, future research will explore this issue and the positive experience of students like Jacinta is likely to be found to be a common one.

Roger, the Racist

A very troubling question for me is the one asked by teachers regarding students they deem to be racist. Many teachers are hesitant to build cross-race (or cross-ethnic) teams for this reason and are clearly missing an opportunity to develop tolerance and acceptance in their students.

At the outset, it must be clearly stated that racism (or sexism) will not be allowed in the classroom. Classrooms must reflect the spirit of the U.S. Constitution and the notions of equality built into our heritage. Respect must be shown for everybody and be expected in all interactions. Teachers need not attempt to build friendships between students, but must work hard to build working relationships between members of all salient social categories in the nation.

Suggestions: With that stipulation in mind, what about Roger? First, the teacher should make clear her commitment to the ideas just stated: Students must work across all groups in preparation for life and in accordance with the Constitution. Students often challenge this idea with unfounded notions about a "free country" and who they will or will not associate with. Teachers must counter that a free country does *not* freely allow discriminatory behaviors, words, and actions. The individual's right *not* to be discriminated against is a higher right than the "right" to publicly disrespect someone.

Second, the teacher would probably be wise to evaluate the level of racism being shown. Many times, this attitude is loosely held and not very meaningful. In such cases, positive interactions between cross-race teams will help to relieve the situation. Placing Roger in a racially mixed group of students will help him; care must be made, however, that others are not victimized by this arrangement. Concern for the recipient of the racism or sexism must be felt.

In some cases, the feelings of racism are deeply held and dangerous. Confrontation within the group is possible. I would advise that these matches not be made until such a time when students are more understanding of the gains to be made by working in integrated settings.

For example, Long Beach, California, has been called the gang capital of the United States. Long Beach has teen gangs built along racial lines, and mixing two members from each gang in the first cooperative experience might be dynamite. However, such a mix might serve well as a stated long-term goal of that particular class; it may also serve as a worthwhile discussion focus for a class.

The movie *Dangerous Minds* portrays a similar situation in Rose-Anne Johnson's class. Early in the year, two of the class's "toughs" *could not* be brought together easily. But by the end of the movie, because of the teacher's interventions, there was mutual caring by the boys for each other.

Although the situation with teenagers needs careful scrutiny, racism among younger students is almost always a thoughtless vestige of adult attitudes and can simply be ignored. Thus if Roger is a 7-year-old who says that he does not "want to work with any of them white kids" one can assume that his hostility is built on ignorance and lack of successful experience. As such, the solution is to provide those experiences in a cooperative learning setting that is gently but firmly implemented.

Attitude change research suggests that the best thing that can happen is the mutually beneficial reaching of a common goal by a diverse team—the exact process instituted by cooperative learning.

Chris, the Techno-Phobe

Several of the studies cited in Chapter 2 indicated that attitudes toward technology improved drastically when students worked together on computer problems. Joint problem solving provided opportunities for modeling and reflection as well as for suggestions and feedback.

Suggestions: The recommendation here calls for a mixing of prior knowledge and attitudes in the teams built for technological work. Teachers should avoid the common tendency here to place phobics together and experts together because the phobics will simply not succeed. Instead, they will share their miseries with each other. The experts will not gain disproportionately by their working with other high achievers and will miss the opportunity for reconceptualizations discussed earlier.

Arthur, the Anal Retentive

The student who drives many teachers crazy is represented here by Arthur, the anal retentive kid who needs to fix every mistake, dot every *i*, complete every task on time, and can stand little ambiguity. Often, teachers fear that real life will play this child a drastic blow, for the real world is not made up of neatly built and easily solved problems.

Suggestions: It is obvious that Arthur really needs to work with some kids who have greater tolerance for ambiguity, a weaker need for completion and who feel less stress at facing complex challenges. These personality issues, described earlier in the chapter, play a central role here.

What may be overlooked in the case of Arthur, however, is the great positive force he would bring to the others in his team. While Arthur may bother many teachers who group students, we do greatly appreciate his perfectionism, his punctuality, his concern for pleasing others in power, and his desire to always do the right thing. If anything, modern society does not have nearly enough of these youngsters and he would model these attitudes and practice such behaviors in front of those in need of them.

While the old saying that "opposites attract" may be debatable, the new saying that "opposites offer options" is not. Arthur will help his teammates stay on task, be serious about their work, and attend to details. Moreover, his teammates will help him see a more tolerant approach to these chores.

People who use the Myers-Briggs personality scale often joke that "SJ's need to run the world." By this they mean that a personality type not unlike Arthur's has a great need to complete tasks and to put closure and structure on everything. These people are often misunderstood by more relaxed types (NP in the Myers-Briggs parlance) who are more fluid in their work, but then again, never seem to get anything completed. Perhaps working relationships that get the best out of these polar approaches would maximize the effectiveness of the team and help each student gain actual experience with other personality types.

Emil, the Alienated

Emil, an alienated 10th grader, represents the many students who simply are not moved by schoolwork or who have emotionally dropped out of the modern society. The truly alienated are often unable to cope and will not be in the modern classroom. But many students who are on this path or who have serious adjustment problems are there and need to be included.

Interestingly, Glasser (1986) in his classic book, *Control Theory in the Classroom*, suggests that 50% of modern youngsters are alienated from the school process and from schooling. *Most* of these, he posits, would profit greatly in team settings. He sees the teams offering some students enjoyment or fun during school, a chance to affect events or power, an absolutely necessary sense of belonging or inclusion, and a sense of freedom to make school personal—these four qualities satisfy human needs.

Suggestions: Many somewhat alienated students will be motivated greatly by the chance to work with peers, even if it is assigned peers. Frankly, Glasser thinks that it is virtually impossible to reach them *without* a team organization in class. Thus, many students like Emil may be turned around to a new positive direction by working with other students, especially if he gets direct contact with others who have high aspirations or who have a sense of the value of schooling.

Paul and Paula, the Parasite Twins

These two students present the biggest problem to novice users of cooperative learning. Students like them are simply the ones who feel that they are along for the ride and need not contribute to the effort. They are students who make life miserable for others in the group and whose advantage-taking cheats and ruins the system. In short, they must not be allowed to succeed without doing their share of the work.

Suggestions: Several things can be done to make sure that they contribute. For one thing, strong leadership or a strong sense of commitment (perhaps Arthur?) should be present in the other teammates. If need be, separating the five students "most likely to be parasites" and matching them up with the five students "most likely to make everyone work hard" might be a productive way to start your team composition process. (The remainder of such a team can be balanced by using other criteria.)

Although this latter matching system is used by some teachers, there are a number of a teachers who attempt to force this type of student's hand by putting them all in one group. In other words, one team is built solely of lazy, diffident, and/or coasting students. Experience shows that these groups are disasters and that little if anything ever gets done. My advice: Do not do it that way.

These students need to do their share of the work and need to be around students who will make them contribute. The teacher must also build in activities to force them from a parasitic mode, a task that is not difficult to do (see Chapter 6).

OTHER USES OF THE TERM "GROUP BUILDING"

The term *group building* has been used in several ways by advocates of cooperative learning. As used here, it refers to the composition process used by teachers to build cooperative learning teams. However, once built, the processes used to help develop that group into a smoothly functioning learning team are also referred to as *group building,* a bonding process that is thoughtfully done and carefully sequenced (Kagan, 1992).

Several strategies follow that will help guide the first few interactions (and, thus, the bonding process) of a newly assembled team:

Hold Every Student Accountable

Some notable cooperative learning models in the Johnson and Johnson tradition call for the group to produce a product or solve a problem worked on by every member. Attesting to the fact of their participation, each signs a pledge the she or he has contributed to the project.

Most teachers do not hold a great level of trust in *all* their students and they also hold legitimate fears of the destructive power of a student regarded as a "parasite" by peers. Thus, ensuring that all students contribute and are held accountable is imperative.

This process can be easily accomplished. Teachers can visually monitor every group during a task and should intervene when they see a nonparticipating member. At the close of the activity, preferably timed to help keep students forging ahead, each member of the team can be publicly asked about the work. Questions should range from "What did your team come up with?" to "Jack, what role did John play as the team did its work?" and serve as a clear reminder that every person is to contribute.

Moreover, a combination of the preceding strategies would see the teacher stop at every group location and randomly call on a member to summarize privately the progress. For example, imagine a team of four students actively arguing or talking. The teacher wanders over, listens, and when things quiet down, asks "What is going on here? How is it going?" This process requires everyone to be accountable and clearly sets the expectation of participation. Moreover, this intervention reinforces the idea that other members of the group are responsible for trying to encourage or demand contributions from all.

Another possibility is to have the students conclude an activity and then individually write down a summary or a description of the event. This may also include a retelling of particular individuals' roles in the process. Again, this would heighten the expectation that all are to contribute.

As simplistic as these suggestions sound, many teachers simply fail to use them. The inclusion of an accountability clause early in the team activity drastically increases the likelihood that everyone will contribute and reduces the chances of free riders or what I call "parasites."

Personalize the First Team Activity

Imagine that a math teacher has announced her teams and has had the students move their chairs into position for the teamwork. Which of the following two activities would more likely involve every student?:

1. The teams are to create a math problem similar to the ones she had done on the board, but they are to use quantities drawn from every member's lifestyle (i.e., if they are doing ratios, use the sibling counts from every member; if simple addition, use the costs of favorite foods).
2. Solve problems 1 through 5 on page 86 of the text.

Obviously, both tasks attempt to improve the same skills and are similar in structure, but activity 2 is a far more common real classroom experience. Note, however, that activity 1, which uses actual student realities, offers a slightly different motivation because it *requires* every student to participate and personalizes the problem. Activity 1 utilizes a much stronger positive interdependence than does activity 2.

Other examples abound. Compare the following pairings to identify those activities that are *more likely to require everyone's contribution* at the outset:

Sixth-Grade Math

1. In pairs, write one description of the classroom using math concepts.
2. Partner X describes the room as partner Y writes the description down.

Fourth-Grade Science

1. Read the passage in the science text on page 124 and answer questions 1 and 2 on paper.
2. Partner X reads the passage to partner Y who summarizes it satisfactorily. Turns are taken after each paragraph but only one passage is provided (the Johnsons call this *positive resource interdependence*).

Kindergarten Language Arts

1. The team is given three crayons and told to draw a story.
2. The team is given three colored crayons, one for each child. They are to draw one story, using every color.

Eleventh-Grade Social Studies

1. Come up with arguments for or against capital punishment.

2. Write a four-part dialogue (each member takes a part) arguing capital punishment.

Notice that in each pairing the second task is structured to force the contribution of every member. While all are sound activities, they are not equal in the ability to involve all.

The earlier every member of the team feels a part of a successful team experience, the better off that team will be.

Praise and Reinforce Good Behavior

For various reasons, students are quite likely to participate in the very first teamed activity. Thus, there will be plenty of opportunities for the teacher to identify and publicly reinforce proper intragroup behavior. The math teacher described earlier could easily spot students working together and contributing. She could also utilize the accountability strategies offered previously to create desired behaviors that could be reinforced.

Imagine that the following rules are written on the board at the outset of the activity:

1. Everyone must contribute.

2. Everyone must encourage others to participate.

3. Stay on task.

4. Disagree with ideas, *not* people.

As the teacher walked around during the session, she could say things like "Janie, it's great that you kept asking Tomas for his ideas," "Your whole team kept working . . . it was neat that you created more than I asked for," and "Chang-Lee, you did a fine job of making sure everyone understood." Each of these statements is designed to keep students on task, reward desired behavior, and maximize student involvement. This simple approach is frequently missing during teamwork, a distressing reality that is easily fixed; its use will help bond team members.

Group building, then, in this second conception, solidifies the team members and helps them develop a positive affect and an identity.

CHAPTER 3 SUMMARY

Chapter 3 provided many ideas about the first necessary structure of cooperative team learning, the grouping policy used by the teacher to construct effective teams. Although the various activities provided opportunities for readers to experience certain situations and to try their hand at applying principles, several propositions guided my suggestions, the research base, and the policies of many practitioners:

1. Most of the time, the teacher should construct the teams and then announce the compositions to the students in a positive light.
2. The teacher should generally strive for a rich blend of diversity within the various teams, using demographic variables such as ethnicity, social class, race, gender, religion, and personal variables such as personality, attitudes, and strengths/abilities.
3. The teacher should design the teams thoughtfully, carefully blending many variables. Note, however, that public announcements of the team should never focus on weaknesses or on issues of tokenism that would reduce individual personalities into token representativeness.

The chapter provided information about the relative importance of many student variables, including ability, perseverance, aspiration, social class, handedness, religion, ethnicity, gender, disability, birth order, learning style, and personality. In general, these qualities should be mixed in a team, or in the case of birth order and learning style, ignored completely.

The chapter also offered several other ideas regarding variations on the group-building theme. For example, a report was made of student preferences in teammates that reveals student desires to be similar to the ones sought by teachers: Students want partners who will enjoy doing their work, will complete their fair share, will include everyone, and who will not cast unfair blame for a failure.

Advice was given on the handling of common problematic situations or special cases, ones involving youngsters who are racist, techno-phobic, frequently absent, class clowns, alienated, anal-retentive, parasitic, new to the class, bullies, or gifted.

Several suggestions were offered regarding the first time a team works together. In a nutshell, all students must be held accountable, the activity should include a personalized and meaningful component, and the teacher should aggressively articulate successful practices actually used (catch them "being good"). The first experience of a team is often its most important one; success then helps build the team's chances for long-term success.

In short, this chapter provided a great many insights to help modern teachers construct effectively balanced and activated cooperative learning teams, a most vital component of the cooperative learning process.

REFLECTION QUESTIONS

1. Some teachers resist the task of assigning teammates and philosophically prefer to allow the students to make their own teams. Take a look at both the six fourth graders and the twelve 10th graders discussed earlier in this chapter and predict the following:

    a. Which students would end up alone if they were allowed to choose?

    b. How much mixed-gender and cross-race mixing would have occurred had students picked their own groups?

    c. How long would it take during the school year before the kids began to mix themselves in the way that the teacher would have done?

2. Here is a list of statements that can be made to classes to help motivate them to work in assigned groups. Please rank order them from 1 to 5, with 1 being the statement most likely to be used by you in getting your students going and 5 the least likely:

   _____ a. "I have built the teams to spread out old friends; this will help keep you at work."

   _____ b. "The way that I have matched you gives everybody a chance to meet new people and have access to skills and experiences that would not be available otherwise."

   _____ c. "In every pair, I have mixed people so that there is a blend of intelligence, hard work, creativity, strength, wisdom, and different perspectives."

   _____ d. "Working together ought to cut the work in half . . . and each of you has been given a partner who can do some things that you cannot."

   _____ e. "It is usually motivating to experience something new . . . so I have given you a new partner to work with!"

3. Clearly, constructing teams is an art, not an exact science. Propositions such as (1) provide females with the support of other females, (2) avoid the feelings of token placement, and (3) work from strengths, not weaknesses, do not give a great deal of guidance. Yet teachers are very good judges of youngsters (Good & Brophy, 1994) and they tend to use personality matters over all other factors anyway. It might be instructive to consider any set of student profiles offered in this chapter and ask others to construct teams using those student profiles. Compare your groupings with theirs and reflect on what their placements said about kids and schooling. (Do not be surprised if the nonteachers use a form of homogeneous grouping or tracking.)

4. Interview a youngster between the ages of 5 and 18 about working with others in class. Include these questions:

    a. If you picked some teammates, would you pick friends?

    b. When the teacher has assigned teammates, what problems have evolved?

    c. Who do you like to work with and why?

    d. Are most of the kids in your class like you or different?

    e. What is the hardest part about working with a partner who is [the opposite sex]?

    f.   What do you say if a teammate is not working or doing his or her share?

5. Interestingly, an Israeli study examined the volatile relationships between Arabs and Jews in a cooperative learning setting much like our hypothetical "Seth" and "Ahmad" (Hertz-Lazarowitz, 1993). Results indicated a positive result for attitudes and understanding in cooperative classrooms. Here is a list of other variables that may have helped these students become more tolerant of each other: (1) age, (2) gender, (3) level of school, (4) length of teamwork, (5) willingness to participate, (6) attendance rates, (7) group size, (8) type of activities used, (9) post–high school aspirations, and (10) social class. Try to predict which of these conditions were responsible for desirable results (i.e., the closer in age the better; the more dissimilar the social class, the better; the longer the group stayed together, the better).

four

AUTHENTIC ASSESSMENT, GRADING, AND TEAMS

GRADING FELIPE

Imagine Felipe as he walks into his sixth-grade classroom on the first day of school. He is a pretty good student, shows up, does his homework, and cares about his grades. His family is proud of him and in the back of his mind he is thinking about college. Teachers see him as keeping up with his work and as a successful student. On that first day, his teacher will tell him about the grading system that will be used to determine his quarter grade in language arts. Without additional knowledge of Felipe, which of the following systems do you predict he would prefer?:

1. a bell curve system, in which the top 20% of students get A's, the next 20% B's, the next 40% C's, the next 10% D's, and the final 10% F's;

2. a system in which all tests and papers are worth 100 points, with the mark for the quarter being a straight average of these pieces of work; or

3. assignment to a team such that all projects and assignments are done in groups with everyone in the team receiving the same grade;

4. an individual contract with the teacher about work expectations and grade possibilities for himself;

5. a system in which 50% of the quarter grade is based on the teacher's interpretation of his effort and his work habits as judged by his homework, class work, and participation; the other 50% of the grade is based on the average of his test scores;

6. a system of no grades for individually prepared drafts of papers, just feedback comments; these papers are individually presented to a team of teachers as a portfolio and evaluated as an A, B, C, or incomplete.

Made your choice? I offered these six choices for several reasons. First, in my observations, they represent the most common ways that teachers attempt to be equitable and fair when assigning grades. These systems are not equally represented in the teacher population but they are the most common. Secondly, these are the systems in place when a veteran teacher has shifted from traditional teaching to the use of cooperative learning, and has attempted to adjust the grading system accordingly. They exist as a baseline for changes and comparisons. Finally, *none* of the systems offered above appears to be the single most effective in conjunction with the use of cooperative learning. Therefore, my intention is this chapter is to describe *alternatives* that will work with teamed systems and will provide teachers with the flexibility they require. Moreover, part of this chapter is devoted to a philosophical discussion of the purposes of grading, which is a central factor in the development of a teacher's system.

As you answered the question about grading systems, you may have assumed the following: Felipe cares about his grades (he does); Felipe perceives that teachers are fair judges of work (they are); teachers care about him (they do); and teachers can clearly state why their grading policies relate well to their work assignments and to their students' needs (they often cannot and do not).

As for the "right" answer, teachers that I have worked with often disagree with each other about Felipe's probable preference. If he were real, we would ask him, but we cannot so let us briefly look at several factors that might relate to various choices:

1. He is doing well, so he might prefer to keep the status quo. The most common system is the second one listed, traditional averaging; that would be a likely choice.

2. He appears to care about grades, so he might be motivated to persevere based on the appeal of higher grades; that speaks to a system where he would gain over less hard-working students such as the bell curve system.

3. He has a lot to lose if he feels that he has been assigned to a team that includes "losers," "slow learners," and "unmotivated kids." These are the very youngsters he has successfully competed with for more than half of his life! Therefore, he might shun group-graded team achievements.

All three of these factors suggest that a student like Felipe, who represents a stereotyped student that teachers like to work with and teach, may not care for cooperative groups or any sort of team grading or teamed effort. In fact, this attitude is also reflected in the general perception of educators. Many teachers have had bad experiences with team-graded projects as students in college and therefore reject cooperative learning because they assume that team grades are the *only* way they can mark. Two issues must be realized as you read this chapter: (1) Team grades are only one option available in cooperative learning, and usually a bad one at that; and (2) many students, represented by Felipe, are fearful of working in teams because they assume that they will be "brought down" by their teammates. This attitude is reinforced by many parents. Teachers must have a solid grading plan (a structure) and they must articulate it so that everyone understands it and knows why the teacher thinks that it is fair and effective for her or his students.

GRADING OPTIONS

Although there are potentially hundreds of grading schemes (and combinations of schemes), I have chosen to describe carefully several that I think have potential for success with a cooperative learning-based system of instruction. Each has several varieties that make it adaptable for all levels of education and for all subject areas. Also, some of these systems can be combined to form even more complex, but perhaps appropriate, systems.

Individual Examinations with Group-Based Bonus Plan

The first grading policy chosen for discussion is perhaps the wisest and most easily adaptable for many teachers. Simply put, this system calls for students to study and work together as teams during class time while carrying some responsibility (or interdependence) into the test arena. Students get to share ideas, help each other learn, and explain and modify their understanding of schoolwork, *but* they test in a traditional manner: Each student does his or her own test alone. However, grades are determined with one twist; each student receives his or her own score and a bonus if *every* member of the student team scores above a criterion mark set by the teacher. Let's look at two examples of this system in operation:

1. Niola is one of four teammates that work together in a third-grade science class. She scored an 83 on the Friday quiz. Her teacher had set the bonus criterion for 78, and when her teammates George (79), Phil (98), and Marcia (84) all reached or surpassed that level, she and her teammates all received a 5-point bonus. Niola's score was recorded as 88. (By the way, the teacher changes the criterion level and the amount of the bonus each week; 2 weeks ago they all had to get at least an 85 because the "stuff was easy," but they did not get the 3-point bonus because George got an 82.)

2. In the 11th-grade math class, Jaime, Rod, Doris, and Martez needed to score above 80 to secure each other a bonus set by Ms. Juhngin. Three of the students were in the high 90's, but Rod's 79 caused them all to miss the extra points.

The bonus system is often seen as the wisest for two reasons:

1. It demands individual accountability, which is a factor that students, teachers, parents, and administrators generally see as the "most fair" and certainly the most traditional way of grading.

2. It does not punish a student for the lack of success of a teammate. Although this may limit cooperation and interdependence a bit, it often keeps the "good" students working. It also lowers the level of bitterness that often ensues from first-time efforts with teamwork. Our earlier situation with Felipe suggests that he may well fear that he would be hindered working with slower or less able colleagues; under this system he need not fear that eventuality.

Please note that losing a bonus is fundamentally different than having something taken away, for instance, if a student's grade is lowered because of a teammate's failure. The philosophical distinction between these two conditions is important and should be made clear to students. A practical example may illustrate this point more than the theoretical explanation given and may well be one that you will choose to use with your students.

The Johnsons (1987) suggest one system of grading in which each member of a cooperative group takes the test alone and then *one* test is randomly selected for scoring and that grade is given to everyone on the team. Thus, Joan, who had answered 95% correct, receives the same grade of 78 as Roland, Marty, and Babs because Marty's 78% was the paper chosen for scoring. This system makes many students howl negatively, especially when this system is first introduced (later, once team learning is accepted and liked, many more judge it as "fair"). It can create bitterness and dissension as well, something the novice user of cooperative learning really does not need.

Compared to this random choice approach, giving a bonus if everyone does well makes more sense and is more like the real world. For example, in professional sports each player signs an individual contract, but is awarded evenly divided portions of extra bonus money for playoff participation, when the team achieves at a high level. Also, many companies have included bonus systems as incentives for employees as evidenced by the numerous profit-sharing systems in corporate America. They are seen as rewards for both individual and group-based achievements.

Another version of the individual test plus bonus system calls for teammates to score a certain total number of points to qualify for the bonus. Thus, instead of attempting to bring everyone up to a certain minimum level of success (i.e., 78%, 80%), it recognizes a wider disparity of ability and sets a criterion of total points. For example, on a spelling test of 20 words, each student receives a score (i.e., 16 correct equals 80%) and each four-person team has a criterion set of 60 right answers for the bonus. Group 1, the Honey Bears, have scores of 20, 20, 18, and 11 for a total of 69 correct; therefore, each member qualifies for the bonus. Group 2, the Sugar Bears, has scores of 14, 17, 13, and 15 for a total of 59, so they do not qualify for the bonus.

This type of system accomplishes its goal of linking students' success to each other and helps motivate them to work together effectively when given the chance. It also helps clarify the students' ability to assist one another by identifying weaknesses and strengths without assigning negative consequences to that action. In the preceding example, if Group 2 were given another attempt at the test and provided 15 minutes to study together, one could picture the students helping one another on the very words that they had missed. This is a form of remediation and individualization that most traditional teachers find very difficult to accomplish.

Individual Examinations

In this model, the students work together as teammates during class time to study and learn in various ways. However, all graded exercises are done individually and there is no interdependence of grades.

At first glance, this seems to be an odd system to use in a cooperative learning setting. After all, there is no built-in motivation to help others. Because others' grades are not reflected in one's own, there is no sense of mutual ownership of the one thing that really counts in school, namely, grades. Finally, it does not seem to reward students for helping others. However, several theorists have argued these positions, including Alfie Kohn, and have based their position on the following premises:

1. Cooperation is its own reward and does not need to be reinforced by "gold stars" or other incentives.

2. The use of incentives such as those outlined in the bonus plan option described in the last section might damage the altruistic developments arising from working together (Kohn, 1994). Rewarding someone for doing something she or he would do naturally makes a mercenary out of him or her; damages creativity (Amabile, 1989); and reduces the frequency of the desired behavior when the reward is not present.

3. Cooperative learning should stress learning, *not* grading. Students should learn together but do not have to be evaluated in a mutually interdependent way.

Thus, the use of individual exams is extremely simple, and has been practiced by almost all teachers during the past several hundred years. However, teachers who opt for this grading system should not forget that the team does study together prior to the individual test. For example, Smith spends at least part of every third-period English class with her teammates Rioux, Mehta, Grando, and Fredericks. Every other Friday they take a test in the course and receive individual grades.

I have little evidence that such a system, while judged "fair" by many, is of any real value to a cooperative learning system. I clearly come down on the side of offering incentives to induce the desired behavior and against the coercion evident in the teacher who says "Here is a list of the words for tomorrow's test; remember that if you fail you will not be eligible for sports." The "no pass, no play" rule is far more coercive than suggesting a five-point bonus for successfully helping a classmate.

Interestingly, many teachers who feel that they are "moving slowly" into cooperative learning, do not like to fool around with their grading schemas and therefore unreflectively and mindlessly opt for this individualist system. However, students like our ubiquitous Felipe who are doing well on their own and have no reason to trust the shift to teamwork may need the bonus system just to sample it. Using *all* individual assignments may well quench any incentive to work together. It certainly negates the philosophical attempts to tie schoolwork to the teamwork present in adult culture such as that found in the contemporary business world. Mixing individual grades *with* other evaluation systems makes far better sense to me.

One final note is offered while we are thinking about the possibility of studying together, but testing alone. Although I do not think that this is a very valuable system, the reverse, studying alone and testing with personal grades contingent on another's work, does have research support! Fraser, Diener, Beaman, and Kelem (1977) conducted a study that used varied amounts of limited student-to-student contact but which tested alone, and graded student A in conjunction with his or her distant partner, student B. For example, Fraser's college students did have some contact with partners, but spent the majority of their studying time alone. Tested individually, the grade they received was the average of the two partners. The study found an increase in the amount of material learned during the course and found higher grades than those earned by students who worked alone the previous year! Apparently, having others depend on one's performance is a motivator to work hard.

Collaborative Testing

One interesting modification of the standard testing package is to allow student teammates to take part of a test or quiz collaboratively in their team. This type of test does not suggest that the students wait for Bobby Bright to decide what the answer to each question is and then all four teammates write it down. Its intent is for students to take a set of essay or objective questions and analyze them together, *without* reaching a consensus. Then each student records his or her answer individually.

I use versions of this system often in my own classes and often add these stipulations:

1. For teams that work hard during a unit and have shown that they can help each other and work effectively, the collaborative test is used as a reward and an incentive to mark the desired behavior.

2. The groups are instructed to discuss items but *not* to rely on any one person to supply the answer. This is checked by teacher observation *during* the test.

3. Questions are used that both review and evaluate important content but which call for divergent, creative, or separate responses.

Here are several examination examples for item 3:

- Every one in the team takes a different item from the list of terms for Unit I. They are to briefly define the concept, explain how it fits into the rest of the material, and create three examples of the concept.

- For a fourth-grade history class, tell the students the following: One of you is a farmer, a soldier, an enslaved teenager, and an elderly grandmother. Briefly write a letter "back home" telling about your perceptions of the Civil War. Be sure to use at least three of the ideas we developed in class.

- For a language arts class, tell the students the following: Because February is Black History Month, each of you is to write and illustrate a Haiku poem about a famous African-American. Design a way to integrate the group's work together. You may use your notes . . . you have 15 minutes. Ready, go!

Please note that the preceding examples are helped by the kind of collaboration a professional writer would have when doing a similar task. Compare them to the following examples:

Which word is spelled correctly?:

1. grungie   2. bouy   3. marchall   4. gymnasium

Please pick out the capital of New York:

1. Albany   2. New York   3. Buffalo   4. Long Island

These two examples might invite simple copying and deter real discussion, whereas the earlier three do not. The first three examples given are far more valuable items for learners' cognitive growth. One advantage to the use of cooperative teams is that students can be asked to do far more complex tasks than usual and this type of testing system takes advantage of that fact.

Group-Graded Projects

Although I started this section by talking about grading structures, what I am really doing is disseminating strategies that can be used within overall systems. Later, I will provide you with some quarter-grade approaches that integrate some of these components and represent what most teachers do: They figure out some formula for tests, quizzes, homework, class work, participation, projects, individual assignments, etc., and weigh each accordingly. However, some cooperative learning teachers omit all of that and simply make the quarter grade dependent on teamed projects, a system that other advocates (Kagan, 1995) and I do not like and suggest you avoid at all costs.

Picture what can go wrong during the first quarter of the school year, when Felipe finds his grade critically dependent on the work of his teammates. If he is a dedicated student, he will find himself doing most of the work—and feeling embittered at his partners for "ripping him off." He might lose motivation and, consequently, if the group-graded project is done solely outside of the classroom, the issue may never be discovered by the teacher if Felipe elects to do all of the work and cover for the failure of the other team members. While Felipe may be trying hard and accomplishing a great deal, his teammates' lack of effort may *lower* his grade significantly.

The issue of group grades is not all one sided, however. There is some evidence that students can learn to like a group-graded system. Johnson, Johnson, Buckman, and Richards (1986) discovered that after a 4-week project, middle school students grew to believe that group grades were fair. Interestingly, work on those projects was done under direct teacher supervision and under a system in which each student had to sign a paper verifying that she or he did indeed contribute. This close monitoring of individual participation mattered to the success of the projects and to the attitude change of the students and is a vital part of the Johnsons' system.

Secondly, a study with college students (Hwong, Caswell, Johnson, & Johnson, 1992) showed that they came to view group-affected grades as "more fair" than individual grades in less than half of a semester. Again, structures were manipulated in the study so that these subjects were made to feel "responsible" toward each teammate.

Thus, confronted with somewhat disparate views on the use of group grades, I suggest that they be used under these circumstances only:

1. Teams are teacher assigned. No self-picked teams for these projects should be allowed.

2. The project is of lengthy duration, has multiple parts, requires multiple skills and talents, and is worked on during class hours.

3. Students clearly articulate the expectations of each teammate and specify individual roles regarding how they fit together. (I like to joke that the second string quarterback on the Super Bowl champion's team gets a ring, even if he does not play in the game. His real part is played during the week and he therefore is no minor part of the team's success.)

4. *Most importantly,* the group-graded project should not be the first activity engaged in by the team. This rule is often violated. A significant portion of the cooperative learning process takes place in team evaluation, self-assessment, and time spent working on varied activities prior to the project. These all help make the project a success.

For example, in a fifth-grade classroom, Ms. Kloinder built four student teams and they worked daily on class activities for several weeks before she announced their big "country" project, a group-graded event. Each team had to submit its plan and had to justify the responsibilities of each member.

At times, groups like those in Kloinder's room that have worked together effectively actually *prefer* being group graded on projects because it is seen as the fairest of all grades! It means true sharing, true teamwork ("Just like in sports!"), true interdependence, and so on; K–12 teams will often opt for group grades if a project is assigned *after* the group has experienced some successes. Therefore, group grading does merit being one of the options here, but it should *never* be the only structure nor should it be the first one used.

Daily Grades

The final alternative I wish to describe here is one that I have regularly used in my teachings of seventh grade through college: I "grade" the students every day, and vary that grade from an individually scored one to a collective group. Several good things happen when teachers fix a numerical value to their perceptions of every students' achievements that day:

1. Teachers become very conscious of every child and more observant on a daily basis.

2. Teachers are more likely to use "good" activities in class so they can witness students actually at work and can see their products at the end of class.

3. The cooperative team is more likely to receive teacher feedback about their efforts if the teacher is in an evaluative mode on a regular basis.

4. Fewer students are overlooked, and this includes the frequently absent, the quiet, the shy, and the females identified by research (Sadker & Sadker, 1994) who are so often forgotten.

With the need to "grade" each student comes the need to observe each student closely. Many teachers have told me that they never understood the cooperative learning theorists' use of the term *facilitator* until they began grading each student every day. They have found that they truly observe and try to record the actions and reactions of students while they are working on projects. Consequently, this process forces them to move around and comment on student behavior. Thus, students begin to take ownership of their own teamed learning, with the supportive assistance of the teacher.

While appearing on the surface to be just a Skinnerian reinforcement schedule ("Nice comment, Bill . . . keep encouraging your teammates, you have a +5 today"), this system is more sophisticated than that. The philosophy expressed is a very blue collar, or "lunchbox," approach that recognizes that each student has his or her own daily work responsibility. Thus team learning can count both as a positive experience and as a positive grade when student contributions are recognized.

In the daily grade system that I advocate, a score from 0 to 5 would be used to register an approximate value for the quantity and quality of the interaction and contribution made on a particular day. Although advocates of this system do differ on the liberality of their scoring system, it seems that a student who tries to work with his or her teammates, engages in the tasks, and sincerely attempts to learn the material, would receive a 4 on a 5-point scale; this is not a norm in the sense of average, but a norm that presents a standard expectation for the daily assignment. A score of 5 on this scale would *not* be reserved for the "best" student that day (a competitive system will destroy the entire team learning approach) nor for the "best" team that day; rather it would be given to a person/team who did the expected, showed a sense of enthusiasm, or had gained insights that helped the others learn or complete the task. A score of 5 is very common in active and engaged cooperative classrooms.

Scores of 2 and 3 reflect behaviors below expectations. A 3 is often the result of a student needing correction or encouragement to return to work; the student then often does so! Scores of 0 and 1 are infrequently given and are marks that warrant serious concern. To receive a 0, a student has to refuse to work cooperatively (i.e., take a "0" on a task) or continue to be disruptive after several warnings and consequently she or he had to be removed from the group.

An absent student receives no points (no learning, no contribution) but should be allowed to do an activity that serves as a makeup effort if she or he wishes to recover the points. This makeup work is often done alone, and is a situation that bothers many cooperative learning teachers. Some of my colleagues deal with this in a way similar to that of missed tests; that is, they give a special, individualized makeup task. Often, this test takes the form of helping someone learn something related to class or helping a teammate improve on a quality related to the missed work. Many districts do not allow teachers to do anything that might be interpreted as "punishment" to a legally absent child. (Note that many teachers think that absenteeism is one of the major obstacles they face.) Every teacher may wish to work out a system that fits her or his local needs, but identifying the standards, or "rubrics," for each grade should be done carefully, publicly, and in writing.

Daily Grade Examples

To gain a little familiarity with the daily grade rubrics that were detailed earlier, I now present several examples of observed student behavior and ask you to grade the behavior on a 0 to 5 scale. Remember that 4 is the level of expectation (the B level). Also remember that for the most part the teacher is trying to sell the students on the benefits of cooperative learning and is using the grade to help encourage them to do the right thing.

1. Stanley is a fourth grader who worked for 20 minutes in his language arts team today. Each of the four members is writing a horror story. His story received high praise from Jessica and Anthony, but fellow teammate Harold kept wandering to another group. Stanley managed to get Harold to read and comment by going after him. Stanley also made sure that his comments about the other papers were understood, especially by Harold. Near the end of the session, Stanley got a neat idea about adding a ghost to one part of the story.

Stanley's daily grade   0   1   2   3   4   5

2. Parvinder is a member of an eighth-grade partnership that is researching local history in social studies class. Today, half the class time was spent in partnerships, devising an outline of their work so far. Twice during the 30 minutes, Mr. Martin had to remind Parvinder to get back to work and help his partner, Sharon. A couple of times Parvinder helped Sharon begin the outline, but she did most of the work. When Mr. Martin was not looking, Parvinder snuck over and joked with Sal. Mr. Martin caught and scolded him.

Parvinder's daily grade   0   1   2   3   4   5

3. In an 11th-grade math class, Ms. Curtaine has asked the students to break into their four-person teams (she calls them *base groups*) and create sets of quadratic equation problems that utilize the principles found in the text examples. She wanted the students to be able to solve their own problems and explain them to others. Gloria worked at these for the entire 30 minutes, as did each of her teammates. The

teacher did wander by, watched, and said nothing (just smiled and nodded). Twice, Gloria noted that a problem being designed had a flaw and was thanked by Jake and Franie. At the close of class, the sheets were signed by all who felt that they had contributed (a technique invented by the Johnsons) and turned in; the next day the groups would solve each other's problem sets.

Gloria's daily grade   0   1   2   3   4   5

4. Kanisha is in a second-grade pair with Gustus. Today they are spending a few minutes "interviewing each other about life and career possibilities for when they are grown up." Kanisha asked a lot of questions, said "good" a lot, and smiled at Gustus's answers; he did the same. She learned a lot and decided that they should draw their discoveries on a large sheet of paper. At the end, the two of them (along with Gustus's friend Dion, who was finished and had wandered over) were on the floor crayoning their findings and, in fact, implementing her ideas.

Kanisha's daily grade   0   1   2   3   4   5

Now that you have evaluated the behaviors of various children in different settings, at different tasks, and in different structures, you have a better idea about the process. In each case, you had to spend time observing the individual and the group. That observation may have led to an intervention (a warning, a smile, or a nod) and thus served as a reinforcer. The grade you placed on the students makes sense now; it is not a simple accounting of participation, but an attempt to put a value on how well the students are fulfilling their obligations and engaging in desired learning behaviors. It also offers an estimate of how much has been learned.

Although many educators have trouble with a system such as this, the vast majority of students see it as the most fair system because they have been graded on their *actual* work in class, as is the case with most of their parents who get paid for the work they do every day. Many students see the system of weekly quizzes and tests as having little to do with their daily classroom experiences and efforts and see no validity in doing them. Daily grades are a truly authentic assessment of desired behaviors.

Those considerations aside, here are the scores that I would have recorded for the four children we evaluated:

Answer Key

1. Stanley certainly did everything that he was asked and actually went beyond the call of duty when he chased his partner down! He demonstrated that he was learning and that he was trying. I would give him a score of 5. If every student behaved like that every day, just imagine how much could be accomplished in school!

2. The best score I could give Parvinder for that day is a 2. He has been off task, negligent about his work, and has hurt the chances of his teammates. Although his behavior is typical of many of our youngsters, it should not be allowed to go

without some form of correction. He did show some signs of cooperating, so I would avoid the score of 1.

3.   Gloria's day was meaningful and suggests that she will have accomplished a lot. I would certainly give her at least a 4, and feel assured that everyone would be better off by her receiving a 5. Gloria's supportive correction of the flaws is a skill that will serve her well in life and I hope that someone has noticed that she has acquired it.

4.   Kanisha deserves a 5 and I would probably give the same score to Gustus even though "more leadership" was shown by Kanisha. This pair worked very well and extended themselves quite a bit. Once again, we find that once they get started, cooperative individuals tend to work very well, exceed the standard expectations of the situation, enjoy themselves, act creatively, solve problems, and learn a lot. Not surprisingly, Kanisha received a 5 and so did two of the other three students. (Although these are fictional scenarios, they do represent observations that I have made in their real-life counterparts.)

One final point before closing this section: A great deal of research suggests that students of all ages like to be active in class; they like to make things or at least have some product of their work; and they like to work with peers (Goodlad, 1984; Grant & Sleeter, 1986). It should come as no shock that most students do well under the kinds of conditions set in our hypothetical examples! They were engaged and active, worked with peers, were busy designing something, *and* received feedback and a rewarding grade for their behavior. Most real students would react positively most of the time—Parvinder's case becomes the exception, *not* the rule. Compare the motivational support of the various activities described earlier with the following examples from poorly run traditional classrooms. (The following examples were also built from actual situations.) Score these students as you did the others:

1.   Juanita is in a third-period science class at Happy Valley Middle School. The first 10 minutes sees the teacher call on students to read the answers to their homework problems. For 25 minutes he then "gives notes," which means that he talks about ideas and points to an outline on the board. Today, Juanita has written down everything that was on the board but has heard little else. During this segment, the teacher asks six questions, four of which Timmy Smith answers. As a matter of fact, the teacher tends to call on the first person to raise his hand and shout out; 90% of the time this is a boy. The last five minutes of class are marked by a few announcements about upcoming events and a reminder to do the homework and get ready for the big test.

Juanita's daily grade   0   1   2   3   4   5

2.   In his sixth-grade class, Johnny finds that social studies is always just before lunch. Mrs. Candrell has them read at home every night and questions them on their reading. They may not use notes in class but they do have "silent time," which is 5 minutes prior to questioning, to prepare. Today, Mrs. Candrell's eight questions and their respondents are as follows:

When did Columbus start his third voyage? (Jill)

Were the reasons the same as the others? (Frank, Lionel, Mark)

Where did Columbus get his money? (Chris)

Was Columbus crazy? (Chris)

Was Columbus a hero? (Thad)

Was Columbus successful? (Brian)

What did the book say about the importance of the trip? (Chris)

Why did Columbus make these trips? (Chris)

This recitation went quickly and was marked by the teacher's use of gesture and posture; she moved around and talked a great deal. However, Johnny did not pay any attention and sat staring at the teacher's eyes. If the great educator John Dewey was correct about "students learning what they do," then Johnny learned no history that day because he never once focused on the teaching–learning process.

Johnny's daily grade   0   1   2   3   4   5

Note that whatever you circled for Johnny's daily grade must be looked at again. I am not sure that Johnny was supposed to do anything during class. Mind you, he certainly did not behave in a way that helped him learn and yet he was not a discipline problem. Compare this boy's behavior with any of the other students—Parvinder included—in the four examples that we scored earlier to establish the effectiveness of the active atmosphere of cooperative learning.

In summary, grading students in their daily cooperative learning work session may be time consuming and intimidating, and it may force students to behave, but it does have the potential to encourage learning and sharing behavior and to lead to

TABLE 4.1   Daily Grade Tally

Student Name	M	T	W	Th	F	M	T	W	Th	F	M	Total = Grade
Marika	4	5[a]	4	5	4	h[b]	3	4	4	5	4	42/50=84
Joshua	5(1)	5	4	5	4(1)	h	3	5(2)	4	5	5(2)	51/50=100[c]
Manny	3	5	4	3	4(1)	h	3	3	4	5	4	39/50=78
Donna	A[d]	5	4	5	4(2)	h	3	4	4	5	5	Incomplete

[a] On Tuesday (week 1) and Friday (week 2) all members of the team scored a +5 for their achievements. Some teachers would recognize this as an event calling for recognition and/or a bonus point or two. This teacher does neither.

[b] An *h* indicates a Monday holiday.

[c] Joshua's teacher would not put a 102 in the book, although his brother's teacher did. In addition, Joshua was not allowed to give his points to Manny, who "needed them." Even though he had already secured a 100, Joshua continued to help his teammates on their assignments.

[d] Absences, like Donna's on Monday, had to be made up by the end of the quarter. Eventually she did some work (helping Manny on a paper) and received a 4 for that absence; thus, her grade eventually became 45/50=90.

recognized desired achievements and actions. To me, it is a wonderful component of cooperative learning.

Finally, one may ask what is done with all of these daily grades? In short, they can be recorded and kept. In time, they serve to form the basis of a test or project grade and can be used as part of the overall quarter grade.

With a 5-point scale, every 2 weeks or so 50 points worth of class time will have been graded. The daily totals can be added and used as a test score. Teams may have members with vastly different grades depending on the scenarios that play out, or they may have very similar scores. Peruse the example given in Table 4.1, which was drawn from a seventh-grade social studies roster. (Note that the extra score in parentheses indicates an optional bonus mark for homework that some students chose to complete.)

SPECIAL SITUATIONS

The concerns about grading bother many a teacher attempting cooperative learning for the first time. For reasons that have to do with past experience, traditional beliefs, and student expectations, teachers need to have absolutely clear policies and rationales. In working with practitioners, it has become clear that many teachers seek to avoid grading teamed work for fear of sabotaging their own efforts; therefore, they use totally individualized grading. Of course, most of these trials are thus sabotaged because without some sort of interdependent grading, students feel no formal obligation to work in teams as assigned. This section looks as several situations— always presented hypothetically—that trouble teachers and have not already been answered in the text. As you read along, you should evaluate my responses and compare them to yours.

High Absenteeism

Each district has a distinct policy regarding absences. Some say that work must be allowed to be made up; others suggest that alternatives be provided; and every district distinguishes between acceptable and unacceptable absences. Let's look at several suggestions that may help teachers come up with reasonable options in the case of legitimate absences.

If the daily work involved group or teamwork, the makeup assignment should also involve similar work. If the missed lesson involved soliciting someone else's opinion or teaching something to someone, for example, the makeup work (either daily grade or quiz) should also require the same. In many cases, helping a teammate master some material is the best solution in a K–6 situation. In grades 7 through 12, after-school makeup work may not be possible although it should be the first option.

Working alone to complete a grouped task can be allowed but it should be the *last* option offered. For example, Rod missed 3 days this week while his teammates completed a project about the life cycle for eighth-grade science class. They received a B+ for their efforts and although he was there on Monday for the beginning, he did not contribute (or attend) enough to warrant being given the grade. He was asked to work on a similar project with Manny when he too returns from illness, but now it appears that Manny will not be back for a month. Rod was then asked to plan and teach similar content to a group of seventh graders who have their esteem period during his study hall time; that did not work out either. Finally, the teacher allowed him to do an individual paper for the grade.

In the case of Rod's peer, Furman, no makeup was allowed. He was present for all 4 days of that project, but was disruptive and bothersome to his teammates: Five times he was warned by the teacher and did not improve or try. Finally, he was asked to do the work alone. He refused to do the project at all and received a 0 for the work. His teammates were graded as a group and received a B for the project, and on the test that covered the material they each received 90%. They did not receive the bonus, however, because Furman did not get 80% or better; his 0 prevented them from the bonus because he was only removed from the project, not the bonus situation. His teammates did speak to him about trying harder next week, mainly because they wanted a shot at the bonus.

No Assignment of Grades

For the most part, teachers must assign grades because evaluation is considered part of their job and, in practice, graded work represents the "real curriculum" and the real work of the school. If the teacher does not grade group-related efforts, but does grade individually completed work, an unfair imbalance exists. Many females and male minority students do much better in teamed situations. It seems unfair to deprive them of opportunities to be graded on learning under the conditions most opportune for them.

Portfolios

The portfolio approach mixes wonderfully with cooperative learning because it supports active learning, and the completion of materials demonstrates success. In a system that requires a portfolio, much of the work can be collaboratively constructed or peer reviewed, and class can easily become a workshop for the completion of submissions; having part (or all) of it teamed should facilitate the process.

When I use portfolios, I identify the assignments that are expected in each portfolio and also allow the students to choose items for inclusion. With regard to the teacher-assigned submissions, some are to be done individually and some done as a team. All of these are required and many are done during class time.

Students Who Want to Work Alone

How should a teacher approach a student who just will *not* work with any others or *insists* that he or she can do all the work alone? This is actually an easy item to answer. Exposure to a diverse set of circumstances and learning styles is critical to individual development. If I had a student who insisted that because of personal style, cultural upbringing, or personal preference, he or she needed to do all work, all tests, and all projects alone, I would say "no." As a teacher, my job is to (1) strengthen student skills in a variety of circumstances; (2) teach students to be tolerant and to work effectively with diverse populations; (3) strengthen student understanding of the principles of the democratic heritage; and (4) maximize students' knowledge bases. I could not do all of these with a teamed study approach *alone.* (Similarly, high stake examinations are individually done, a fact I cannot change, and I do have to prepare students for them as well.) Studying in isolation is not in the students' best educational interests, as inclusion projects can attest. Likewise, I would say "no" to the student who wanted study only in same-sex pairs.

I am the teacher and have a great deal of power over my professional decisions about grading policy. I seek to be fair and I seek to use broad and diverse approaches to student assessment. If I am fair and up front about my intentions, I am taking a *legal* position. Thus my grading schema and expectations *require* students to work in various arrangements.

One quick anecdote: I once had a student tell me that she would not watch a film required in a course because she does not watch films. I told her that I had a lot of kids who "do not read" but that I was still assigning reading! As a teacher, I want all of my students to succeed, regardless of background, beliefs, and styles. I honestly believe that it would not hurt anyone to do part of a course with others and thereby be required to learn to interact effectively.

Lazy Students

To no one's great surprise one of the popular questions regarding groups and grades is this one: What if I use a 50–50 split between individual grades and team grades, and I have many lazy students who seem to get higher grades than they should? It reflects in part, the belief that a group grade gives something for nothing. It also shows a disproportionate faith that tests and grades for individuals are good indicators of what one has earned, and group projects are not.

Frankly, I think that most teacher tests are not valid indicators of what has been learned and therefore an individual score is at best a rough guess. If teamed grades are higher than individual grades and the teacher is actively monitoring the group (to avoid simple outright copying) then two explanations come to mind quickly:

1. The teamed part provides a good forum to incorporate all of the students' ideas and helps them make more unified sense of what they know.

2. The teamed part provides cues that some learners need to recall and formulate ideas that are not available when they are working alone.

In both of these cases, the grade given has been *earned.* The grade is also an indicator that the student can offer something that he or she has mastered, unlike, for example, with the multiple-choice test situation, which essentially attempts to identify what the students do not know.

Finally, this question often masks concern about an easy A or B, a factor that bothers many teachers. (Note the resistance to Glasser's Quality School, 1990, which demands that students do B work by eliminating the C option. This has been met with firm resistance from teachers who wish to have a low pass option.) To them I say that it is highly unlikely for a student to get an undeserved B or A simply by being part of a group that does well on a team part of a test. My guess is that such a student does not traditionally do well on standard tests, does well in the teamed condition, and thus receives a more accurate score on an individual part because of his or her participation or the teamed component. For example, if one gets a 45% with his team on part 1 of a test, and then a 20% on part 2, he deserves to pass and has not received an unfair grade. Moreover, another student who gets that 45% on part 1 and then gets 38% on part 2, ends up with a 73, not an unduly high (or low) grade for his knowledge and his effort. (A grade of 73% looks like a C to most of us.)

Use of Authentic Assessments

Much has been written about making assessments of student learning more authentic (Armstrong, 1994; Wiggins, 1994) and this has resulted in a great increase in the demand for student portfolios and a backing away from the single-minded use of paper-and-pencil tests. As an operating principle, any evaluation that does *not* require a paper-and-pencil test is often seen as moving on the continuum toward "authenticity." Thus, those parts of the curriculum that are taught with cooperative groups have the potential of being assessed authentically. The entire daily grade structure described earlier in the chapter is a strong form of authentic assessment: The teacher takes note of the learners' efforts at learning together (process) and the results of that daily work, the achievement (product). In this way, the daily grade is a more authentic assessment than is a paper-and-pencil test.

Also, once groups work harmoniously, teachers will assign them projects and assignments that frequently result in a product other than that offered by a paper-and-pencil test. The resulting grades also count as more authentic assessment. Actually, without the use of teams in a classroom, teachers could assign projects that are authentic, *but* would have a very difficult time assessing the processing efforts students use to complete them. Many of the opportunities to judge student knowledge, effort, and perseverance would be lost. Synthesis, analysis, and application skills could only be judged by their eventual product and not by their developing use by learners.

The next decade will surely find us assessing students using formats other than paper-and-pencil tests. Even in New York State, home of the famous end-of-the-year all-size-fits-one regents test, is witnessing a change: The State Education Department is aiding districts who are seeking "variances" from those tests in their development of alternative forms of assessment (many of which involve grouped activities). New York also added a question on its sixth-grade PEP tests (evaluating the effectiveness of programs) that requires a group planned project! Finally, New York has changed its certification testing for teaching to involve a videotape of a teacher teaching along with paper-and-pencil instruments. A teacher teaching . . . sounds like a pretty valid and authentic assessment of . . . teaching! (Incidentally, the lesson is judged by a group, a board of examiners.)

In summary, authentic assessment goes hand in hand with cooperative learning. As we continue to move toward clarifying our outcomes and away from single-minded reliance on standardized tests, we will create a more user-friendly classroom, a more engaging curriculum, and a more meaningful set of learning experiences for all students.

Parents Who Dislike the New System

I have heard teachers ask "What if the parents do not like the new grading system?" Without belaboring the point, this question sounds like the teacher believes that the parents currently *like* the system in use. Clearly, that assumption may be true for the students who are doing well, that is, those like Felipe who flourish under the status quo. These families are certainly going to be in favor of a system that profits their children, even though a new one (i.e., cooperative learning) may help them even more. There is a great risk in change, but thoughtful change can be well received if it is packaged correctly. I suggest that letting parents know how and why a grading policy is being changed is important for students below the 10th grade. These parents will be less critical if they understand the rationale behind the switch (see Chapter 1 again) and especially if they see that the teacher's commitment and expectations as strong (Vermette, 1994).

Like most new things in life, the sooner successes are realized with the new system, the better everyone will feel about it. Moreover, parents often reflect what students say at home. If they are coming home saying things like "Our teacher made us into teams like Little League and we all win or lose together," "I can help my friends learn and if we all do well on the test, we all get a bonus," "We all work together and the teacher helps us do it right so that we can get good grades," and "Billy, Tommy, and Juanita helped me get the spelling words right," then most often the parents will accept your system and thank the stars that their child has you for a teacher.

Nothing succeeds like success so my advice is to make the system work for most kids right away! Very few students actually lose ground under this system and therefore the parents' thinking will come around to that of the teacher more often than not. I strongly suggest that the teacher notify parents when any new system is used; *grading policies* are only part of a cooperative system, but one that has great emotional potential. Perhaps a "letter home," similar to the generic sample presented in Figure 4.1, will head off some difficulties. As you read this draft, identify the components that you would change *if* you were sending it home to your students' parents.

Teacher Acceptance of Different Grading Norms

Another often asked question is that of "What if I am a new teacher and I sense that the school grading norms are different than mine?" This final question in our discussion of special situations is very common and also very complex. New teachers must

Dear Parent or Guardian:

This year, we will be using a rather interesting and innovative approach in our social studies class: It is called "cooperative learning" and its central theme is that each student benefits from working in teams during class time. As you well know, many of the students here in school have participated in sports teams and after-school clubs where they learned to appreciate the values of unity, loyalty, challenge, and cooperation built into working with others. In many cases, involvement in these "team" activities/settings not only helps the individuals learn more about the sport or club, they also enjoy it more and work harder at it. I wish to use classroom teams to help my students realize these advantages on a regular basis and in my regular classroom.

By the way, cooperative learning has been used successfully in many subjects and at many grade levels, but I feel that it is especially crucial in the social studies. In social studies I wish for learners to understand their own country's heritage, their own individual lives, and the problems and patterns of civilizations. They also need to learn to think critically and responsibly, and they must develop democratic skills and attitudes and learn to appreciate diversity from an individual approach to a cooperative team learning system.

1. *Construction of the Teams.* Approximately once a month, students will be assigned to stable three- or four-member teams. They will not pick their own teams, for in adult life we are expected to work effectively with all different types of people. Here at school I did not pick my colleagues or my students and their parents, yet I must work with them effectively. I am sure that this is true for you in your daily lives as well. We seldom pick our neighbors, our extended families, our workmates; however, we are expected to interact with them in a productive manner.

   Moreover, the point of teamwork on a daily basis is *not* to have students make friends out of all their classmates. Thankfully, this outcome does often happen, but friendship is not as important a goal as the development of the ability to work with people of different beliefs and backgrounds. Students learn to accept each other and help each other now to prepare themselves for similar roles as future citizens.

2. *Daily Activities.* Every day in class, at least some time will be spent in teamwork. On some occasions, groups will be completing worksheets, creating interpretive projects, rehearsing (quizzing) each other, or doing practice tests.

   While these activities *could* be done individually, they will be more productive when done by groups. Moreover, there are some new and exciting activities that can *only* be done by teams. In these lessons, students take responsibility for mastering the material, teaching it to each other, and/or meeting each other in tournament-type play. (Two of these plans are called Jigsaw and Teams–Games–Tournaments.)

   Since social studies also involves the discussion and analysis of issues, problems, and current events, each student is expected to contribute ideas and opinions from his or her perspective. The skill of solving problems in *groups* is one that modern business also requires of its workers; we will also be doing this as we prepare the students for the demands they will face as adults.

   As you can see, we are planning many different types of activities, some short and some long, some typical of school, and some not. We intend to utilize the many different

FIGURE 4.1   Sample Letter to Parent Regarding a Change in Grading Policy

types of skills and talents that team members possess so that each student will learn some new skills from teammates and broaden his or her understanding of human intelligence and abilities. In this way, every single student will gain knowledge and an appreciation of others' talents.

3. *Grading.* Students *do not* receive team grades or take *team tests* on all assignments. Just as some adults bargain for their own wages, and some have groups (e.g., unions) do it for them, we will use diverse types of grading structures. I want the students to understand different reward systems and have them evaluate each.

   Moreover, students need to experience the fact that they do better individually as their peers (teammates) succeed; and this reflects real adult life. Thus, we will use bonus systems if group members score well on tests, complete their assignments, or finish their assigned work.

   There will be group-graded projects, but most of the work will be done here in school so that we can monitor progress. I want to make sure that every student is encouraged to contribute and does his or her share of the responsibilities. Doing the work here in school also helps make all groups more equal; it would not be fair to all students if only some teams get together regularly outside of school time or if one person in a team were saddled with all the work. Democratic systems seem to flourish when all citizens take their responsibilities seriously.

4. *Rules for Teamwork.* Since so much time will be spent in group work, students will be asked to help formulate the *rules* they will follow when working together. This practice, too, is consistent with the democratic principle called "consent of the governed."

Of course the teachers and the parents have a say in this self-governing exercise as well. This is similar to the system of "checks and balances." We will be sending home the list of student-generated rules soon and ask that you discuss them with your youngster. This investigation into laws, governance, and opinions will help the students understand and appreciate these aspects of their democratic heritage.

In conclusion, I would like to add that we are very excited about this new approach and look forward to your discussion of this letter with your youngster. We have every hope of seeing it work as well here as it has in many other places. Students have learned more, learned to get along better with each other, and felt better about themselves under this system. The demands on future citizens to be knowledgeable, dependable, flexible, tolerant, and cooperative are clearly stated and widely acknowledged; with this new system, students will learn these traits in the classroom as well as on the athletic field and in after-school activities.

Cordially,

cc: Administrators
    Students

try to fit into an existing social reality; it is very difficult for them to be change agents in stable institutions and yet they often want to practice the new techniques they have just acquired.

Everyone knows that different schools have different policies regarding grading, such as these:

1. School A requires that there must be a range of grades for every class, although this never mandates F's (failures).

2. School B mandates common multiple-choice final exams, made up collaboratively by five teachers for all the students in one grade.

3. School C requires individualized service learning programs *and* assures that no more than 25% of any quarter grade comes from a teamed project.

Such policies do exist, as do ones that have courses that are "worth more" than others (i.e., honors classes that count as 105% of regular classes). These practices come from philosophies of the desirability of competition between students, from beliefs in low expectations for the "forgotten half," from a strategy that seeks to bribe students into doing what they should, and from a fear of innovation. Novices must respect and react thoughtfully to both the existing practices of the school and the philosophies that support them.

However, there is good news. Today, cooperative learning is not a fad; it is a reputable, accepted, and respected instructional practice. Moreover, institutions from the Marines to General Motors are expecting schools to graduate students who can work together in teams and who are evaluated as a collective. A new teacher who implements teamwork will find herself or himself far more in the mainstream than he or she would have been just a few years ago. Finally, I cannot imagine that many teachers are being hired today who have not shared a willingness to experiment with cooperative learning and who do not possess some knowledge of its practice.

With that said, a "lone ranger" approach that sets the new teacher against the world will have negative and damaging ramifications. If the novice user of teams has prepared a thoughtful and supportable grading plan, especially one that recognizes a variety of strategies, he or she will be in a strong position to approach parents, colleagues, students, and administrators. The use of portfolios, projects, some tests, bonuses, team projects, and daily grades all offer the promise of fairness and objectivity desired by everyone and can be welded into the existing mores of most contemporary schools.

THE USE OF GRADES

We now need to step back from the grind of setting up a scoring policy to reflect on the basic purposes of grading. This section provides an opportunity to analyze common beliefs about grades, the demands for fairness, and their implications for cooperative learning.

Imagine for a minute that you have walked into a noisy and crowded faculty room in a contemporary American middle school. It is the day after the grades for the first quarter went home to parents. A new report card is being tried and it provides comments and particulars about individual behavior as well as the traditional letter grade. On this day, the stark reality of the grading process is visible in the strained voices of the teachers talking. As if in a round-table discussion, eight teachers take turns venting their beliefs as you listen. On a separate sheet of paper, jot down your responses to each comment.

Mr. Smith: "Grading is inevitable; it is part of our job to determine how much the students know and what exactly they can do. Not everybody can master all of this, either, so the bell curve is nature's way of providing stratification."

Ms. Goldbrick: "Since I can never make tests that are completely fair, I give them many chances to take and retake a test. There is no way that I can fairly build in any sort of grouped grades with regular grades."

Ms. Fancy: "All of life is group graded: Unions all negotiate the same raise, all the guys at minimum wage get the same amount. It is very rare that two people doing similar work would receive different wages (to start). Therefore, group grades are the only way to go for work done together."

Mrs. Dowzer: "Any test or part of tests taken together . . . well, I consider that to be cheating, plain and simple. There is no way that one could take a collaborative test and see the value of the grade as anything but invalid. Studying together is OK, but a teamed test . . . can you imagine group questions or group projects on any high stakes test? Besides, where in real life does business treat its people as a unit?"

Ms. Lavell: "The only fair grading system is a contract one, whether or not it involves portfolios. All A's are not equal; all B's are not equal; and all kids are not equal. We should use a system in which grades are used as motivators, and let them strive and persevere toward goals."

Mr. Polica: "In my system, homework and participation have always counted as much as test grades because they are better indicators of what the student has learned. In that structure, there is no room for group efforts. How could one judge how well a group did on something?"

Mr. Franklin: "Grades do two things: They stratify the kids for society and they send messages home to the parents about the efforts of their kids. Both of these must be done by schools or the politicians will never be able to justify their school spending! School is the social agent to sort out the kids at government and taxpayers' expenses. If some are hurt by it, it is justified by the end result."

Miss Feldman: "The only real grades are pass and fail: Either the students got it or they did not succeed. Discrimination between 79 and 81 makes little sense and certainly does not indicate a great difference. Since the students' classroom behavior *does* affect other students, I say that we should put them in groups when we can and let them sink or swim together."

Answer Key

Because of the volatile nature of the whole grading process, I have chosen to close this potentially challenging chapter by providing one set of responses to the positions forwarded by these teachers. Be assured that this set is *my set* of answers, as opposed to the only right set of answers. As with most difficult and real problems in the world, there are no easy solutions and no universally accepted right answers. On the other hand, those who wish to implement cooperative learning teams as described here would be wise to examine my answers because they were formed with the distinct purpose of advancing the process as smoothly as possible. Comparing them to your set should prove to be a valuable exercise in reflection.

Response to Mr. Smith: "While I agree that grading is inevitable, it is because we have conceptualized schools to develop a product, not to confer a process. I sincerely believe that there is no bell curve for learning, and that we can almost ensure that if something is truly important, we can teach it to everybody and skew your 'bell.' For political reasons, we teachers have to show that learners are mastering something, and tests or portfolios can demonstrate that fact. It sounds like you want grades to stratify society: I would like school to bring everyone up to a certain level—and allow for greater growth beyond that level; teams help me do that."

Response to Ms. Goldbrick: "You sound as if students can learn to answer the questions that are on tests, but today's battle over IQ revolves around that very issue. My reading of it is that people can and do learn things and thus improve their abilities (Fraser, 1995). Group grades can and should be a *part* of that process: Some students have their major intelligence in that area and to not utilize them would be paramount to structuring their failure in the process. It may well be that a group-graded project is a better indicator of Tony's knowledge than, to use your words, an 'unfair' paper-and-pencil test would be."

Response to Ms. Fancy: "Although I agree about the cooperative nature of our society, within that collective product must be a process that ensures individual accountability and individual effort. Group grades can be the most unfair of all; especially if they reward nothing or punish great accomplishment. Group-graded projects and cooperative tests must be well structured, be fair to all, and balanced against individual assignments."

Response to Mrs. Dowzer: "I think that you and I are far apart on this issue. I agree with Ms. Fancy; for the most part, we are all in life together. A collaborative test can measure collaborative skills. How could you authentically assess them any other way? Often students know more than they can demonstrate on a regular paper-and-pencil test. The collaborative aspect gives them a chance to cue their recall, make connections, and function like people do in the real world. After school is done, no one *anywhere* in life takes tests to measure success; in life, regular assessments are authentic. Almost all jobs in our nation are collaborative, so where do the students learn how to function that way if not in school?"

Response to Ms. Lavell: "I agree that contract grading is fair and for the most part motivational. I also suspect that many students would do better if they could make those contracts, or build those portfolios, as part of teams. Working into the contract/portfolio approach a series of group or team activities is a very simple process and it would broaden the set of skills being assessed and expected of learners. You seem to have in place a system that could easily adopt a teamed component."

Response to Mr. Polica: "One could measure a group's achievement easily. For example, you could set the expectations for each person on a project and then watch and assess how each one fulfilled those expectations! Moreover, you already said that participation is important; my guess is that you place import on the learning process and the effort expended. Both of these would be helped by cooperative learning teams and in all cases individual performance could be easily assessed."

Response to Mr. Franklin: "Howard Gardner rants and raves about the 'uniform nature of schooling' (1993) and suggests that there is little content that everybody *needs* to know. Therefore, stratifying students for colleges, for jobs, for the military, and for awards is difficult to do since every person learns different things, using different intelligences. The use of cooperative teams gives many students their best shot at getting good grades both because they actually do the things in class that *cause* them to learn more, and they are far more likely to be motivated to try than they are usually (see Glasser, 1986). I personally do not care for schools and, hence, teachers as stratifying agents. I am much more comfortable seeing ourselves as agents of change, as trying to reach all kids and exposing them to modes of operation that they would not encounter elsewhere in life. We should strive to make them all successful learners and able to make good decisions about their own futures."

Response to Miss Feldman: "I do think that students' grades are heavily touched by other's work—everything from how students behave in class to asking good questions, and to the enthusiasm level of the teacher for that particular group. Like most everywhere else, we do not operate as individuals in a classroom. On the other hand, grades can motivate and they can be indicators of mastery, of achievement, and of success. Most of us who work for a living would behave differently if we were never paid for our achievements. If students received no grades at all, we would have to find other forms of recognition like Bob Slavin does with his school newsletters and awards! Moreover, there actually might be a difference between 79 and 81, as manifested by the difference in perseverance, in deciding whether or not to help someone else, in checking one's work, or in studying a little harder, with the latter behavior helping a whole team qualify for the bonus set at the 80 level. The difference might appear to be minor at first glance but it has the potential to reinforce desired behavior and attitudes and lead to higher expectations and achievements."

Please note that my responses reflect the ideas that have been developed elsewhere in the chapter and reflect a commitment to utilize the grading process to strengthen the use of cooperative teams. Each of these teachers' comments reflects a common belief or practice and each provides us with a chance to reflect on our own systems and structures. I would hope that the readers vicariously engaged in the mini-debates provided here so that they will be better able to give a clear, clean, and carefully worded grading rationale to their students. Mistakes in the development of a fully articulated grading process have ruined many attempts at using teams and have left bitter tastes in the mouths of many students regarding working with others. It is critically important that this grading structure be implemented well, and rationally defended, if the novice user of cooperative teams is to be successful.

CHAPTER 4 SUMMARY

Chapter 4, a lengthy and detailed piece, described various grading models that teachers could utilize to help build a coherent and acceptable grading policy of their own. Five specific grading alternatives were examined.

The first, the use of individual exams with group-based bonuses, has much to offer. It motivates students to work together and share in a bonus if individual criteria are reached. In addition, it does not damage an individual for a "weak" team effort.

The second, pure individualized testing, recognizes that students can learn together but not be made to feel part of a larger group through grading. While it is used often, this is seen as a weak system that does not help force students to maximize their interactions or their feelings of interdependence toward each other.

The third system, collaborative testing (full or partial), suggests that students can both study or learn together and also test together. This system recognizes the validity of teamwork and also has variations that do not allow the "straight copying" that most teachers would foresee in such a condition.

The fourth system, group-graded projects, is commonly used but raises several concerns. Like team testing, group grades invite some students to coast and some to do more than their share of work. These concerns can be mitigated easily and suggestions were offered to that end.

Finally, the fifth model calls for the use of daily grades that are either individually based or team earned. Such grading recognizes that students can be assessed authentically beyond the regular use of tests and projects. The system suggests that students should be graded every day while they work, indicating that engaging in the process of learning is analogous to the completion of the products of learning.

Teachers' philosophical concerns over grading were also dealt with; an examination of the reality of assessment resulted in an acceptance of a system that calls for grading as a useful tool. Rationales for team-based components of individual grades were advanced as well.

The remainder of the chapter dealt with the major, typically thorny issues of grading, including the fact that some team members are frequently absent, some teachers must reconcile their own grading strategies with school-based demands such as the use of portfolios, some students are just plain lazy and will not participate, and the issue of parental concern. Suggestions for these dilemmas were offered along with a quiet plea that the use of portfolios with both individual submissions *and* team-based submissions be seriously considered for the future.

REFLECTION QUESTIONS

1. Throughout this chapter, the author has utilized some underlying assumptions that are worth deeper analysis. Evaluate your perception of each of the following beliefs:

   a. Students are motivated by the very possibility of receiving higher grades, especially if they are attached to meaningful activities and are conducted with peer help.

   b. Students can be motivated by working with peers who are *assigned* to them, instead of *chosen* by them.

   c. Paper-and-pencil tests have only limited validity and often they do not measure what a student "knows" about a topic.

   d. Daily assessments are far more genuine and therefore more authentic than are end-of-unit paper-and-pencil tests.

   e. Working with others is more prevalent in the real world than is working alone.

   f. Students should be required to try to learn and to be assessed in a diverse set of styles and under diverse conditions, both to utilize their strengths and to develop their weaknesses.

   g. Grading policies are heavily controlled by the teacher, and thus the grade a student "earns" is heavily dependent on the teacher's perceptions of a fair and just system.

2. Throughout this chapter the author has been dealing with both concerns for maximizing the workings of the cooperative team (an empirical question) and the fairness of a grading system (a philosophical issue). To assess how well I have conveyed these issues, I offer a small quiz—a true paper-and-pencil test dealing with what the teacher has taught.

   Below are the descriptions of three tenured science teachers working with the seventh grade in a local middle school. Each has a different system, believing that he or she is using cooperative team learning, and has had the system accepted by the administration. Each is therefore "legal" and in operation. Please rank order these from 1 (highest) to 3 (lowest) with regard to how you think that I, the author, would rate them. This is a prediction activity, because I will offer my answers in time. As you read, predict how I would (comparatively) rate them and, later, after checking your perception and my answers reflect on how well (or poorly) I was able to make the case for particular evaluation practices.

Ms. Konrad: During 10 weeks of science, Ms. Konrad's students are placed in three-person teams. They do daily science activities such as compare notes, complete worksheets, answer questions, and solve problems. They are given a teamed, "contribution" grade at the end of the quarter. These are individually based, accounting for such variations as absences and effort. About half the time the teams all receive the same grade. The other half has members receiving disparate grades. This grade is one-third of the science quarter grade.

Another one-third of the quarter grade is based on weekly, 20-item "objective" quizzes that are taken and scored individually. No bonuses are offered and there is little pressure put on having students encourage their teammates to study for quizzes.

The final third of the grade comes from one big team project, which is also an item given a group grade. Generally, students are put into teacher-built teams (the same ones used for daily work) and at the half point of the quarter are assigned a topic (e.g., our muscles, how the telescope works) and each topic is split into three parts: One student does one part *but* the grade is an overall rating of the three parts and how they are integrated. Konrad gives the students 20 minutes on each of 4 days to help them pull their parts together 1 week prior to the due date.

Mr. Feinblatt: Feinblatt builds his quarter grade on just two components: assignments and tests. Students are placed into randomly built teams every Monday and complete daily activities in teams. The products of these activities (notes, pictures, descriptions, etc.) are scored on plus or minus basis. Individuals are scored, *but* most of the members of a team end up with the same grade.

The other 50% of the grade is built on tests and quizzes (a quiz is a test that counts half!). These are almost always store-bought 25-item multiple-choice questions, and he does offer a bonus: If a team has one member with at least 88% and no score lower than 60%, every team member gets a 4-point bonus. Truthfully, this happens almost every time so that members do feel some sense of urgency to help (at least enjoin) others. Interestingly, there is only a low correlation between high rankings on one part and high on the other; in other words, students scoring high on assignments probably do not do well on tests. The system is seen as disjointed and the students themselves often say that they get two grades averaged in their "two" science classes.

Mr. Sheehan: A strong advocate of cooperative learning, Sheehan gives three tests during the quarter and assigns daily homework that accounts for the other part of the score. The first test is unique in that it is taken twice. The first administration is individual and does offer a 4-point bonus if all members of a team score more than 75%. However, the test is then readministered and taken collaboratively; that is, students take the test the second time in their teams and may discuss answers before putting their 50 true/false choices on paper. Students are asked to pick, prior to getting the grades, which test they wish to have count. The other two tests are normally taken individually and do offer a bonus.

The daily grade/homework grade reflects the idea that they are in school to work, to interact and to share and by doing so they will learn. Homework is seen as individual time to practice and understand class materials. Daily homework is collected at the start of every class and is graded on a 0, 1, 2 scale.

Ranking (1, highest; 3, lowest)

Konrad   _____

Feinblatt   _____

Sheehan   _____

Answer Key: The ranking process is easy for me because the criteria I wish to use involves two questions: (1) How does the system motivate students to master the material? (2) How does the system encourage students to help each other? I sense that Sheehan's system does this the best and actually allows the students to take one test together, quite a radical idea today.

Feinblatt's system ends up being half-good, which is better than not good at all. To a large degree, the students will end up trying to help each other, but they must have time to do so.

Perhaps surprising to you, I ranked Konrad third. I fear that the system that requires a group-graded project—but shows disdain for teamed activity on a regular basis and on regular tests—ends up as a paradox. The students are receiving mixed messages; they are asked to work together and yet are really unable to be effective as teammates during the project. More than the other two, Konrad appears to be using cooperative teams as just another strategy, *not* as an organizing philosophy to run the classroom. My guess is that the system is pretty messy in practice and that many students end up with bad feelings about "working together."

3. Several case studies follow of children receiving grades from teachers experimenting with cooperative learning. For each case, identify aspects that you (a) consider fair or unfair and (b) expect to be effective or ineffective in making the teams work. I will do the first one as a model:

Debbie: Debbie is a fourth grader at Competitive Valley School. In her arithmetic class, the teacher assigns daily homework and weekly quizzes. Grades are marked on the curve so that about 20% of the kids get A's, 30% B's, 30% C's, 10% D's, and the bottom 10% fail. In her class of 30, this translates to three failures and six A's. The teacher, by the way, has no explanation of why this system differs from the traditional statisticians' curve, but does not seem to worry very much about that part.

At the end of the 10 weeks, Debbie's scores looked like this: 13, 15, 9, 22, 21, 17, 14, 11, 14, 10, a total of 146, placing her 16th from the top and getting her a C in Math.

Answer Key: This system, and those like it are travesties for several reasons. First, the grading system shows no relationship between achievement and scores. We have no idea how much Debbie learned, just that she was in the bottom half of her group. The structure also does not allow any accountability for the teacher, who may or may not be doing a good job. Frankly, bell curve systems are the curse of our educational system and should be outlawed! Worst of all, college instructors are the biggest users of them and they are the models provided to novice teachers.

Second, the curved system invites students to tear down the achievements of others and to create divisiveness between students and between groups of students. Competition is supposed to be the result of a curved system and it may occur; however, competition rarely maximizes performance and focuses on relative gain, *not* overall achievement. To finish first in a spelling bee does not mean one is a good speller, just that one did better than rivals. Likewise losing a spelling bee (or four Super Bowls like my beloved Buffalo Bills) does not indicate a bad speller or poor team, just a less able one that day. Moreover, such competitions hurt members of some groups, like females, disproportionately hard (Weisfield, Weisfield, Warren, & Freedman, 1983).

Interestingly, Debbie's teacher tried cooperative learning on the day before one of the tests, but it did not work very well. Frankly, the students did not appear eager to help each other, which is no surprise when you realize that they are hurting themselves in *relative ranking* every time they help someone else learn something!

Last, all the advantages of cooperative learning are usually lost when teachers attempt to make teams compete. Many teachers disliked Slavin's somewhat successful STAD and TGT because they contained aspects of required losing. (TGT includes a tournament round that pits the weakest members of every team; the person who loses that round stands out as the clear choice for "Least Able Student" in the class. That is a pretty tough load for most children.)

Newman and Thompson's (1987) analysis of cooperative programs for grade 7–12 students showed no disadvantages when completely noncompetitive systems (like the ones the Johnsons advocate) are compared to Slavin's. The affective results, of course, favor total cooperative inclusion rather than winner–loser competition.

Three more case examples follow for you to examine:

Frank: Frank is an eighth grader. His social studies teacher has assigned him to a four-person team for the entire quarter. His quarter grade will be composed of the following marks, all on a 0–100 scale:

a. his three individually taken plus bonus point for team achievement tests (90 + 5; 88 + 0; 76 + 5) = 88 average;

b. his one group/team essay test = 85;

c. his individual project = 78; and

d. his team project, a group grade = 85.

This quarter average, with each of the four units counted once, equals 84, which rates a B.

Guillia: Guillia is an 11th grader who is taking a heterogeneously mixed course in English from Dr. Patrick. Her quarter grade includes work done in two different base group teams, one for daily discussion and a different one for an interest-based research paper. The interest paper is a required option for those who wish to try for an A but it must be done in pairs or teams. The grade is composed of the following marks:

a. three tests, each containing 50% individual and 50% group problem-solving components (95, 87, 69);

b. daily contributions totaling 200 points over 10 five-day weeks, a daily average of 4, rating a B; and

c. satisfactory completion of the interest paper, including the planning and assignment of responsibilities, resulting in an A.

Her three areas result in a B, a B, and an A, for a quarter score of B+.

Theodore: Theodore is a fifth grader taking language arts from Mr. Johnson. Three scores averaged for the 6-week grade, a formal report card that is sent home. The first area, written expression, is graded on the quantity and quality of his individual work, as negotiated with the teacher. However, it does involve peer writing (a la Atwell's writing workshop, 1987). Peer review is expected but is not done by assigned permanent teams. This time, Theodore has done two short papers and a research paper, for which he supplied adequate modifications, and received a B for the work.

The second area is spelling. Johnson, a traditionalist, adds required tests of new words on a weekly basis and tries to get students to use these words in their writing. The weekly 10-item quizzes are individually graded but include two team study periods per quiz and involve bonuses both for team achievements and whole-class achievements. Here is how this quarter's scores look for Theodore (bonus in parentheses): 9(+1), 6(+0), 7(+0), 9(+2+1), 10(+0), 10(+2), 8(+1), 6(+0), 7(+0)= 82 = B−

The third part of Theodore's grade is the two group-graded projects completed by his team. The first was a 15-minute taped skit based on the favorite part of a short novel that they read. The students had to design the skit, write a dialogue, rehearse, practice, tape, and then revise based on the taping. This went well and was given an A.

The second team project in language arts involved the group inventing a project based on some aspect of modern society. They chose O. J. Simpson's trial and included interviews, the writing of a song, a presentation of their theories, and other aspects of the case. The project was designed such that all team members were directly involved, and it had to use all seven of Gardner's intelligences. It was far too much work for the relative amount of value it contributed to the overall grading system and the students in Theodore's group were disappointed that their A did not carry more weight on the overall quarter grade.

Thus the grades that Theodore attained on the three parts, B, B−, and A resulted in his getting a B+ for the quarter.

CHAPTER *five*

GOVERNING THE GROUPS

The focus of this chapter, the construction and implementation of an effective governing policy, is often the most poorly practiced component of cooperative learning. Approaches to it vary from a comprehensive "teach the social skills" plan (Johnson, Johnson, & Holubec, 1994) to a laissez-faire, "leave 'em alone" approach seen in many high school teachers. To my mind, the teacher must have a clear set of expectations for teamed behavior, the students must be aware of and able to follow it, and the students must generate and receive feedback as to their performance. It is the goal of this chapter to (1) convince teachers of the need for a governing policy and (2) offer suggestions as to the formation and use of such a policy.

If students are totally left to their own devices, little will get done and if they are placed under the total control of the teacher, their creativity and motivation might die. Students need clear directions and successes, and they need to generate a personalized understanding of their behaviors—these form the essence of governing group work.

The chapter opens with an extensive look at the complexities of rule making in cooperative learning classrooms. This discussion should instill a deep understanding of the formal and informal rule-making and rule-enforcing processes that are at work as students are forced out of externally enforced, quiet, passive, and isolated individual settings into largely internally monitored, noisy, engaged, and interactive teams.

The closing sections offer a series of assessment forms that can be of immediate use in helping students improve their cooperative and interactive skills and increase their achievement during teamwork.

Imagine that you are a visitor to Bill Kennedy's eighth-grade American history classroom. It is first period and the students are energetically chatting, awaiting the onset of class. You are sitting next to a girl named Mary, whose schedule you are "shadowing" (Stevenson, 1992). She is unaware of your observation of her and you are settling in as Kennedy speaks:

> OK, you guys know the routine. Get in your pairs and start that interviewing process that we're working on in both Social Studies and Language Arts. This period, I will give you about 15 minutes, but I want a written set of notes to take with me. As always, follow the rules (waves at front wall) . . . you don't have to like each other, just work together . . . and treat each other with respect. I will be around to see how things are going.

You turn and see Mary scanning the room and then smiling as a big boy shuffles in late. As he walks in, he notices the room being rearranged (into pairs) and his eyes find Mary's; he begins a slow walk to her. They then sit, desks touching with the students facing each other. You decide to observe the session and think about how they behave toward each other.

Vignette 1

WILLIE:	"So what are we supposed to be doin' this time?"
MARY:	"Willie, Kennedy's got us this time. We have both English and Social periods back-to-back to do this interview thing . . . we're supposed to gather our notes during the two periods . . . and then write it up during esteem . . . I got esteem last period today."
WILLIE:	"Interview . . . I don't want to do any interview."
MARY:	"Willie, I interview you . . . you're supposed to take notes and then write a description about how I did my job . . . sort of watching the interviewer thing. Remember he said that we were supposed to be working on our 'interpersonal' skills."
WILLIE:	"I gotta be telling you all about me? . . . Why me? . . . I didn't do anything in my whole life."
MARY:	"I guess we each get our turn . . . but . . . you know that I think that everybody's life has its own history . . . how come you're named Willie? . . . he said that we should start with names . . . "
WILLIE:	"Do you have to tell? . . . my real name is Willing . . . ain't that something . . . it's funny . . . I was a twin with Harmon . . . his name is really Harmony . . . my Mama was special about names."
MARY:	"Any other interesting names in the family?"
WILLIE:	"You mean different from your family's? I guess so . . . I got three sisters . . . April, May, and June . . . my Aunt Wanda said 'good

	thing we don't have any December babies'. Anyway, my brothers are Sylvester, Rodney, Maurice, and Harmon . . . my last name is Newman."
MARY:	"I didn't know that . . . they call your name as 'Walker.'"
WILLIE:	"That's my Ma's new name since my Dad died. . . . I still want to use Newman . . . I think we had a relative who got to be a freed slave and took on that name so he wouldn't have to be named after the master."
MARY:	(writing furiously) "Fascinating . . . kind of neat . . . you got your own history . . . my last name is hyphenated on my mother's diploma . . . I haven't decided what I'll use yet . . . especially if I should ever get married."
WILLIE:	"Oh . . . you'll get married . . . most girls want to have a family . . . but be careful about babies' names . . . they stick . . . my brother would kill me if he knew you know he's Harmon-y."
MARY:	"What else do you know about the slaves in your family?"
WILLIE:	"Little bit . . . (turns and shouts across the room) Hey, Harmon, you got the pictures with you?" (Harmon walks over and gives Willie a battered small blue book.)
MARY:	"Hey . . . is Harmon an identical twin or just fraternal?
WILLIE:	"Well, I came first . . . him about ten minutes later. Sometimes I can think what he's thinking . . . and we're really something on the fast break. . . ."
MARY:	"How do you guys do when you're apart? I'd feel funny being split from . . . from . . . part of me. . . ."
WILLIE:	"My Mama used to tell me that twins got a good price during slavery . . . but sometimes white folks thought that they were like a curse . . . a bad sign. . . ."

Just then, Kennedy walks over, clutching his clipboard. The students pause as he hovers: "You guys looked busy. Everything going well?" Before seeking an answer, he turns to *you* and says, "You've been observing. Name three things that you think were positive about their interaction." (Use a separate sheet of paper to list your three answers.)

After the initial shock of being put on the spot, answers come readily to mind. You articulate a few sentences based on those answers, nodding and smiling to the students as you offer the feedback. Importantly, the students probably understand and accept your answers because they have been through the reflection and analysis process before. They are used to both explaining their own behavior and having it analyzed by others. Moreover, their response seems to indicate the internalization of a set of expectations that they follow.

The question looming behind the observation is "How did the kids learn the rules they followed in Kennedy's class?" Several plausible answers come to mind, each important in its own right:

1. The students have been trained by teachers, parents, and others to act in a socially acceptable way: namely, with respect, tolerance, equality (the values of the U.S. Constitution), enthusiasm, and perseverance.

2. Kennedy has taught them to develop a healthy attitude toward interaction, and their behavior in the various roles shows his influence.

3. The students invented the behaviors on their own and are simply following their internal dictates.

Aspects of all three answers ring true in our hypothetical example. Previous socialization had acquainted them with acceptable norms for interaction, Kennedy had posted the Johnsons' eight rules (discussed later) on the board and enforced them, and the students have modified their behaviors to fit the circumstances that they have encountered.

Moreover, Kennedy approached the external governing of groups with several clear beliefs:

1. Since his students were in eighth grade, they "knew" how to act correctly. Johnsons' eight rules were *not* new to the students.

2. Most of the time, students behave appropriately and thus most of his remarks are positive and supportive in nature.

3. Kennedy believed that he must make his presence "felt" in the room; he neither abandoned nor ignored the teams, but assessed their efforts at completing the assigned tasks.

4. Monitoring the groups was like governing the groups. Kennedy saw his job as helping the students do what was right and desirable by most everyone's common standards. He was filling the role of executive officer of the class, facilitating effective interactions.

Note that Kennedy did teach the social skills and the desired behaviors, but did so by catching students being "good." If he were teaching younger students or those who did not understand the rules (expectations) of society, he would teach them as he would any other skill (demonstration, explanation, practice, and more practice as advocated by Johnson & Johnson, 1987). But a close look at the actual rules being utilized that day suggests that the students probably do know the rules:

Johnson and Johnson's Rules

1. I am critical of ideas, not people.

2. We are all in this together.

3. Everyone is encouraged to participate.

4. I listen . . . even if I disagree.

5. If I don't understand, I ask for a restatement.

6. I try to understand all sides of an issue.

7. I must have good reasons for changing a position.

8. First, all ideas are brought out . . . and then I put them together (Johnson & Johnson, 1983).

If, in the hypothetical observation, you had used these eight rules to assess the interactive process, what would have resulted?

For me, I think Mary and Willie's discussion was splendid and I would be thrilled to have my students work at this level of effectiveness at all times. (By the way, given the grading policy advocated in Chapter 4, these students would have received a 5 for their achievements.) There was disagreement, but it was resolved gently and did not cause personal attack. Secondly, there was a clear feeling of teamwork in the effort, probably spawned by the strong positive interdependence required by Kennedy's interviewing task. Third, both students shared, listened, and sought clarification and elaboration, and while there was no conflict to be resolved, the students managed to synthesize a few ideas to connect to their own. Finally, recall that Mary did do as she was directed, taking the copious notes required by the teacher! Thus, I could have found much to praise in their teamwork and would have addressed my comments to how well they interacted and showed interest in each other's diverse experiences.

Earlier you were asked for your immediate responses to Willie and Mary's efforts. You have since been exposed to some of my thinking, Kennedy's beliefs, and the Johnsons' rules. Because the teacher's recognition of the students' work is central to the success of cooperative learning, the teacher's comments should be carefully offered; therefore, given the opportunity, what would you have said to the students? (Use a separate sheet of paper to record your thoughts.)

It is the thesis of this third structure of cooperative learning—governing—that both teacher recognition and student recognition of desired behaviors are the engines that drive successful interactions. Thus, at some point, students must be asked to reflect on their own behaviors and make judgments about their effectiveness. Thus, Willie and Mary could have been asked "How well do you think you guys worked together today?" Their answers, drawn from analogous real-life observations in an urban setting, are interesting:

WILLIE: "Aw, Mary is a good partner . . . she is always helpin' me. She makes it fun to be doing history."

MARY: "Willie always does his work. And he has got an interesting life . . . it gives me a lot to think about . . . like coming from slaves and everything."

Note several critical things about these comments:

1. The students are able to see for themselves the value of working together and across what in the past has been restrictive lines of school achievement (Mary is an A student and Willie is a C), race (Willie is African-American

and Mary is Caucasian), social class (Mary is from a professional family, Willie is working class), and gender.

2. Although they did not refer directly to the Johnsons' eight rules, they seem to have internalized several of them in their comments.

3. Although the comments are brief and anecdotal, the process of commenting on their performances seems natural and common to them. They are used to reflecting on what they have learned *and* how they interacted together.

A system that I have been using in my own class asks students to identify specific positive qualities about their partners that were evident to anyone who might have observed them working together. After having the students write their responses privately, I have the partners guess what positive thing was said about them. They then check their answers, sharing with each other the positive attributes demonstrated. It is amazing to see what impact this has had on students of all ages: Human beings love to hear good things about themselves and they really appreciate having someone else see their value. If Willie and Mary had given their responses in this way, they might have said things like "she's always reliable and pleasant" and "he's always patient and has a good sense of humor."

For many teachers, this practice is often off limits because it asks student 1 to say something positive about student 2 and vice versa. Many teachers seem reluctant to do this, fearing that students will not do it well or simply refuse. Yet if the group is going to learn to govern itself, such assessments will have to be made and, eventually, they will include negative as well as positive assessments. This positive-first approach is very safe, fun, and effective. To make it even easier, one could include a list of "desirable partner qualities" as a kind of a check sheet rather than have the students generate their own comments.

Figure 5.1 is a 40-item checklist of partner qualities. It was formed from the actual workings of the Waterville, New York, secondary faculty in October 1994. These are the actual qualities shown by partners during a brief task completed by the faculty pairs. The items were tabulated and are currently used as follows: When teachers ask students to work in teams, they are expected to demonstrate as many of these listed qualities as they can. The list works both as an instructional guide and as a quasi-assessment form. The teachers possess these qualities, model them, and are now in a position to reinforce them in the students! As you read through them, ask yourself two questions: (1) Which of these would have been identified by Willie and Mary about the other? (2) Could this checklist be used to record observations about particular students during teamwork in my own classroom?

RULES FOR EVALUATING GROUPS

Numerous effective systems have been developed for recording and assessing interactive data in the literature (Aronson, Blaney, Stephan, Sikes, & Snapp, 1978; Marzano, Pickering, & McTighe, 1993; Kagan, 1992; Johnson & Johnson, 1987;

Name _____

Date _____

Analysis of Self _____ or Teammate _____ (Name)

Waterville CSD Teachers
October 1994

Partner Qualities

1. ____ good listener	21. ____ open to new ideas
2. ____ accepting	22. ____ concise and thorough
3. ____ explained clearly	23. ____ articulate
4. ____ made situation comfortable	24. ____ asked creative questions
5. ____ made feel successful	25. ____ curious
6. ____ followed directions well	26. ____ kind
7. ____ provided thoughtful input	27. ____ intelligent
8. ____ enthusiasm for working with a partner	28. ____ competent
	29. ____ good artist
9. ____ cooperative	30. ____ pleasant
10. ____ gave clear directions	31. ____ smart
11. ____ supportive	32. ____ paid attention to detail
12. ____ gave positive feedback	33. ____ positive in spirit
13. ____ patient	34. ____ encouraging
14. ____ caring	35. ____ adaptable
15. ____ good sense of humor	36. ____ honest
16. ____ gave guided practice	37. ____ had creative ideas
17. ____ repeated directions	38. ____ sensitive to my ideas
18. ____ helpful	39. ____ considerate
19. ____ nice smile	40. ____ showed leadership
20. ____ inquisitive	

FIGURE 5.1   Checklist of Partner Qualities
Courtesy of Waterville CSD Teachers.

and, best of all, Clarke, Wideman, & Eadie, 1990). All are similar in that they call for students and teachers to evaluate the effectiveness of team efforts based on some specified criteria. Establishing those criteria, or setting the rules, can be traced to three distinct strategies:

1. The teacher hands them down.
2. The students invent them at the outset.
3. They evolve out of actual interactions.

Let's look briefly at each of these rule-setting strategies:

Rules Are Handed Down by the Teacher

In my own experience, the most common approach at all levels of schooling is that of the teacher handing down the rules. On day 1 of the school year and at any grade level, the teacher posts a short list of rules that need to be enforced if the class is to be a success. (In the classrooms of cooperative learning teachers, the rules for team-work are often separated from the rules for other types of learning, a practice that I think of as unfortunate.) These rules, often fewer than six in number, are usually concerned with talking, touching, punctuality, preparedness, and tolerance of others. Often the teacher's explanation links them to school rules or practices and to the notion that school is a community (or an institution) that needs to have rules to protect everybody.

Several years ago I taught a high school class. Here are the six rules I handed down then and still use today:

Rules for Dr. Vermette's Class

1. *My turn, your turn:*   Everyone must be quiet and attentive when one of us addresses the entire group or team. It shows concern, increases learning, and helps us relax while we're together.

2. *No put-downs are allowed:*   You can think what you want in a democracy, but the intimacy and safety of this diverse group *requires* that we keep some thoughts to ourselves. Bad words *do* hurt and will not be used in class; here, we address each other in a respectful way, telling the truth but not hurting others. (The term *respectful* should be defined during a class discussion.)

3. *Encourage others to succeed and share with them:*   Life is composed of people working cooperatively and effectively; these are the attitudes that support all successful efforts.

4. *Be on time and be prepared to stay until the end:*   The rest of the class *needs* your insights, ideas, and suggestions and you *need* to be here to understand others' contributions.

5. *Be responsible for your duties:*   Cheating on or ignoring work eventually hurts you and hurts other people as well. Each of us is unique and special and yet responsible for many things and we need everyone's contribution.

6. *Act as if today mattered:*   Because it does! We should behave in class and in our teams in the way that we believe is right and we should be proud of ourselves and our efforts (life "counts"). Make the most of every day's opportunities.

As is typical, I posted one set and discussed them with the class on the first day. What was perhaps unusual was the manner in which the class discussed these rules. Each student was asked to read the rules silently and then rank order them as to their importance to a successful class. Concepts were classified in a large group session, with special attention paid to the use of the term *respectful*. (We wanted agreement on that meaning.) Students were then teamed up to compare their rankings, specifically to identify the most commonly held beliefs. Interestingly, all six rules were thought to be "pretty good rules" and yet there was some disagreement about their relative importance. I had the chance to point out to them how well they had done in their discussions; I had caught them "being good." This fact was most helpful because I now had my own vision of their group work abilities *and* a real live demonstration of their entering behavior. I also had evidence that they understood my rules and their behavior indicated that they owned the same rules. It was a neat package: I knew that they could function together and so did they!

By the way, there was agreement that the least important rule was rule 6. They differed in their beliefs that school mattered much and they certainly did not believe that school was part of the real world. I pointed out that our discussion of the rules had been of both the school world and the real world. . . . they really had done some thinking and decision making. They were not totally convinced but we had established that we were going to work together effectively and that we knew how to do so. I had used a brief team learning experience successfully and had shown that I would actively monitor the group based on the established rules. They understood that this process could be effectively implemented.

Rules Are Invented by the Students

In this approach, the students offer their ideas about what the classroom ought to look like and which rules should be followed. In some conceptualizations, punishments are also listed although the severity of their typical draconian suggestions has dissuaded many of my colleagues from following that practice.

Teachers who use such an approach are usually adept at making kids understand the need for rules and show that they care about the student's opinions. Moreover, such an approach clearly establishes a shift in the teacher's role. She or he goes from knowledge and rule giver to offerer of ideas ("facilitator" of learning), a shift that is necessary in cooperative structures.

At the younger ages, students will often offer rules they experience at home as policy at school. Modifying such offerings into acceptable statutes for the entire class is a skillful procedure for most teachers and goes a long way toward connecting the two major institutions of a child's world, home and school.

For older children, having a say in the rule-generating process carries an internal monitoring whammy that is often *not* anticipated. Violation of other people's policies can be seen as youthful rebellion, resistance to unfair authority, or simply growing pains. Violation of one's own rules hits hard: If it is not seen as hypocritical, it is seen as true failure to live up to one's own expectations. There is no more teachable moment for teens than being confronted with a failure to live up to their own self-expectations. Truly, in this scenario, the teacher is an enforcer, but one who is acting to help the youngster be all that she or he wishes to become and expects to become. "Discipline" under such a condition becomes a more tolerable matter for all parties.

A quick note to those who would experiment with having students generate their own rules: Students may not have worked in groups before, so make sure that they understand the implementation of their rules in a teamed scenario. For example, if they say "Take turns talking," the teacher should help them understand that there will be six or seven groups going on in class at any one time and overlap is likely. If they offer "Students should always try hard," the teacher may offer "What would we say if teams were working well?" Finally, teachers should suggest that students think about a rule that describes what is expected of members of a group when that group successfully finishes its work before the allotted time is over.

Teachers who allow students to make their own rules run many risks, *but* they have much to gain: Students tend to believe in and follow rules they make. Ownership is wonderful.

Once again, please look at my six rules, which were used in a hand-me-down fashion. These rules were actually culled from a series of discussions with inner-city high school *students* in New York State. I found their rules to be meaningful and interesting, and probably better than the ones that I had been using. They are still "hand-me-downs" to my classes, but I do emphasize that they were generated by other students. This is an obvious attempt to help legitimatize their authority and it often works.

Rules Evolve As a Result of Actual Interactions

Surprisingly, many teachers do not provide rules and expectations at the outset of a class. Some teachers proceed in this way because they assume proper behavior will be forthcoming. Others do it this way because they have not thought through their own vision of the cooperative classroom. For others still, they wish to have it learned as a topic as the course evolves. Let us take a look at how one such evolving system could operate.

Note that the Johnsons' use of specific roles is built into their system very carefully. They hand down the roles, define them, have students experience them, and then practice them. They typically teach students that someone should be the leader, another the encourager, another should keep a record of the session, and perhaps the fourth person could be the summarizer for the group. These roles are fixed, transmitted, and practiced.

However, the teachers who fit in my third category use roles in a different way. Without specifying how the group is to function, several days of projects or tasks are assigned and completed with little monitoring by the teacher. Then, the groups analyze their efforts using roles to assess its workings and to evaluate its effectiveness. Students should develop their own personal plans to monitor their own behaviors, independent of teacher expectations.

Luczkiw (1995) has provided a comprehensive list of desirable and undesirable roles that would be very helpful to teachers hoping to have students "discover" their own behaviors. The following list describes some of the roles you can expect to see emerging in groups. (Note that each of these roles represents one character trait that may be displayed by an individual and does not represent the entire personality of the individual.)

Leader	Organizes the group and chairs the meetings. Gets the discussion started.
Peace Maker	Calms members who disagree. Suggests compromises to solve disputes.
Blocker	Has a fixed opinion that cannot be changed. Will not listen to other members. Disagrees with solutions that are not his or her own.
Joker	Fools around and wastes time. Sidetracks other members.
Competitor	Vies for the role of leader with others. Pushes his or her own ideas to the exclusion of others. Tries to control the group.
Problem Solver	Suggests creative solutions to problems. Looks at the situation in a variety of ways.
Resource Gatherer	Gathers materials helpful in solving the problem. Knows where to find data required by the group. Generates ideas and opinions.
Clarifier	Asks for definitions or explanations of terms or ideas. Raises questions to reveal all sides of the issue.
Sympathy Seeker	Criticizes his or her own abilities. Claims to have nothing to offer. Makes excuses for failure to participate.
Withdrawer	Refuses to participate in the group or to take responsibility. Leaves early or does other work during group time.
Tension Reliever	Finds humor in difficult situations. Senses difficulties and suggests solutions.
Follower	Agrees with the group decisions. Accepts others' ideas and works along with them. Assists in completing the required tasks.
Consolidator	Tries to put together different ideas or concepts.
Summarizer	Forms conclusions based on group ideas. Checks on agreement within the group.
Encourager	Listens carefully to the group. Encourages participation by all members. Invites members to give their ideas. Supports weaker members.

Source: Reprinted with permission from Luczkiw, G. (1995). Personal communication about the Institute for Enterprise Education, St. Catharines, Ontario, Canada.

Frankly, I do not advocate the use of this type of evolving approach (although the 15 emerging roles are helpful analytical tools!) because it allows the students to work without direction for too long. Whereas it does offer some of the advantages of a discovery (or inductive) approach, it takes the great risk of producing dysfunctional, ineffective, divided, and hostile teams. A highly skilled teacher may be able to reunite some teams that have started to split apart, but too many of us would simply be lost in such a chaotic scenario. It is far better for most of us to articulate the clear vision first, and then have the students experience the expected successes.

In closing this section on the origin of the rules, it is instructive to look at the practice of two successful practitioners. The first is a highly skilled high school social studies teacher, Doug Van Vliet of Averill Park, New York. Doug is creative and innovative, never content to let things stay as they are. For several years, he followed a procedure that was hard for me to classify into one of the three categories for rule setting. I suspect that many readers will think of him as handing down the rules, but as you will see, he leaves a lot of the decisions to the students and offers them great room to "evolve" as a team.

On the first day of school, Doug sits his 11th graders in straight rows to observe, take notes, and evaluate a real demonstration. Four students from his previous year's class arrive and he gives them a task or a problematic situation and 15 minutes for a team interaction. His new class observes the old group and he then coordinates a larger group discussion about effective and ineffective behaviors that they saw. Doug does not generate a mandated set of required behaviors (or rules) but simply exposes students to the real example and then lets them discover their own.

In the following days they begin to work in groups and begin to evolve their own rules for governing their own groups. Doug has always seen his role as helping them to stay on task and encouraging them to learn the material; he is far less enforcer or evaluator than many of us, and the system does work well for him. When entrusted with the responsibility, his students generate a workable system to monitor and govern themselves—in spite of many of our fears of a *Lord of the Flies*-like outcome.

The second professional is Sharon Sorensen, an elementary school teacher in Toronto, Ontario. Sharon has videotaped periods of group work done by various teams of 6- and 7-year-olds working at different projects. Using commonly accepted criteria (as judged by the various forms offered by selected authors), some of the teams work cooperatively and some do not. That is, some work effectively and some require the use of intervention strategies. Sorensen does not tell her young charges which teams are working correctly, but lets them watch the tapes and judge for themselves. (They use forms for this peer evaluation.) Even at that young age, the children demonstrate a clear knowledge and preference for the behaviors labeled "desirable" by adults.

Thus, Sorensen encourages the desired roles or social skills, but in a way that actually affirms the choices that the students have opted for. In this way, she shows them great respect and finds herself in the position of supporting and reinforcing their behaviors by her monitoring efforts. Later, they use role play to help them clarify their understandings.

Like Van Vliet, Sorensen recognizes that the students need to have ownership of their own processes and actions. They also discover that it feels good to help and be helpful to others—a behavior that we wish to continue to reinforce throughout group work.

THE RELATIONSHIP BETWEEN RULES AND SOCIAL SKILLS

As you will see later in the chapter, almost every researcher who has written about cooperative learning in the schools has had plenty to say about how teachers could go about discovering how well the group is working as it attempts to reach its goals. One conceptualization (Johnson, Johnson, & Holubec, 1994) makes a huge issue out of the teaching of a social skill. They suggest that teachers need to teach these skills at the outset, as they would any other content. Another author, Elizabeth Cohen (1994), is far more worried about the perceptions of low-status students held by others and suggests that we not care about skills but concern ourselves instead with how students regard each other. Other authors focus on other aspects of the interactions.

When trying to implement any of these systems, a teacher still has to have a pretty clear vision of what is "supposed" to happen if the session is going as designed. Thus the rules governing the group work are comprised of the social skills being practiced in a productive group. If that statement is difficult for you to accept, try to picture it as a metaphor: The group that is doing well can have its skills assessed via the rule-evaluating documents that are about to be presented. If a group is successful, it is most likely following the rules; if it is following the rules, it is most likely practicing the actual social skills being developed, the ones that are most productive outside of school as well.

Interestingly, there are theorists who have made available many conceptions of social skills. While I do not conceive my team learning system with social skills in mind (I use the six rules and Glasser's ideas), I offer you an interesting and useful list of skills drawn from Clarke, Wideman, and Eadie (1990). They consider two kinds of skills necessary for successful cooperative learning: task skills and working relationship skills. These skills can be taught or used as concepts to be evaluated in an interaction. We discuss these skills in the following section.

Examples of Cooperative Skills

There are two kinds of cooperative skills. *Task skills* are used by group members to complete the assigned academic work. *Working relationship skills* are those that help build and sustain the group's disposition and ability to work together. Examples of the two kinds of cooperative skills are given in the following lists:

Task Skills

- asking questions;
- asking for clarification;
- checking for others' understanding;
- elaborating on others' ideas;
- following directions;
- getting the group back to work;

- keeping track of time;
- listening actively;
- sharing information and ideas;
- staying on task; and
- summarizing for understanding/paraphrasing.

Working Relationship Skills
- acknowledging contributions;
- checking for agreement;
- disagreeing in an agreeable way;
- encouraging others;
- expressing support;
- inviting others to talk;
- keeping things calm and reducing tension;
- mediating;
- responding to ideas;
- sharing feelings; and
- showing appreciation.

Frankly, the distinction between skills and rules is not worth losing sleep over. If you decide to ignore the suggested approaches offered here and generate one of your own based on Clarke's set of skills, you and the students will most likely be reinforcing the desirable qualities that will make the cooperative learning system work. If you opt to adopt my system based on the six rules, you should expect to accomplish exactly the same thing.

There are many roads to the center and it just takes a clear vision to know if you are getting closer! Once again, any articulated set of rules should contain the social skills being advanced.

MAKING A FORMAL ASSESSMENT

Think back to the beginning of the chapter. You were asked to observe Willie and Mary (and catch them "being good"). You were asked what you would say to them about their performance(s). I also mentioned that Willie and Mary would be asked what they thought about their performance and the suggestion was made that they might want to set goals for their next teamwork project. These items form the elements of a successful team learning assessment and in the next section you will be provided with a sample application of a system based on a set of rules and a set of teacher behaviors.

Before proceeding, however, read through the following two additional vignettes of teamwork in Bill Kennedy's eighth-grade classroom.

Vignette 2

MARY:	"Does everybody understand about the 14 points? Billy, you look awful confused."
BILL:	"Huh? . . . naw, I'm just . . . just. . . . "
GREG:	"C'mon man, you so stupid. . . . "
MARY:	"Greg . . . Billy . . . we're all supposed to be able to state them using our notes. . . . "
GLORIA:	"*With* notes? Who you be kidding . . . Kennedy never say that. . . . "
GREG:	"Ah . . . let's find out what the. . . . "
BILLY:	"Go ahead ask him . . . sshh" (pointing at Mary who is trying to get their attention by raising her hand).

Vignette 3

TIM:	"This poster thing is looking pretty good . . . don't ya think?"
ROGER:	"Damn . . . it looks good . . . what next?"
BRIGID:	"You know that none of our ideas (looking directly at Cathy) . . . *none!* . . . got into the actual final product. . . . "
ROGER:	"Well, they weren't any good. . . . "
TIM:	"Ha! . . . You know that girls are only good for one thing . . . ha" (laughing, high-fiving Roger with his right hand and grabbing his crotch with his left).
CATHY:	"You guys are pigs . . . like all males. . . . "
TIM:	" . . . snort . . . snort . . . soooeee . . . soooeee."
ROGER:	" . . . bacon . . . I smell bacon . . . ha ha ha."
BRIGID:	" . . . OK, OK . . . calm down. . . . "

As you have discovered, both of these team sessions are dysfunctional. In the first, the students are taking forever to get started, and in the second, the rivalry between genders (and the outright sexist behavior) is killing any chance for successful learning. On a separate sheet of paper, record at least three violations of Vermette's six rules and then continue reading.

There were many violations that you could have listed. Clearly, there were put-downs that had to be stopped. There was also little sense of student encouragement toward others in the group. Third, it appears that there was little concern for taking turns.

Reflect on the process of applying Vermette's six rules for analysis that you just used. That is precisely the practice that I advocate for you to use formally. Take a moment to look at the team reflection forms shown in Figures 5.2 and 5.3. Figure 5.2 is for use by children in grades 4 through 12 and Figure 5.3 is used for kindergarten through third grade. Note that these forms are simply designed, match up conceptually with the six rules, and provide the respondent with a continuum of choices.

Before we discuss who fills these forms out and when they do so, let's talk about why we use the forms. If I had seen and heard Tim (in Vignette 3), I would have been quite upset and would have intervened. The nature of my handling of the case would have begun immediately in the teamed setting and would have started with his apparent violation of rule 2 on Figure 5.2 ("We settled disagreements in a tolerant and supportive manner."). If I had witnessed Vignette 2, I would have noted that at some point, I would like to talk with the group about rule 4 regarding getting to work effectively.

As you read through the evaluation form shown in Figure 5.2, note that its use of a continuum and not a categorical yes/no approach allows respondents to make careful judgments if they wish. Behavior is seldom an "all or nothing" thing; it tends to run in patterns with some deviations. This form is sensitive to both fluctuations and improvement of performance as it occurs.

The form of Figure 5.3 is designed for use by younger children. It allows the children simply to circle the categorical response. (Willie and Mary, if they were 6 years old, would have both circled "Yes" for "we took turns and shared.") Or the child might opt to make a mark estimating how close to "Yes" they felt they were.

Note that the two forms mirror each other so that a similar set of expectations (rules) can be reinforced all the way through a K–12 program. Remember, however, when preparing forms for use by small children, that the forms should be big enough to allow space for a child's handwriting. Also note that the six rules are *not* age specific; they are commonly held and universally acknowledged in Western culture. Enforcing and reinforcing them at every level will certainly help children internalize and practice them.

Completing the Team Reflection Forms

Recall that the structure of Form B suggests that students fill the form out by themselves (that is, by circling the best response). For Form A, I spoke of "when the respondent" fills it out, but what does that mean? Who fills these forms out? How? When? These are natural and important questions that must be answered as you develop your governing policy.

Form A and Form B, as well as the other forms discussed later in this chapter, are used to gather data in three typical situations. First, the teacher has to observe the teams every time they work in class and occasionally should do a formal observation that includes filling out the form and giving it back to the students. If Form A had been used by you on Willie and Mary, how would you have rated them?

FORM A

Team Name _____ Teacher Rating = ____

Members Present _____ Date _____

Task _____

1. We took turns sharing ideas and attended to each other.

   ◄───►
   never   seldom   sometimes   often   frequently   always

2. We settled disagreements in a tolerant and supportive manner.

   ◄───►
   never   seldom   sometimes   often   frequently   always

3. We encouraged everyone in the group to focus, share, and succeed.

   ◄───►
   never   seldom   sometimes   often   frequently   always

4. We got to work, did our work, and stayed focused.

   ◄───►
   never   seldom   sometimes   often   frequently   always

5. We made sure that everyone contributed to our efforts.

   ◄───►
   never   seldom   sometimes   often   frequently   always

6. We were proud of our effort, enthusiasm, and achievements.

   ◄───►
   never   seldom   sometimes   often   frequently   always

(OPTIONAL)

1. Compared to our past teamwork, today was _____

   _____

2. The single best part of our teamwork today was _____

   _____

3. One key thing to focus on to improve our group next time is _____

   _____

FIGURE 5.2   Team Reflection Form for Use with Children in Grades 4 Through 12, Based on Vermette's Six Rules (Form A)

Team Reflection Form (Vermette's 6 Rules)

Team Name _____   Teacher Rating =

Members Present _____   Date _____

Task _____

NO   **YES**

1.   We took turns and shared.

2.   We treated each other nicely.

3.   We encouraged everybody to try.

4.   We did our work and met our goals.

5.   We made sure that everyone helped.

6.   We were proud of our effort and the result.

FIGURE 5.3   Team Reflection Form for Use with Small Children, Based on Ver-mette's Six Rules (Form B)

#1   Today our team was

_____

_____

_____

_____

_____

_____

#2   The single best part of today was

_____

_____

_____

_____

_____

_____

#3   Next time, our team will

_____

_____

_____

_____

_____

_____

Second, the team can fill out the form together as part of an analytical sharing session that seeks consensus about their behavior. If the optional section is also filled out, consensus can be reached about what they need to do next to improve their functioning.

Finally, the form can be filled out by individual students working alone, providing the teacher with information that can lead to the teaching of necessary behaviors or to the careful observation of particular persons. Completing the form as an individual suggests that the group would not profit from discussing various viewpoints at that time, a scenario that many of us can easily envision. For example, recall Vignette 3, and imagine Tim, Roger, Brigid, and Cathy having a consensus-bearing "discussion" about their situation. Such a discussion will eventually have to take place as they resolve their conflicts, but to try to force a team self-assessment in their current situation would probably have been nonproductive.

The bottom of Form B (Figure 5.3) attempts to get at the same type of brief analytical questions that are offered to the older youngsters who use Form A. However, while some space was allowed for printing a reaction, space was also left for the students to draw their reaction or response to the items.

For example, one group of children drew a sun to show how they felt (positive, happy, like a sunny day) about themselves. Often, children enjoy themselves so much in groups that they get startled by question 3; they want next time to be like this time. The teacher might allow them to draw the same picture there (a sunny, happy, day).

Do not let yourself fly past the point being made here: Cooperative learning can be successful with the youngest of children in kindergarten and also with the honors class in the 12th grade. Although the products of these team sessions would be vastly different, the interactive processes would have interesting similarities. Use of the same six rules spiraled throughout the K–12 experience is plausible and practical.

Children between 5 and 7 years old are learning to decenter and to help and share with others. Teacher expectations are embedded in statements such as "Kendra, please go help Arma with his boots," "Jacinta, could you help Martha find the place where the crayons go?," and "Louie Jones, could you please be a good boy and go show Louie Herst which name is his *and* tell him the story of the big brown bear. He missed it and he would *love* to hear it." These types of statements are among the most commonly heard in the young childhood wing of the elementary school and reflect a cooperative community environment. Very few teachers at this level would find the six rules dysfunctional.

Children between 8 and 10 years old are often caught between pleasing the teacher and peers and the structure of Form A reinforces behaviors that will satisfy both. Moreover, teamwork at that age should serve as an intervention to help motivate those students beginning to "learn" to fail at school by creating a larger unit, the team. Obeying and appreciating the rules makes sense to these youngsters.

Children between 10 and 14 are incredibly busy changing identities every moment and trying out new abilities. The behaviors and skills reinforced by Vermette's six rules are especially helpful at this age, when so many structures are under revision, rejection, or renewal. The cross-gender relationships between children are often so tenuous at this point that many teachers fear cross-gender groups will not work or could lead to cases of sexual harassment. The students need to work together successfully, to see each other as people and *not* as stereotypes. They need to encourage each other as they develop. Using the six rules to form a vision of their individual and interactive behavior should help these youngsters in their development.

Finally, some teachers believe that cooperative learning cannot work with *teenagers* because they are "too cool" to care or to work hard with or without peers. But, again, because they are closer to adulthood than younger children, they should have begun to see the ultimate value in the ability to interact, to work hard, to be tolerant and caring, and to see the relationship between school and the outside world. The values inherent in the rules are mainstream and offer a great payoff in the adult world. School for older teenagers can be seen as a type of apprenticeship for a later life in which nonadherence to the six rules has more dire consequences.

How Often to Use the Forms

Groups should complete self-assessments regularly, a murky concept for sure. Let me clarify:

1. The first time a group works together, some reflections on observational data should be gathered. Most likely, a teamed self-assessment would be most helpful.

2. For teams working a portion of each day together, one group-processing analysis session led by the teacher and one self-assessment per week is not too much to keep everyone apprised of progress.

3. For sporadically meeting work groups, there is little sense of continuity in interaction being developed. Perhaps one thing that can help hold the group together as a team is a brief assessment at the end of most work sessions. For example, in a traditional daily 40-minute art class in the seventh grade, Dever only has her teams work together five times in the month. If assessment only takes place two or three times during that period, few of the instructional or psychological advantages of working in teams will be realized. In this case, assessment on all five days is warranted.

External monitoring by the teacher should be a regular component of every activity done cooperatively, with some groups being assessed each session and every group being monitored within a regular period. Secondly, internal monitoring, preferably done by the team *as* a team, should be a frequent component of the team process. While some teachers grade such teamwork (see Chapter 4 for a system), others simply expect it to improve by assessment and intervene as the team's data suggest.

GLASSER'S ROLE

In 1986 one of the best educational books ever was written by William Glasser. Entitled *Control Theory in the Classroom,* Glasser provided a strong explanation of why more and more students are "turned off" and "tuned away" from trying in school.

He paints a bleak picture of school as an institution that consumes youngsters' lives but provides *no satisfaction* to them as human beings. He articulates a clear vision of one approach (perhaps the only approach) that can change the inevitable mental deaths of most students. His approach involves the use of learning teams in school!

From a psychological perspective, the use of teams and group work offers students the four satisfiers that they, as human beings, need. In a nutshell, these four satisfiers are *fun, power, freedom,* and a *sense of belonging.* Most students report enjoying their teamwork (fun), feel that they have made a contribution (power, a nonexistent possibility in a traditional class), feel that have had options and alternatives provided (freedom), and felt that they actually were part of something (belonging). Glasser would say that because real possibilities exist for experiencing these four qualities, students like teams, work harder, and learn more.

As students age through their K–12 years, enthusiasm drops and apathy increases, which is why Glasser's book focuses on secondary youth (grades 6 through 12). However, there is evidence mounting that younger students feel less connected to schooling than in previous years and are alienated from the process. In either case, helping students to see and feel Glasser's four satisfiers may help them develop as people and motivate them to succeed.

With those purposes in mind, I offer you a second evaluation form, called Team Reflection Form C (Figure 5.4), which is to be used in conjunction with the Forms A and B discussed previously. Take a moment to peruse this form. This one does not focus on the collective behaviors or attitudes of the team but on the individual team members. It is to be filled out by the youngster or by the teacher. As constructed, the four spaces for names allow a teacher to record information about each team member at one sitting, but the teacher may opt to use it for just one student at a time.

When Form C is used as an internal monitoring device, the students can use check marks or a narrative to log their impressions of themselves.

The first eight items shown in Figure 5.4 are standard fare for team learning. They focus on skills/rules including encouraging, helping, handling conflict, keeping focused, working, leading, showing respect and caring, and the ability to recognize and react to others' nonverbal behaviors.

The second batch, delineated by the dashed line, includes four items that attempt to capture Glasser's insights. As written, behavior 9, "Helped others feel like they belonged to the team," hopes to assess both the individual's efforts to include others and to determine whether or not the person feels included. Data gathered on that line will indicate how students feel about the group and how they think others feel, an empathizing procedure that is not easy but which is central to the success of adults in the contemporary world (Goleman, 1995).

Behavior 10 asks about fun and about helping others enjoy themselves. Behavior 11 is the freedom measure. It attempts to assess whether choices were generated and made or whether the group experienced a very restricted environment.

Finally, behavior 12 is the power measure, the satisfier that Glasser thinks is most motivating and least likely to occur. You may recall that in Vignette 3 Brigid was upset that the girls' contributions did not make it into the final product, meaning that Tim and Roger's sense of power had come at the girls' expense. This item

FORM C

Teacher/Grade Level: _____ Date: _____

Group Observed: _____

Task: _____

Length of Observation: _____

Student Names

Desirable Behaviors   _____   _____   _____   _____

1. Encourages others
   to offer ideas or give
   feedback.
2. Provides help to those
   who want or need it.
3. Handles conflict in
   approved way.
4. Keeps team focused
   on task at hand.
5. Actively engages in
   necessary learning
   procedures.
6. Interacts with patience,
   tolerance, respect, and
   caring behaviors.
7. Provided leadership to
   team when necessary.
8. Utilized supportive
   nonverbal messages.

- -

9. Helped others feel like
   they belonged to the
   team.
10. Helped others have fun
    and/or enjoy the team-
    work.
11. Helped learning team
    see alternatives, options,
    and decision points.
12. Provided contributions
    to the final form of the
    product.

FIGURE 5.4 Team Reflection Form C

suggests that everyone needs to have some sense of ownership, some sense of power over the final product, a sharing of the resources and of the input. The second part of my proposed intervention to that group would have focused on the sense of power needed by all.

In cooperative learning, the actual activity of the group is the focus of the class and thus power has shifted from the teacher to the students, where it belongs. They must actively learn and resolve conflicts. In such a nondictatorial (i.e., democratic) system, compromise becomes an important concept, an important skill, and an important philosophy. Both noun and verb, *compromise* is at the heart of the actual interactions of a successful team.

Team Reflection Form C complements Forms A and B in that it allows a deep look at a single child either externally by the teacher, or internally by the student. Used properly, information on the 12 items ought to help a student see why the team is working so well because of him or her or how it could improve because of him or her. The strong sense of internal attribution built into this type of assessment makes it a powerful device for improving cooperative learning and for the social psychological development of young people.

INFORMAL OBSERVATIONS

There is a great scene from the best schoolteacher movie ever, *Teachers* (1994), in which the stodgy and miserable English teacher has the students so regulated that they come in silently, pick up their seatwork quietly, complete their seatwork quietly, and exit quietly, placing the completed work quietly on his desk. It is such a well-regulated and totally useless system that when the teacher dies at his desk, sitting quietly behind his newspaper, no one notices. In fact, classes continue for several more periods before his death is discovered. Unlike that teacher, the effective cooperative learning teacher cannot be "dead" on his or her feet, but must be active during the teamwork, walking around the room, cajoling and exhorting the students to do their best work. Some call this cheerleading, facilitating, or hovering, but for the most part, it is an important piece of the process.

Conducting a Walk-Through

Imagine for a minute that you are teaching the 20 students shown in Figure 5.5. As shown in the figure, the students are spread across the room, working in four-member teams with the teacher's desk in its traditional frontal position. During a 20-minute work period, where do you walk, stand, hover, and sit? How many groups do you observe? To how many groups do you actually talk? Should some groups be observed silently, or acknowledged with only grunts and gestures? What do you say, if you do talk? When would you leave a team alone? Trace your imagined steps on the figure, starting at TD, the teacher's desk. This represents your path in this teacher behavior called a *walk-through*.

The preceding questions are the types of questions often asked by teachers new to a teamed system. Interestingly, teachers who use teams frequently tend to answer them all with "It depends!" This answer suggests that informal observations not requiring the completion of the previously described forms are situational in nature and are part of the "art" of teaching. If this is true, then each teacher must define and develop his or her own style of external monitoring. While I tend to agree with this notion that each of us has to develop our own individual monitoring style, there are some common tendencies or approaches that the reader may wish to reflect on, as discussed in the following paragraphs.

Every team should have the teacher physically near them at least once during a session and therefore teachers must do at least one walk-through during the session. Often, important questions or problems will be shared with the teacher, but only if she or he is near enough to be called over unobtrusively. Most of the time, teams answer their own questions, but at times, having a teacher nearby helps.

Moreover, most of the time students do good work in groups. If the teacher does not come close, some participants may feel that he or she does not understand or appreciate their efforts. Having the instructor walk by, smiling and nodding at their efforts, is a tremendous reinforcer for groups.

Also, some groups do *not* work well or they have trouble getting started. The presence of a teacher in physical proximity is a nice motivator to prod reluctant (or lazy) teams to begin their assignment.

Thus, if I were to trace most successful teachers' paths onto Figure 5.5, their walking path lines would be all over the place, crossing each other on several occasions and seldom returning for very long at the teacher's desk.

The quick bursts of verbal and nonverbal communication that transpire during walk-throughs are thought to be very important to many effective practitioners. For instance, many teachers recommend that one student in each of groups VI, IV, and II (see Figure 5.5) needs to move his or her position so that he or she is more

FIGURE 5.5   Team Seating Arrangements: Trace the Walk-Through

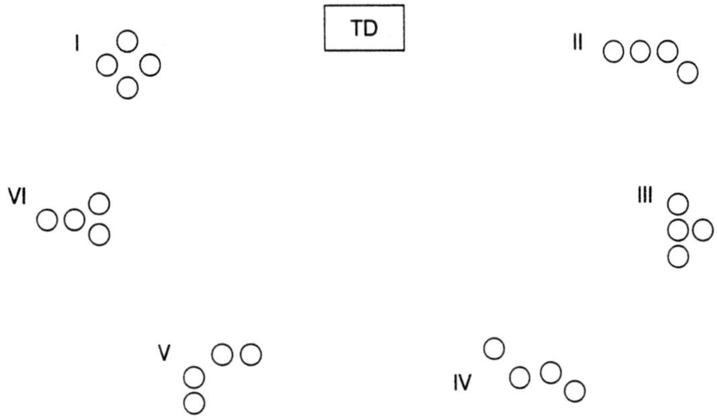

involved with the flow of information. Some teachers demand that all teams sit like group I does. Here are some common verbal ways to help that change happen, with Sal representing the students most set apart from the others:

1. "Hey, Sal, move your chair over here."
2. "Would you guys please move your chairs so that they face Sal better?"
3. "Is this the most effective seating arrangement you could invent?"
4. "Sal, are you able to interact from over there?"
5. "Sal, I've watched your team for a few minutes now . . . it doesn't look like you can talk to the rest of them."
6. "Sal, whasamatter . . . you got B.O.?" (*Note:* This is one that I've heard, but would never use!)
7. "Pretty hard to get involved from out here in the outfield. . . . "
8. Bending over, whispering privately in Sal's ear, "there is no way that you're going to get anything out of this . . . move your chair closer and get involved."

Nonverbally, the teacher could gently push Sal's chair into better position or signal the same result with the use of a finger pointing or a hand gesture.

Which is best? Which is a bad move? Those are clearly situationally related questions, but do notice that the teacher's quick, informal intervention is focused on helping the group stay on task, getting everyone involved, and improving the team's effectiveness. Such informal interventions are common and helpful and much less cumbersome than is a formal assessment.

It is useful to envision another application of informal teacher comments during a walk-through. Here are several other examples of potentially productive teacher comments that may have been appropriate during the very brief exchange between Mary, Bill, Greg, and Gloria in Vignette 2:

1. "Mary, it was wise of you to check on how the others are doing."
2. "Gloria, did you notice that I was right about the fact that being in a team helps you guys review and clarify what is supposed to be done?"
3. "It is worth the time it takes to get the task clarified."

Take a minute and place these comments where they seem best suited, given the short dialogue that you have available.

Take another minute and ask yourself these two questions: (1) How would the rest of the team dialogue have changed if the teacher had actually intervened with a verbal comment? (2) What nonverbal gestures could have accompanied or replaced the verbal ones that have been offered in Vignette 2? (Nonverbal comments may have also changed the flow of discussion, but are generally less obtrusive.) Answering these two questions should help you develop the art and science of your intervention, since you will be clarifying a vision of the group work *and* your role in the classroom by answering them. Some who have played with these ideas have asked a third question: "Why does the teacher say anything at all? Why interfere?" (Note the choice of the concept interfere, not intervene.) These teachers generally think that the process works better with little intrusion by the teacher.

Reflecting on these issues should help clarify your vision of the effective group and may also help you define your own style of informal intervention.

The third and final consideration is that the teacher may play the role of a genuine and effective catalyst far more than is often suspected. Many team learning teachers actually sit in the working group and participate; they do not assess or reinforce. That is, they become a de facto member and contribute. When this happens, the teacher is often still perceived as an authority but one whose ideas now appear as suggestions or new data, not as directives.

Some comments from several teachers as they sat in various teams follow. Some are "suggestions," offering alternatives or serving as a catalyst for the team, whereas others are related more to data transmitting and are likely to be received as "orders" or "directives." Knowing the difference between the two types should help you determine the role you prefer to play.

Please classify each of the following teachers' comments as *C* for catalyst or *D* for directive. Also please identify which of these items you think you would use consistently.

_____ 1. *Shuman, 4th grade:* " . . . 'receive' is spelled wrong . . . and you cannot ask the mayor for that . . . it is illegal and she can't do it."

_____ 2. *Shockley, 1st grade:* "You have several more crayons. Any chance you could get them involved?"

_____ 2. *Sheeran, 7th grade:* "People almost always think of writing a letter . . . what are some other legal ways that people could show their disapproval?"

_____ 4. *Samms, 10th grade:* "You cannot use that verb in that way in French. It is just wrong."

_____ 5a. *Smythe, 12th grade:* "No one would ever look at a resume that included a family picture. Take it out."

_____ 5b. *Smythe's team teaching partner, Smits, when he sees the resume a minute later:* "That's different. What might the employer think about it? It is unconventional, you know?"

_____ 6. *Snyder, 3rd grade:* "Nice job . . . anything else that could be added?"

Those teachers wishing to play a catalyst-like role probably identified statements 2, 3, 5b, and 6 as "catalysts" and also preferred those comments over the remainder.

Behaviors to Observe during a Walk-Through

Here is an abbreviated list of things that teachers often notice and comment about, verbally and nonverbally, as they do their informal monitoring of group work via a walk-through:

1. group activity when the task is compete;
2. a particular rule or social skill being demonstrated;
3. the rotation of leadership (or dominance) during a task;
4. the physical positioning and nonverbal gestures used as students interact;
5. the acceptance or offering of "help" during tasks;
6. the concern for the quality of the work by the students;
7. the contributions of low-status students (a la Cohen);
8. the use of language within the group; and
9. the attention and/or participation of each member.

Although these concerns are for the most part self-evident, item 5, regarding "help," warrants a bit of elaboration. It has been suggested that this is one expectation or rule that teachers must overtly teach and overtly demonstrate and reinforce as often a possible. Research by Webb (see Chapter 2) suggests that under certain conditions, boys will not help girls, a special concern for middle school teachers since that is the age at which girls begin "dumbing down" (Sadker & Sadker, 1994). Thus, even though it will lower their own score or damage their own product, boys might not help girls. Keeping this in mind may help teachers more easily spot instances of "failure to help" and/or "failure to seek needed help" during an informal observation.

Furthermore, a study done by Ross and Cousins (1994) suggests that students want to help and are willing to help but are confused about how to help and how to know that help is needed. Thus, in peer-tutoring activities that concentrate on simple problem-solving, rote memorization, or low-level understandings (such as those found in STAD, TGT, and part of Jigsaw), students may not be clear on how or when to help. They might need formal instruction. In more complex and free-flowing activities such as the ones obviously favored in this text (see Chapter 6), students are more likely to know how to help, that is, how to engage others and share ideas, and they will improve with the use of the governing strategies offered in this chapter.

Conflict Resolution

Compared to peer teaching-type tasks, open-ended tasks can lead to a different type of problem: conflicts that arise from differences of opinions. Interestingly, while most such disagreements are positive because they force students to think, react, and see alternatives, some can create dysfunctional teams. Numerous effective conflict resolution models are on the market and many are familiar to teachers (the best, perhaps, is Johnson & Johnson, 1995). Common to most of them are several valuable ideas that may help teachers deal with team-related conflicts:

1. Students need to be able to explain their positions.
2. Students need to paraphrase others' positions to their satisfaction.
3. Agreement must be reached on the point that agreement must be reached; a permanent state of stalemate cannot be allowed.

4. Alternatives must be generated that satisfy the goals of each party and they must be weighed until one is reached that satisfies the goals of the various parties.

While this is not a model of conflict resolution, it does capture the essence of the interactions that take place when a team in conflict resolves an issue. The teacher will often play a role in such developments, especially if the conflict is heated and is preventing the group from continuing. Most often, however, conflicts are easily resolved internally by students using a process that corresponds well with the four factors just listed. In fact, just as teachers are not aware of most of what happens inside of a particular team, teachers are usually unaware of the frequency with which dilemmas are handled successfully by team members. Once again, students intuitively know that disagreement is not bad until it becomes dysfunctional—that is, they know that it needs to be resolved when it endangers the effectiveness of the group.

An Example of an Informal Walk-Through

Let us take one final look at Kennedy's classroom. In Vignette 4, four students, Damian, Lynn, Harmon, and Fern, are working together as they have every day for 3 weeks. It has been a good group, one that has worked hard in class and is now facing their last piece together, an open-ended project that relates to the Colonial period.

Before you read the vignette, I suggest that you review the assessment forms offered so far (Form A for teams and Form C for individuals) and put them aside. As you turn your attention to Vignette 4, picture yourself as having casually walked by the group and stopped. Having listened, prepare yourself for the type of informal feedback that has been discussed in the previous section.

Vignette 4

DAMIAN: " . . . then you guys think that a travel folder for Williamsburg would be cool?"

LYNN: "Let's do it full color, fold-out . . . the whole package."

HARMON: "Neat . . . got any ideas about what aspects we should exclude from all of our stuff?"

LYNN: "We probably have to keep slavery stuff . . . and about the daily life. . . . "

DAMIAN: " . . . all that stuff about women's lives was . . . pretty boring . . . glad I didn't live then."

FERN: "It wouldn't have been so bad if you were white and had a family . . . men may have had it tougher?"

LYNN: "Why do you think that? They were in charge . . . owned property . . . did what they wanted . . . and didn't face childbirth."

HARMON:	"Childbirth . . . that's women's own fault . . . they only get pregnant so that they can keep a man . . . it's like that now in my neighborhood."
FERN:	"No way . . . in the old days . . . women got married . . . and then got some importance. All the kids I know that got pregnant just got lots more problems and the guy . . . he just dumped them . . . anyway . . . making a baby is a big deal . . . raising a baby is a load."
LYNN:	"Hey . . . want to try to do a 'Williamsburg Now and Then' . . . or like America 1760 and 1995? I know that I'm glad to be alive now . . . but not sure that this life is better . . . even though now I'm free . . . and can even try for any job I want. . . . "
HARMON:	"I don't know . . . that sounds like a good idea . . . but awfully hard."
FERN:	"Hold on . . . sshhh . . . I got a great idea . . . if I can just get it out. . . . "
HARMON:	"Fern . . . your head is full of lots of things . . . but ideas I don't know . . . (smiling) take your time . . . what's the plan?"
FERN:	"I GOT IT! We can do a video ad or a tape comparing the two . . . it'll be living, moving . . . not like a paper structure."
DAMIAN:	(High-fiving Harmon) "I told you that she was smart . . . pretty good idea for a girl that can't kiss worth a damn."
FERN:	"Hey . . . you so ugly . . . you'll never. . . . "
LYNN:	"Hey guys . . . let's get back to that idea that Fern had . . . what would it take to put together a documentary?"
DAMIAN:	"A comparative documentary . . . awesome. . . . "
LYNN:	"Let's keep our heads out of the gutter long enough to act like a team: Harmon, make a list of these ideas. Everybody ready? Let's get them down . . . Fern?"

Answer Key

By now you have seen that many of the activities and reflection questions in the text have no single "right" answer. This task is a classic case of this practice. Yet I feel compelled to provide the reader with some feedback, especially if she or he is not in a position to discuss this example with a partner.

As I watched and listened to these students, I thought of many things that they should consider. How many of these I would actually offer is unclear—if I had interrupted, I might have changed the remaining dialogue! If I chose to wait until the session was over, the opportunity to do "good" might have passed. I might decide to wait until another time to offer a specific idea, for fear that I may overwhelm them with too much feedback at one time. Thus the actual discussion is just a vision, but here are the items that I had generated and from which I would choose several to discuss with the four students:

1. This group effectively builds and connects each other's efforts.
2. This team really praises its members, but some of the language use could be seen as offensive outside of the group (Harmon, line 13).
3. The put-downs that arose may have seemed funny, but in time, they might prove divisive and should be withheld (Damian, line 16; Fern, line 17).
4. Lynn (line 18) has the ability to pull people back to work and to help them focus and will probably become a successful adult because of it; she should try to show the others how to do it.
5. The generation of the "Now and Then" and documentary idea is brilliant and certainly speaks highly of their ability and they should be told.
6. This group's ability to engage everyone is superb.

The agenda that is formed by all six of these observations is too extensive for a brief conference such as the one available to the teacher on a walk-through. Selecting the one or two items (if any) that can be touched on "depends" on the larger picture that we have open to us. Perhaps some of us see one issue as so important that it over-rides all others. That issue is most likely the put-downs or "ragging" on each other that is a fact of life in contemporary adolescence and that shows up here. While the badgering might seem friendly and bonding most likely it is *not* totally appreciated by every member and, therefore, potentially divisive. However, there is so much "positive" happening in this group that to note only the put-downs might do the students a disservice. If mention is made of that aspect, at least one positive aspect should be noted as well. My choice for that role would most likely be a mix of praise for brilliant teamwork to generate a project and for the role played by Fern in keep-ing the group on task and harmonious. With this balanced approach, the put-downs can be correctly included as part of a total community effort and not as an isolated incident taken out of context.

OTHER ASSESSMENT FORMS

As mentioned previously, several famous theorists have offered teachers very useful observation and evaluation forms. In its own way, each provides a valuable and well-structured alternative. Like the ones seen earlier in this chapter, each reflects the vision of successful cooperative learning espoused by its maker. Moreover, by its exis-tence, each reinforces the notion that internal and external monitoring are essential steps in the team learning process.

Aronson et al. (1978)

The first of the forms (Figure 5.6) is from Aronson's research team and was built for his Jigsaw strategy. It is to be used at least in part on a daily basis and is an

---

GROUP PROCESS SHEET

Note to the teacher: This sheet is designed as a handout for the students to help them become familiar with some important aspects of group process. You may also want to use some of the ideas from this sheet in a "Group Process Bulletin Board."

Some important things to remember about group process:

It is important to let the person who is talking know that you are listening to what he or she is saying. Some ways you can do this are nodding, smiling, and asking questions.

There are some other ways you can show you are listening. Can you think of any?

When you are using the Jigsaw method, you do many different things every day, and you need to have time for each of them. Try and keep an idea of how much time is left so you do not run out before you are done with everything.

At the end of each day you will have a process discussion. You will answer several questions about what happened in your group that day and discuss them. These discussions are important because how well you will be able to learn the material depends on how well your group works together. Try to help see what problems your group is having, and come up with suggestions for solving them in these discussions.

This is a list that you can use to have students process what happens in their group each day. Have them discuss the first three questions most days. The other questions provide additional focus on specific issues. You may want to do one a day, or whatever you have time for.

(1) What one word would you use to describe how the group was today? _____

(2) What one word would describe the way you would like the group to be? _____

(3) Is everyone participating?

Yes, always _____ Usually _____ Occasionally _____ Rarely _____ No, Never _____

If not, why not? _____

FIGURE 5.6 Aronson's Group Process Assessment Form

internal monitoring device designed to help students reflect and improve their own behaviors.

As you review the document shown in Figure 5.6, note Aronson's emphasis on the traits of listening, praising, and sharing talk time and on the use of nonverbal communicators. Also, note that the form forces the team (not individuals) to answer the questions after a discussion session. This suggests that assessment should urge a team consensus about the process, rather than simply establish a pure evaluation.

Johnson, Johnson, and Holubec (1994)

The second form is from the work of Johnson, Johnson, and Holubec (1994). The Johnsons' many publications offer a host of useful instruments but the one displayed in Figure 5.7 has been chosen for several reasons. First, it is very similar to Team

---

(4) Are you (everyone in group) trying to make each other feel good? If not, what are you doing?

Yes, always _____   Usually _____   Occasionally _____   Rarely _____   No, Never _____

(5) Are you trying to help each other feel able to talk and say what you think?

Yes, always _____   Usually _____   Occasionally _____   Rarely _____   No, Never _____

(6) Are you listening to each other?

Yes, always _____   Usually _____   Occasionally _____   Rarely _____   No, Never _____

(7) Are you showing you are listening by nodding at each other?

Yes, always _____   Usually _____   Occasionally _____   Rarely _____   No, Never _____

(8) Are you saying "That's good" to each other when you like something?

Yes, always _____   Usually _____   Occasionally _____   Rarely _____   No, Never _____

(9) Are you asking each other questions?

Yes, always _____   Usually _____   Occasionally _____   Rarely _____   No, Never _____

(10) Are you listening and really trying to answer these questions?

Yes, always _____   Usually _____   Occasionally _____   Rarely _____

(11) Are you paying attention to each other?

Yes, always _____   Usually _____   Occasionally _____   Rarely _____

(12) Is any one person talking most of the time?   Yes _____   No _____

(13) Is there a way to have a group where everyone talks about equally?   Yes _____   No _____

Source: Aronson, E., Blaney, N., Stephan, C., Sikes, J., & Snapp, M. (1978). *The Jigsaw classroom* (pp. 161–162). Beverly Hills, CA: Sage. Copyright © 1978 by Sage Publications. Reprinted by permission of Sage Publications.

Reflection Forms A and B that were culled from Vermette's six rules. Second, since their research has clearly demonstrated the power of group processing (Yager, Johnson, & Johnson, 1985), it was wise to include the very tool used in those experiments. Third, their form can easily be used in the three different ways that were described earlier: (1) by the teacher to gather data for assessing the privately held opinions of class (or team) members, (2) for observational analysis by the monitoring teacher in a formal session, or (3) as the focus of an intrateam discussion for consensus-building purposes. Theirs is a simple but clear and usable tool.

Marzano, Pickering, and McTighe (1993)

The third form (Figure 5.8) is one that Marzano's team included in their work on outcomes assessment. This single sheet, pulled from a much larger packet, focuses on

Write Down Two Ways Each Member Helped The Group Today!

Name	Helpful Action	Helpful Action

Group Processing

Agree On Your Answers and Write On Your Group Paper:

1. What are three specific actions we did that helped us do well on the assignment?
   a.
   b.
   c.

2. How did each of us contribute to the group's success?
   a.
   b.
   c.

3. What is an action that would help us do even better next time?
   a.
   b.
   c.

FIGURE 5.7   The Johnsons' Group Processing Form

Source: Johnson, D. W., Johnson, R. T., & Holubec, E. J. (1994). *The nuts and bolts of cooperative learning.* Edina, MN: Interaction Book Company. Reprinted with permission.

the individual contributions of a particular member of a team. It can be used as an evaluative tool by the teacher *or* by teammates *or* by the individual privately.

One thing that makes this single page so powerful is that it attempts to define qualitatively different levels of contribution on each of four identified aspects of team learning: (1) working toward goals, (2) demonstrating interpersonal skill, (3) contributing to group stability, and (4) ability to do various roles.

By overtly setting these standards, called *rubrics,* the form helps the teacher convey the differences in observed behaviors that students often demonstrate. It articulates a top-level performance (a rating of 4) for those students who seek excellence; it also defines the most ineffective behaviors (a rating of 1) for those who need an explanation of their failures.

Student Name _____   Total Points _____

A. Works toward the achievement of group goals.   Points____

_____ 4 Consistently and actively helps identify group goals and works hard to meet them.

_____ 3 Consistently communicates commitment to group goals and carries out assigned roles.

_____ 2 Sporadically communicates commitment to group goals and carries out assigned roles.

_____ 1 Rarely, if ever, communicates commitment to group goals or carries out assigned roles.

B. Demonstrates effective interpersonal skills.   Points____

_____ 4 Consistently and actively helps promote effective group interaction and expresses ideas
        and opinions in ways that are sensitive to the feelings or knowledge base of others.

_____ 3 Consistently participates in group interaction without prompting and expresses ideas
        and opinions in ways that are sensitive to the feelings and knowledge base of others.

_____ 2 Sporadically participates in group interaction without prompting and expresses ideas
        and opinions in ways that are sensitive to the feelings and knowledge base of others.

_____ 1 Rarely, if ever, participates in group interaction without prompting or expresses ideas
        and opinions in ways that are sensitive to the feelings and knowledge base of others.

C. Contributes to group maintenance.   Points____

_____ 4 Consistently and actively helps the group identify changes or modifications necessary
        in group processes and works toward carrying out those changes.

_____ 3 Consistently helps identify changes or modifications necessary in group processes
        and works toward carrying out those changes.

_____ 2 Sporadically helps identify changes or modifications necessary in group processes
        and sometimes works toward carrying out those changes.

_____ 1 Rarely, if ever, helps identify changes or modifications necessary in group processes
        and seldom works toward carrying out those changes.

D. Effectively performs a variety of roles within a group.   Points____

_____ 4 Demonstrates an ability to perform a wide range of roles within a group.

_____ 3 Demonstrates an ability to perform different roles within a group.

_____ 2 Demonstrates an ability to perform a restricted range of roles within a group.

_____ 1 Does not demonstrate an ability to change roles within a group.

FIGURE 5.8   Outcome Assessment Form

Source: Marzano, R. J., Pickering, D., & McTighe, J. (1993). *Assessing student outcomes: Performance assessment using the dimensions of learning model.* Alexandria, VA: ASCD. Reproduced with
permission of McREL Institute, 2550 S. Parker Road, Suite 500, Aurora, CO 80014. Copyright © 1993
by McREL Institute. All rights reserved.

Kagan (1992)

The fourth document (Figure 5.9) is an adaptation by Spencer Kagan (1992) of a form originally generated by the Saskatchewan Department of Education in 1983. It is very easy to use, adaptable, and very helpful to the teacher who wants the students simply to estimate their daily effectiveness as a team. By using a 7-point Likert-type scale replete with clarifying statements (a rating of 6 suggests students did "just what

---

Evaluate on this form the functioning of your group on the task just completed. Make a mark (x) on each scale to show which statement most nearly described how you regard the performance of your group. You may mark halfway in between two statements to get a shading of meaning, if you wish.

1.   EFFECTIVE USE OF TIME:

1	2	3	4	5	6	7
Much time spent without purpose		Got off track frequently			Did well, once we got our ideas clear	No wasted effort— stayed on target

2.   DEVELOPMENT OF IDEAS:

1	2	3	4	5	6	7
Little done to generate ideas		Ideas were imposed on the group by a few			Friendly session but not creative	Ideas were encouraged and well explored

3.   ABILITY TO DECIDE ISSUES:

1	2	3	4	5	6	7
Poor resolution of difference		Let one person rule			Made compromises to get job done	Genuine agreement and support

4.   OVERALL PRODUCTIVITY:

1	2	3	4	5	6	7
Did not accomplish our goal		Barely accomplished the job			Just did what we had to	Held a highly productive session

---

FIGURE 5.9   Group Effectiveness Form

Source: Adapted with permission from Kagan, Spencer. *Cooperative Learning.* San Clemente, CA: Kagan Cooperative Learning, 1994. (This is a later edition of Kagan's 1992 book.)

they had to do"; a 3 suggests that students "got off track frequently"), this form helps the students gain a realistic assessment of their effectiveness and actually record a score for their daily efforts.

One suggestion for those teachers planning to utilize this form: Because of its nature, it is ideal to use as a comparison tool. That is, both team members and the teacher fill out the form during group work and then share their perceptions. If they match, agreement would suggest that perceptions are accurate and appropriate. If there is disagreement between teacher and teammates, an appropriate discussion can be held to help clarify perceptions, set directions and establish future possibilities.

Clarke, Wideman, and Eadie (1990)

In their excellent book *Together We Learn,* Clarke et al. (1990) offer teachers some valuable advice about group assessment. Their text provides many forms that are easily adaptable for use with the types of lessons suggested in this book. One interesting form is ideally suited for student use at the end of a week spent working on a large-scale project. This weekly progress report, shown in Figure 5.10, can be filled out by individuals working alone or by the group as a whole.

The form calls for a review of the progress of the main activity, the next step, and tasks needing help. It is essentially a data-gathering device to aid the teacher in keeping the team on schedule. It also clarifies expectations and achievements and helps the team focus on the next appropriate step for their work.

Cohen (1994)

The final form (Figure 5.11) is a sample student questionnaire drawn from Elizabeth Cohen's *Designing Groupwork* (1994). It is meant to be used as a data-gathering device for teachers using her Complex Instruction project approach (described in Chapter 1). Although it is not suitable for teams seeking to improve their own work by internal discussion, its implementation does force individuals to be analytical and reflective about the actual realities of their team interactions.

Because she is so concerned about the participation rates of low-status members, Cohen designed this as an instrument that allows clear analysis of the perceptions of those students' efforts. While it differs from the other observation forms in purpose and ease of use, it can be a helpful tool for students in the "fourth grade or beyond" (Cohen, 1994). Her Section B consists of open-ended questions that can be used or ignored as necessary.

All in all, these six forms provide options for the assessment process, both internal and external. Combined with those offered earlier in the chapter, they ready the practitioner for the necessary applications of his or her governing policy, the third essential structure of effective cooperative learning.

Please use your Project Checklist as a guide in filling out this progress report each week. These reports will help the group to plan weekly work.

What is the current main activity of group members?

_____

_____

_____

_____

What will be the next step?

_____

_____

_____

_____

Is there a task with which you need help? Please describe.

_____

_____

_____

_____

_____

_____

_____

_____

Cooperation in Our Group

One cooperative skill we are using well:

_____

_____

One cooperative skill on which we need to work:

_____

_____

Date _____

Group Members   _____   _____

                  _____   _____

FIGURE 5.10   Weekly Progress Report

Source: Clarke, J., Wideman, R., & Eadie, S. (1990). *Together we learn.* Englewood Cliffs, NJ: Prentice Hall. Reprinted with permission.

Name:_____

Please mark an "x" on the line to the left of each answer that is most like how you feel for each question. Remember, this is not a test. There are no right answers. I want to know what you think.

Section A

1. How interesting did you find your work in the group?
    _____ a. Very interesting
    _____ b. Fairly interesting
    _____ c. Somewhat interesting
    _____ d. Not very interesting
    _____ e. I was not interested at all

2. How difficult did you find your work in the group?
    _____ a. Extremely difficult
    _____ b. Fairly difficult
    _____ c. Sometimes difficult
    _____ d. Not too difficult—just about right
    _____ e. Very easy

3. Did you understand exactly what the group was supposed to do?
    _____ a. I knew just what to do
    _____ b. At first I did not understand
    _____ c. It was never clear to me

4. *For Multiple Tasks*
    a. What abilities did you think were important for doing a good job on this task?
    b. Was there one ability on which you thought you did very well? Yes ___ No ___

5. How many times did you have the chance to talk during the group session today?
    _____ a. None
    _____ b. One or two times
    _____ c. Three to four times
    _____ d. Five or more times

FIGURE 5.11   Sample Student Questionnaire

Source: Reprinted by permission of the publisher from Cohen, E. G., *Designing Groupwork: Strategies for the Heterogeneous Classroom,* 2nd ed. (New York: Teachers College Press, © 1994 by Teachers College, Columbia University. All rights reserved.), pp. 183–184.

6. If you talked less than you wanted to, what were the main reasons?
    _____ a. I felt afraid to give my opinion
    _____ b. Somebody else interrupted me
    _____ c. I was not given the chance to give my opinion
    _____ d. I talked as much as I wanted to
    _____ e. Nobody paid attention to what I said
    _____ f. I was not interested in the problem
    _____ g. I was not feeling well today

7. Did you get along with everybody in your group?
    _____ a. With few of them
    _____ b. With half of them
    _____ c. With most of them
    _____ d. With all of them
    _____ e. With none of them

8. How many students listened to each other's ideas?
    _____ a. Only a few of them
    _____ b. Half of them
    _____ c. Most of them
    _____ d. All of them, except one
    _____ e. All of them

Section B

1. Who did the most talking in your group today?
2. Who did the least talking in your group today?
3. Who had the best ideas in your group today?
4. Who did the most to direct the discussion?
5. Would you like to work with this group again?   Yes ____ No ____
    If not, why not?
6. How well do you think the facilitator did today in his or her job?

FIGURE 5.11, *continued*

CHAPTER 5 SUMMARY

This chapter focused on the third essential structure for team learning, the development and application of a governing policy. The internal and external monitoring of the teams' efforts and achievements should follow a clearly articulated vision of how teams should be operating while working.

Six rules that spiral their way through the K–12 school years were offered as the basis for team assessment and instruments to aid the teacher in that process were provided. An additional form for evaluation was shown, one that focused on individual contributions and that flows directly from the work of William Glasser. That instrument suggests that his notion of the four satisfiers (fun, freedom, power, and a sense of belonging) is a central explanation of the success of cooperative team learning. The presence of these factors in a learning interaction should be enhanced and/or reinforced.

The chapter also attempted to analyze some of these ideas in action via the inclusion of sample activities and hypothetical vignettes drawn from an eighth-grade social studies classroom. Although suggestions about implementation difficulties were offered, great room was left for each individual teacher's style and implementation.

Finally, it was noted that some of the biggest names in cooperative learning (Aronson, Johnson and Johnson, Cohen, Marzano, Clarke, and Kagan) also stress the importance of monitoring group work. Examples of some of their assessment forms were included to provide alternatives to the teacher wishing to experiment with the group governing process.

REFLECTION QUESTIONS

1. Peruse the 40-item "partner qualities" list generated by the Waterville teachers (Figure 5.1). Read Vignette 5, entitled "Sisters," which involves an all-girl group that has worked as a team before. What qualities would each girl identify for the three others? If you had them identify positive qualities, would it be done openly in words or in a private writing? Why?

Vignette 5: Sisters

SETTING:	Four girls have just arranged their chairs in a perfect square and begun discussing the assigned task. Maria, Lupe, Shandra, and Kelly were in many classes together during the previous year and know each other. This is the third week of school in September and the second set of teams for the students.
LUPE:	"Well, I feel that we should be OK. I think that he wants us to . . . what did he say, Maria?"
MARIA:	"I think . . . didn't he tell us to use our books and stuff . . . and design a new monument?"
KELLY:	"Did he mean statue?"
MARIA:	"I think . . . I feel that that could be our choice. What do you think, Shandra?"
SHANDRA:	" . . . uh . . . " (eyes go to floor).
LUPE:	"Well, let's make it our call . . . for three weeks he told us that social studies is for learning to be a 'decision-making' citizen . . . let's make one."
KELLY:	"Do you think we should ask? I mean, do you feel we . . . ?"
MARIA:	"Lupe's right, Kelly . . . let's do what we think is right. He won't hurt us for it."

KELLY:	"OK . . . OK. . . . "
LUPE:	"My brother Vincent had him last year and he said that . . . "
MARIA:	"Your brother isn't in this group!"
LUPE:	"Don't get sore . . . I'm just saying . . . "
MARIA:	"Lupe, let's do our thing . . . forget about the other stuff . . . you guys are smart . . . and we can have a lot of fun with this . . . let's pick . . . "
KELLY:	(coyly) "Do you think we could pick a bad President? I knew a class had to make 0 cent stamps for Jefferson Davis . . . it'll be cool."
SHANDRA:	" . . . uh . . . never mind . . . "
MARIA:	"What is it, girl? You never say. . . . You look bad. . . . "
SHANDRA:	"I always prefer to work alone . . . usually teachers let me."
LUPE:	"Nothing wrong with us . . . you'll be OK. Group stuff can be fun . . . and I hear that Kennedy lets . . . "
KELLY:	" . . . right . . . he said that there won't be a competition or a tournament like last year. . . . We gotta get started. . . . What are you good at? Hey . . . you're on the singing team . . . why don't we make our monument with a rap song?"
LUPE:	"Salsa's better, but I'm OK with rap, too . . . pretty good idea. Shandra can you help us get the ideas in the right form?"

2. In Vignette 5 (see Question 1), four girls are working in their team. For this question, assume the four girls are working as a team *for the first time*. Analyze their interactions using the various ideas presented in the chapter and prepare either an informal (walk-through) discussion or a formal teacher observation using Vermette's Form A (Figure 5.2) or one of those offered by other theorists.

3. Refer back to the list of 15 roles that was provided in the chapter. Read the following brief dialogues (Vignettes 6 and 7) and identify examples of the roles at work. (1) Determine if roles are personal traits or contextually based functions, (2) whether they change between ninth grade and college, and (3) speculate on the importance of the distinctions made.

Vignette 6

SHARIL:	"What other rituals . . . do we need to surface?"
MARAL:	"Moslem prayer follows conventions . . . I guess that they are rules. But I don't like the word 'rituals' . . . makes it sound like a show . . . and not very meaningful, too."
TONY:	"You know I'm a Catholic and we have lots of bending, kneeling, hands up . . . but I don't think that they're bad. But, Maral . . . they are rituals."
KENDRA:	(interrupting) "A book I'm reading calls it common practice . . . thus showing others that they are *holy* . . . and showing their own members that they belong."
TONY:	"You know that Protestants take communion like we do, but it has a different meaning to them."

SHARIL:	"When I report this time, I think that we're supposed to stick to ritual, but if we want to drift in that direction . . . Mrs. Kelly will let us discuss meanings, too."
MARAL:	"What about the religions you guys read about in the homework?"
SHARIL:	"My stuff about Hinduism was OK . . . I discovered Jains have great detail about the use of broom and bowl, but that Hindu . . ."
TONY:	"What are they for?"
SHARIL:	"Wait a minute, Hindus refer to the Vedas . . . V–E–D–A."
KENDRA:	"Is everybody allowed to read them . . . or just men . . . or Holy Men?"

Vignette 7

SETTING:	Written on the board is the following request: "Identify six arguments from King's 1963 letter."
RONALD:	"Well . . . I think . . . that we're supposed to . . . describe the six key points in (letter) . . . is that what you guys think we're supposed to be doing?"
LaSHWANDA:	"Yeah . . . like I thought that when Martin says that he's in the middle . . . between Old Negroes that have quit . . . and Malcolm . . . you, know, more radical guys."
MARTIN:	"Good point! . . . that painted him as a moderate . . . not an extremist."
RONALD:	"Hey . . . slow it down, I gotta record this. Let me get that point that LaShwanda just made."
SUSAN:	"Ron, you got it OK? Well, Martin's right . . . King didn't feel that he was an extremist . . . except if you also want to call Jesus and Socrates and those other guys he cites extremists, too?"
RONALD:	"Well, I think he was going way too fast back then, but it was a huge change that he was seeking. I guess this ain't the point, though. We don't have to argue this, just get down that we have two of the key points summarized. You know, though, it seems important to note that King used all that religious stuff back in the sixties; it sure made it hard for the police to club singing and praying Christians over the head."
LaSHWANDA:	"Didn't seem too hard back then . . . boy, didn't you see the film she showed last week? Those people were singing, praying or just sitting quietly when the cops beat 'em. They're supposed to protect us, not attack us. The police were . . . uh . . ."
MARTIN:	"That's why that Rodney King shocked us so much . . . what a disgrace . . . I know that you (pointing at Ronald) think that the police are always in danger and should be free to fight crime any way they can . . . but . . . look, things today aren't really any better than they were in sixty-eight . . . and more blacks are in jail than in college . . . or poor . . . or . . ."
SUSAN:	"You know, it did confuse me . . . King also said that economic exploitation . . . and lack of jobs . . . those things are holding back blacks. It does seem that those same things are there today."

RONALD:	"You know, maybe I didn't read this letter as carefully as I should have, but I don't think King really said that about jobs. He's talking overall conditions. It was getting better in the U.S. until Reagan came in . . . and just killed poor people . . . Clinton may well give us some more hope."
LaShwanda:	"I get confused by some of this stuff. That political . . . look, racism has always been a truth in our history. You didn't see Jefferson freeing his slaves, holding the Bill of Rights to the sky, did you? The article says that white moderates have been a problem . . ."
Susan:	"Quick, that's another of the points we're supposed to record. Got that one, Ronald? Here comes Washington . . . Martin, show her the list and tell her what we have."
	(The professor approaches, all four students turn to look at her. Martin takes the list from Ron and starts to hand it to the tall figure.)
Dr. Washington:	"I want to see your list, but first that point about Reagan that I heard come from here . . . why don't you discuss it more . . . see it through . . . I'll be right back to see what you came up with."
	(Dr. Washington turns and moves toward a loud group at a nearby table.)

(Vermette & Erickson, 1996)

4. Have young children "draw" some of the 40 desirable qualities. Most likely, these will show that the children have a meaningful conception of the various items and do indeed prefer them to their opposites. (Listen carefully to them as they work.)

5. A hypothetical couple, the Drs. Jurasciewicz, teach in the Smallville, Ontario, school district. She teaches 12th-grade physics and 10th-grade biology and he teaches the 2nd grade. Both were smitten by the notion of daily grades as explained in Chapter 4.

They perceive the six rules embedded in Forms A and B (Figures 5.2 and 5.3, respectively) as potential rubrics (standards) by which they can better quantify, and thus explain, their daily grading scores. Unfortunately, neither Vermette's six rules nor the 12-item assessment form, Form C (Figure 5.4), matches perfectly with the 5-point scale. (Notice that the 4-point scale on Marzano et al.'s form shown in Figure 5.8 *does set rubrics*.) Design some clearly stated rubrics based on Forms A and B that could be structured into a 5-point rating scale for the Jurasciewiczs' consistent use in class.

Hint: It is easy to turn the daily scale into a 6-point scale, and have an instant match! However, doing so suggests that each item is equally valued—an assumption that might be inaccurate. Take the challenge and write rubrics for each of the possible scores (0, 1, 2, 3, 4, 5) offered in the chapter on grading.

DESIGNING ACTIVITIES FOR CLASSROOM APPLICATION

Two scenarios are presented in the following paragraphs that should alert you to the final critical component of a sound team learning program. We will observe Timmy, a middle-class youngster returning home with news for his parent about "what he did today." We will get a glimpse of an elementary school at work and step inside several of its classrooms to see what actually happens when students learn. Both of these lengthy scenarios point out that it is what the *students* do—not what *teachers* do—that results in learning. We will see that teamed activities are more active than is traditional class work. It is the generation of these good learning activities that provides the focus of this final chapter. Several systems are offered to help new users of cooperative learning take advantage of the power of the technique on a regular basis.

Teachers who have carefully (1) constructed balanced and effective teams, (2) articulated a wise grading policy, and (3) developed a system of governance *must* still plan and implement engaging and meaningful activities every day. To many teachers this is surprisingly difficult, and many have resorted to a rather passive and uneventful routine of just having students "study" together. As will be shown, this seldom provides the spark that catches the interest of diverse learners *or* takes advantage of the different perspectives, skills, and abilities of the group. When constructed properly, a good activity sells itself to learners. Their involvement then seems to go beyond schoolwork and into the realms of real-life problem solving, critical thinking, or construction. The various systems presented in the chapter provide both structures and suggestions to help make this vision of student team engagement a reality for your class.

Let us take a look at Timmy and his elementary school to set the stage for the four approaches we will use to analyze and generate activities.

Timmy's Day

The scene is terribly familiar, but also somewhat passé for our current troubled times: It is 3:15 on a warm and glorious October afternoon and young Timmy is entering the front door of his single-family home in bucolic suburbia, Colorado. His parent, Chris, is at the desk working on a real estate case and looks up:

"Hey, Tim. Have a good day?"

The response is anticipated: "Yeah, it was OK. . . . I got all my work done, so can I go over to Gloria's and Latricia's for an hour?"

"Sure, son. What did you do in school today?"

At this point, Timmy's answer will depend on a lot of things, including his temperament, his relationship with Chris, his feelings of security with his classmates, his disappointments in his personal relationships with other students, his sense of efficacy, etc. However, I would like to think that Timmy's answer to this question is also dependent on the behavior of *his teacher* and his or her selection or design of activities during the day. For example, check the answers that may have been provided by Tim in this situation:

_____   1. "Nothing."

_____   2. "Watched a science movie about . . . something."

_____   3. "Interviewed Latricia about her dog."

_____   4. "Completed our billboard on Argentina's agriculture."

_____   5. "Worked on our play about ancient Greece."

_____   6. "Screwed up the math problems."

_____   7. "Wrote an essay about pumpkins . . . actually, a horror story!"

_____   8. "Drew some pictures to match the story by the baseball player."

_____   9. "Won our basketball game."

_____ 10. "Pretended we were in a French restaurant and had a hundred dollars and we could order anything . . . and if we do it right tomorrow Smith will actually bring stuff in and we'll all cook something different and have a smorgasbord or a buffet that's French. . . ."

Obviously, this text is biased toward cooperative learning, but that bias is rationally based on motivational and cognitive principles. Learners are more likely to want to engage in grouped activities, enjoy them, and work hard at them as long as peer influence is positive. They also will learn more when they discuss and exchange ideas, when they practice those ideas, and when they are expected to think deeply about those ideas. As you read through Timmy's possible responses, could you predict which ones took place in a cooperatively teamed classroom and which ones in a traditional operating mode?

Cooperative learning by its nature forces students to engage in learning activities, conditions which increase learning and long-term retention (Semb & Ellis, 1994). Although many of Timmy's activities could have been done alone, some probably were not. For example, in statements 4, 5, and 9, the term *our* is used, suggesting that he worked in a peer-related fashion. Note that he recalls these activities, and is not sour about them; it sounds like he is pleased or at least neutral about them. There is obvious cooperation built into his interview with Latricia, although he does not sound ecstatic about it. He clearly enjoyed his French class, perhaps most of all. It sounds like the class was broken up into teams, assigned a dollar amount, and then required to do some group planning . . . with overall reward contingencies that have obviously interested Timmy.

Note the other responses; science films, universally despised, seemed to have failed again. (Is there something that teams of students can *do* in conjunction with science films?) The math comment is interesting; if his team had failed, would Timmy have used the term "we" and thus helped share the blame and the burden and lower his own sense of failure? He did not, implying that he worked, and failed, alone. The response "Nothing," which almost always draws a laugh by middle school teachers, certainly indicates no commitment, no engagement, no personalization, and no meaningful interaction. Could that have happened in a day filled with team activity?

Finally, note the other two responses, writing a story and drawing pictures. Many of us assume that these are solitary activities done by individuals. But assume a team structure for a minute; even if these were created by individuals, could peer editing, the building of an anthology, or the pairing of illustrations be included in the lesson? Could the drawings be sequenced for storytelling? Could they serve as illustrations for someone else's writings? Could they be integrated into a collage? Would this litany of activities be meaningful and engaging and result in learning? My guess, of course, is that these would be very powerful learning activities, and would allow the blending of individual activities into teamed projects that would realize all of the benefits offered by cooperative learning strategies.

SOME SAMPLE CLASSROOMS

Let us shift our orientation toward an elementary school. Imagine that you are walking down the corridor of a typical suburban elementary school somewhere in a southeastern state. The hum of the air conditioning permeates everything, yet the sounds of excited children's voices can still be heard, along with several commanding sounds of teachers barking orders. Along with the aural "white noise" comes a visual opportunity to peek into the classrooms of the various doors opening onto the thoroughfare of the hallway. What do you see as you look into those rooms?

As a firm believer in active learning, my first look would be directly at the children in the classroom. I would try to determine what they are doing and what they are trying to accomplish. I would also try to judge the "meaning" of the activity as it is reflected in the nonverbal facial expressions and gestures of students. I would also sneak a glance at the teacher and try to read his or her interest in the proceedings and I would try to evaluate the activity by his or her actions. Given that, here is what we see:

In Room 101, a first grade, youngsters are sitting in pairs, talking excitedly back and forth. A number of students look happy, several are laughing and gesturing, and only one looks sad and confused. As they talk, one partner in each pair stops frequently and draws something on paper. The teacher, face spread wide in a smile, is moving quickly from group to group.

Interestingly, like corn popping in the pan, one by one a member of each pair jumps up and begins to move arms and legs in a strange, but careful pattern. The unfamiliar movement is clearly meaningful to the child and the partner, but not to the observer.

In Room 102, students sitting in threes are spread out all over the kindergarten floor. Laughter, movement, touching, and pointing all stand apart from the smiles, frowns, and puzzled looks shown on the faces. The teacher (the largest person at 4 feet, 11 inches) is sitting on a chair next to one group, holding a little boy who appears very interested in the proceedings. In front of each group is a large piece of paper and three colored pencils. Each paper has been partially transformed into a drawing of sorts.

Finally, Room 103 offers a contrasting view. Each child sits silently, in straight rows. Many appear to be reading the books held before them, some do not have books, two have their heads down on the desk, and one, a large boy, is staring back at the observer at the door. (He also whispered something to a neighboring boy while looking.) The teacher is sitting at the teacher's desk and is also reading (a magazine).

As the observer heads back to the faculty room, one more open door beckons invitingly. In this class, Room 104, students are sitting on the floor in many circles. In each one, students are taking turns talking and making hand gestures to their peers. One group is very animated, but has one member who is not participating verbally. In this room the teacher is standing at the back and simply watching the proceedings. As I watched, on two occasions, students went up to the teacher, spoke, and returned to their group.

These observations are not very exciting and do not show a whole lot of detail about students learning, but they do reveal how active the learners were during class time. You may have attempted to determine what they were doing in the various activities. Here is what later discussions revealed about each observed classroom:

1. In Room 101, pairs of first graders were creating a story and preparing to act it out, like a kind of a miniplay. The story had to do with farm animals and, in effect, the students were role-playing the animals' behaviors.

2.   In Room 102, the students had seen a short video of a zoo in France and were now drawing a picture of their favorite part. Each drawing had to involve three pencil colors, with one color being used by each teammate. (The teacher was holding a child who tends to get overaggressive and needs to be comforted at times.)

3.   In Room 103, the students have silent reading every day at 10:30 and the observation was during that time. The teacher believes in competition and has a large wall chart, graphing the number of books read by each of the 23 students; currently, the range is from 16 (Jenine) to 0 (Brian, Aurtey, and Butch).

4.   In Room 104, the first graders were sitting in their teamed circles, an idea stolen directly from the title of the Johnsons' seminal work, *Circles of Learning* (Johnson, Johnson, & Holubec, 1984). The students were busy practicing American sign language. The teacher had thought it was a good idea for the class to learn sign language anyway, but the inclusion of Dorothy, a child with hearing disabilities, into class this week sparked the project. Dorothy was cast in the role of observer and helper and she had taught some of the signs before. (Her team, the Sugar Bears, will become specialists soon and will help other classmates as need arises.)

By the way, the two students who approached the teacher during the observation were asking how Dorothy was feeling about all this activity and were satisfied when the teacher said that Dorothy thought it was a neat idea.

Once again, these classes show the potential strengths of cooperative learning. In the three teamed classrooms, students were actively engaged in the learning process as they received encouragement and help from their peers and from the teacher. While they directly interacted in the lives of other kids they were reaching outcomes that were larger and broader than they could have reached alone. Their classrooms were noisy, filled with the energy of learning and true engagement and they were purposeful; it was easy to determine if they were reaching their goals because the overt behavior was easily assessed.

Although there is nothing wrong with silent reading, its use in Room 103 provided an interesting contrast. The teacher of the class, ironically, uses cooperative learning frequently, but also uses silent reading daily. On this day, the observation suggested that all the students were *not* actively engaged and the competition showed that the students were negatively interdependent: The more one student read, the worse it was for others. This class is likely to have many students who do not like reading and will not learn to like reading during the school years.

It was also clear that the students who had gained something from their reading (i.e., had become excited) would *not* have a chance to share any of their ideas with peers. There was no place in the teacher's reading program for sharing, beyond a required 30-word written report.

I have offered you these two glimpses into modern life, one in the home of a suburban family and one in the wing of a public school, to prepare you to read this chapter about cooperative activities. Having created good groups, invented a solid grading plan, and designed an effective assessment plan, the teacher is not finished: He or she *must* present viable and interesting activities for the teams to engage in during class time. When Timmy said he had done "nothing," he indicated that nothing had been expected of him; he did not need to write, draw, design, tell, question, illustrate, create, build, share, construct, or identify anything. When he talked of his team project in French, he suddenly found that he had had a lot to do. In Rooms 101, 102, and 104, the teams had been challenged to act out a play, draw a story, and talk without speaking—all interactively and with other people. The result was students who were cognitively busy. In Room 103, some were reading silently and may have been gaining a great deal from the activity. But it was hard to determine if that were indeed true, and many students were not engaged at all. The activity, reading a story, can be very valuable, but should not serve as a powerful all-purpose diet for school children's cognitive growth.

By the close of the chapter, the reader will have had a chance to assess several systems for building activities for the classroom and she or he will have had a chance to evaluate individual lessons for classroom use. The generation of good activities is crucial to all school success and is the vital final cog to the implementation of effective cooperative team learning.

In the next section, you will have a chance to scrutinize 10 different classroom activities closely and to see their relationship to these successful planning systems:

1. Project or task?
2. Bloom level?
3. Multiple intelligences?
4. CREEEPP level?

EVALUATING CLASSROOM TASKS

Here I provide a series of one-paragraph descriptions of some classroom activities at every level for K–12. They are all occurring at the very same time on the very same day across the district's many buildings. Please rate them (i.e., judge them), giving them your personalized evaluation on a scale of 1 (poor, waste of time) to 7 (excellent, valuable lesson); the midpoint score of 4 indicates an acceptable lesson.

Let me model one for you:

   _____   **Sample 1:** Today in class, Franglois has described famous sea monsters to her class of 27 fourth graders. They were all asked to listen to all of the descriptions and then were required to work in their pair partnerships to draw a sketch of a section of the sea with all the monsters involved! They also somehow have to indicate which culture generated the monster and whether it was real or mythical. Finally, they have been asked to plan to tell one sea monster story to a first grader tomorrow and also had to plan their corresponding nonverbal teaching gestures as well.

Now, personally, I do not know much about the sea monster curriculum, but if it had to be taught, this seemed to be a pretty good way to teach it. There was some positive interdependence in that the students had to work together to build the sketch and to give the next day's presentation to the younger children. They were given a pretty clear objective and task and the teacher was monitoring their work. My guess is that they will do a pretty good job, recall their monsters and culture, invent a creative new one, and do well with the first graders. They will have used a variety of skills and would have tapped into several of Gardner's intelligences: No one student could probably have done it as well alone as with "help." I think a score of six is warranted here. What was your rating?

Here are some more tasks. Please score them on the 1 to 7 scale given earlier:

_____ 1. Ms. Dukior has set aside 30 minutes every day so that her first-grade teams can continue constructing their team billboards entitled "Our Communities." The billboards are an attempt at visually representing what the team members think about their neighborhoods, their school, their classroom, and their lives. As they work, songs of different rock groups play in the background.

_____ 2. In Miller's 12th-grade biology class, pairs of students take turns reading from the text and summarizing; these two activities are done as turns by the partners. If one partner makes a mistake, the other corrects it. This continues for the entire class.

_____ 3. In Gavin's sixth-grade class, each four-member team was provided with a fictional $5000 and told to plan a 2-week trip to Mexico. The document to be produced is a travel plan, detailed in every way. Teams have their 40-minute period for the next 5 days to complete the task, which also includes planning the tapes that will be listened to at various times in the trip.

_____ 4. Koelle's third graders have been studying animals and have completed booklets with knowledge about the various animals detailed. Today they are given all morning to plan a videotape presentation about all the "stuff" that they learned. Every team member must be included and everyone in the team will get the same grade.

_____ 5. After hearing about the various food groups, Soarte's kindergarten pairs are making giant posters showing what they eat and how it matches these groups. Students are encouraged to help each other across groups, but most of the time the students work within pairs. Last year's posters are still up in the room, but the students are told "not to do the same thing."

_____ 6. Carpenter's History 11 class has been in study teams for 2 weeks. Now, at the end of the unit on the Gilded Age, they have five class periods to design, build, and field test a board game that shows what they know about the period. During these class days, Carpenter roams around the room suggesting ideas and giving feedback as to how they might improve their product. (One day next week, teams will exchange and then play the games).

_____ 7. In Ms. Rozina's French 1 class, seventh-grade teams are writing dialogues (scripts) that will be acted out on tape. Teams can write as many as 10 scripts for the tape, and each script must include all team members. All vocabulary words learned so far (the list is on the wall) must be incorporated at some point.

_____ 8. In learning about Africa, Unger's fifth graders became interested in *her* background, which had been traced to Ghana. Unger challenged her students to do a project on their interests and built five-member teams to do this. The students have been given 50 minutes a day for the next 2 weeks to complete their projects. One student (chosen by lot) will orally report on the team's work at the parents' meeting at that time.

_____ 9. Forston's fourth-grade teams are preparing for a math quiz on which their bonus points will be tied to their teammates' achievement. Three-member teams are using 20-minute sessions to solve practice problems together.

_____ 10. Sitting with index cards marked *encourager, summarizer, recorder,* and *gatekeeper,* Gadsen's eighth-grade teams are discussing what could be done to end poverty in the United States. Each student attempts to stay within the role assigned and recorders will be responsible for turning in the results. At this moment, the five recorders (Sherri, Latryce, Denise, Vicky, and Claire) are writing feverishly as the students talk.

Several things may become obvious as you reflect on the meaning of your scores:

1. Cooperative learning tasks can take many forms.
2. Not all cooperative learning activities are equally engaging or equally well constructed.
3. Different activities tap into different types of abilities (and intelligences) and are liked differentially by students.
4. Activities can be of various lengths and complexities.
5. Some, but not all, team activities can be done individually.

SOME ANALYTICAL FRAMEWORKS

Having determined that not all activities are equal, it becomes useful to take a long look at several systems or taxonomies that we could use to sort or invent activities. Certain qualities of tasks can make them more or less useful to us and they can help us thoughtfully generate alternatives.

Project Versus Task

If students work on a challenge for several days (or more) and/or need to take home components for refinement or perfection, then they are typically dealing with a team project. Many teachers use cooperative learning only for projects, a mistake from my perspective.

Projects are great for several reasons: They are complex, they can be motivating, they develop perseverance and loyalty, and they demand attention over time. On the other hand, students distrust projects because they fear the parasite student or a partner that will not do his or her share. Projects are also feared because they usually have a greater "cost" in grade points and because the teacher does not get an opportunity to observe the individual contributions or the interaction.

Projects are best suited for teams that have successfully completed many activities in class and ones that have shown they are indeed cooperative. Of the examples examined earlier, the best pure example of a project is example 8, which the teacher, Mrs. Unger, has even called a project. It is relatively ill-defined, unclear, and long term: The students need to work out the details and get themselves started. In many ways her requirement is similar to Sharan's (1992) Group Investigation method because it places so much of a burden on the students.

Note, however, that unlike most teachers, Unger has set out a great deal of in-class time to work on this project. In this way, she can overcome some of the shortcomings of typical projects: She can observe the teamwork, she can assess their progress *and* individual contributions, and she can inspire/motivate/cancel necessary parts of the project. In a regular classroom, terrible projects are not discovered until they are turned in, at which time, of course, it is too late.

Note that the criterion of "time allowed in class" changes the conception of a project to a more complex task, done over time, with many parts, but one that can be done in school. In this way, Dukior's billboard (example 1) and Carpenter's board game (example 6) become projects.

Also, there are possible take-home parts in Gavin's Mexican trip plan (example 3) and in Koelle's videotape (example 4), but most of this work is completed in school.

Tasks, then, are the activities expected to be completed by students during class time. They are frequently called *learning activities* and they are critically important. For the most part it is the engagement in the task—solving a problem, writing a poem, picking out the flaws in a film, dissecting a frog—that triggers the cognitive growth needed for intellectual change. The fact of having teammates provides motivation, reinforcement, feedback, new ideas, and a realism that are not there otherwise.

From our examples, note that Miller's teams are reading and summarizing (example 2), Soarte's are making posters (example 5), Rozina's are writing French dialogue (example 7), and Forston's are solving problems (example 9), all very different activities but ones that force the students to do something with content and with somebody else. They also result in a tangible product that can be assessed at the end of the class period. It is the planning of these types of activities that will produce the most effective learning for the most students in teamed systems in the long run.

Bloom Level

The most familiar of all planning taxonomies is Bloom's cognitive taxonomy, which has six levels (Arends, 1994). In ascending order of importance and impact, they are as follows:

1. *knowledge,* which asks learners to be able to recall or remember material;
2. *comprehension,* which asks learners to be able to restate or transform an idea into new words;
3. *application,* which asks students to solve problems with standard strategies or to use knowledge in a new situation;
4. *analysis,* which asks learners to be able to identify ideas or to compare/contrast certain content;
5. *synthesis,* which asks students to design, construct or build a new entity by combining other components; and
6. *evaluation,* considered the highest level since it asks students to judge, evaluate, or rank and defend their choices or decisions.

Note that levels 3 through 6 are considered upper levels.

Most of you are very familiar with this taxonomy, so there is little need to go into great detail about it here. However, it is important to say that classroom activities that challenge learners at the upper levels require the deepest cognitive processing and result in the best learning and the longest retention. If a teacher were to plan cooperative learning activities using the six Bloom levels, I would advise him or her to use the highest levels with perhaps the greatest focus on synthesis: When student teams are asked to build or design something new, they are asked to bring together all of their various insights and interpretations and experiences and come up with a group-based plan unique to them. Usually, such a task takes advantage of the greatest number of contributions of individuals and involves the greatest number of acceptable contributions.

Among the activities you rated earlier (which happened to be a level 6 evaluation exercise), the synthesis level was being sought in example 1, building a billboard; example 3, planning a trip; example 4, producing a videotape about animals; example 5, constructing giant food posters; example 6, inventing a board game; and example 7, creating French dialogue. If you rated these activities highly, there is a suggestion that you see a great deal to be gained by having students use their ideas together to create new products or new ideas.

Note, too, that the first taxonomy, project versus task, also seemed to favor the synthesis level. Frankly, any good project is somewhat complex and asks students to create something new out of many old ideas and concepts. A lower level project is a waste of a team's time. Moreover, many good in-class tasks are generated by a desire to tap the creativity of students working together. In fact, some teachers who use teams frequently, do most of their planning by simply asking the question: "Since we are studying [topic], what can the students *make* today that would force them to use the knowledge in a new way?"

One could use the other Bloom concepts to identify the various levels at which the other classroom tasks are operating. From my view, none of the examples involves only the knowledge level. Comprehension seems to be utilized in example 2, the reading and summarizing tasks. Application seems to be at work in example 9, in which students are helping each other solve problems. Analysis, the second of the upper levels, is at work in example 10 in which students are comparing poverty solutions. Finally, none of them appeared to be at the evaluation level, but the original task I gave you—to rate these from 1 to 7—certainly was!

The utility of the Bloom taxonomy for designing classroom tasks is enormous. It helps us come up with new, meaningful, and creative ideas that are complex and cognitively rich and it helps us sequence our activities for maximum effect.

Imagine for a minute, a week's worth of sixth-grade lessons on Brazil. The students could locate and recall locations on a map (knowledge), transform graphs of imports and exports into prose essays (comprehension), predict the weather from past records (application), compare and contrast its governmental forms with those of Argentina, Chile, and San Salvador (analysis), plan a trip there (synthesis), and tell why it would or would not be an enjoyable place to live (evaluation). In each case, the task's verbs guided the teacher's planning, ensuring that a variety of experiences would occur and increasing the likelihood that long-term retention would come from the experience.

Bloom's taxonomy is also a very useful analytical tool for understanding what goes on *inside* the group while the task or project is being completed. It allows us to analyze and understand the thinking going on inside various individuals. Look at the comments of the four students in this base group and *identify* the cognitive levels of each of the students' comments:

1. PAUL: "OK. We have to plan a trip to Brazil for the four of us."
2. OSCAR: "A trip . . . you mean like a week's stay and that stuff?"
3. JOAN: "Brazil . . . or Argentina?"
4. PAUL: "Brazil, and he has given us about $1000 to use."
5. KORA: "Let's see travel, food, clothes . . . tips. . . . When we went on our trip, we also had to plan for medicine."
6. PAUL: "I'd prefer only to see big cities."
7. KORA: "Me, too . . . the countryside is boring!"
8. OSCAR: " . . . yeah. . . . "
9. JOAN: "You mean the rural areas are like ours?"

Without getting too complex or too disheartened at the apparent lack of intellectual vigor in this realistic dialogue, note several things about the internal discussion of this group. When students get clarification from each other, they often work at comprehension (Joan, line 9) or literal knowledge (Joan, line 3) levels. When an idea is offered, its acceptance or rejection (Oscar, line 8) suggests that the student has been working on the evaluation level for that moment: Oscar's agreement is evaluation. Ideas offered are either routine solutions, applications, or syntheses (Kora, line 5).

Notice, too, that the very nature of this beginning discussion means that students (1) take *control* over the flow of ideas and the speed of interaction and (2) will move the Bloom levels up and down rapidly, meaningfully, and successfully as they need to.

I wish I had a nickel for every time a teacher told me, "I can't get my students to work with each other at evaluation level," and then had another teacher agree with the statement. I point out that the second teacher, by agreeing, has taken the statement, understood it, reflected on it, and has agreed—basically an *evaluation* process. The point here is that every time we dialogue, we evaluate. Every time we do an upper-level task in a group, we do ourselves cognitive good. When we finish a task that all have worked on, we are changed for the better.

Finally, recall or review the research cited in Chapter 2 that was conducted by members of the Johnson and Johnson teams. Many of their studies have been conducted at the synthesis level of Bloom, with four students generating a new entity to demonstrate their completion of the task. At times, the form of this research has been criticized because the very act of completion of the task by the team was counted as success for all individual members; literally, individual members were not tested for their individualized achievement separately from the group. This academic debate will not be solved here or elsewhere in the near future, but I offer a suggestion that you can test for yourself to see whether you trust team completion as indicator of individual gain.

1. Give a group a task that calls for students to take a variety of ideas and build or construct something new. (From our examples, Carpenter's board game and Koelle's videotapes provide models.)

2. Tell the group that at completion, one of them will randomly have to explain it alone. Each is to contribute and each is to master the whole thing.

3. Have them sign the finished product. Their signatures on the product show that they have understood the work, the rules, and their contributions.

My guess: When it is over, *every* member of the team will be able to explain the project. They will have all worked at synthesis and all will have grown. Students probably *liked* the synthesis activities the Johnsons gave them during the studies, no small matter for schoolwork. They liked the challenge of putting old into new and they enjoyed working together with others. Finally, I am sure that most of them liked putting their own stamp of freedom and pride on the newly designed entity that they had produced together.

Intelligences Utilized

A rather new and very useful planning approach can be linked directly to the work done on multiple intelligences by Howard Gardner of Harvard. In several interesting books (Armstrong, 1994; Gardner, 1983; Lazear, 1991), the theory of multiple intelligences (MIs) is cogently spelled out and sample applications to K–12 classrooms have been provided. In short, the theory holds several key tenets:

1. In the West, a useful understanding of intelligence has been limited by its conceptualization as an overall, immutable, and genetically based reality.

2. Every culture places different emphases on individual traits and the key ones are actually "intelligences"; that is, they are fundamental and important potentialities of every individual.

3. Currently, at least seven intelligences have been identified in the West and they need to be nurtured and developed by educational innovations throughout schooling.

4. A more realistic understanding of human potential and human abilities would be gained by seeing people as combinations of their various intelligences rather than identifying them solely by a single measure of ability (IQ).

Thus, planning with the seven intelligences would result in taking greater advantage of student strengths and backgrounds and would provide every individual a richer and more potent exploration of talents. Although few teachers or teacher educators currently plan their lessons using the MI theory as a basis, it is quite likely that this will become a prevalent pattern in the future. Of course, the planning of projects and tasks with an eye for utilizing the multiple abilities is a natural for cooperative learning teachers.

Let us briefly discuss the seven intelligences in the following paragraphs.

Logico-mathematical: One of the standard school skills (and IQ measures), this is the ability to follow or build sequential and structured ideas such as those found in mathematical problems, arguments, and scientific experiments. It involves the ability to discover and use patterns.

Verbal-linguistic: The second of the two pillars of school curriculum and standard measures of IQ, this is the ability to use words to convey ideas and to use the written symbols of the professional culture. The ability to make an argument, present a case, fashion a profound concept or articulate an idea are all found in applications of this intelligence.

Note that Western standardized tests usually include just these two intelligences. The quality called g (general intelligence), represented by a score (i.e., 100 as average), dominates our understanding of ability and shapes our schooling. Gardner's research has added the next five and will redefine how we plan our team lessons.

Visual/spatial: The ability to use space, understand structure and form, and manipulate the background is fundamental to the work of architects, designers, and other professionals. It is a highly valued intelligence and yet is one rarely treasured in a school setting. Students with an artistic eye are often able to use their intelligence to produce meaningful and wondrous constructions, but seldom get asked to do so in the traditional K–12 classroom. Students who can image and vision are not as respected as those who can write.

Musical: The ability to produce and generate musically related products is respected and highly valued in Western culture. However, music and art programs are often the first ones "cut" by school boards anxious to reduce the costs of schooling. Gardner, of course, sees these as vital and important qualities and rightly stresses their utility in the entire structure of schooling.

Very often, teachers of children older than 10 ignore or forget about the positive aspects of this intelligence. Rarely do older kids get to experience, understand, produce, or analyze music as a regular part of the curriculum, and students blessed with gifts in this intelligence are often undervalued in the classroom.

Kinesthetic/body: Western culture places a high value on athletics and athletes, sports being one of the most fundamental activities of the society. We also respect actors, actresses, and dancers; the ability to move one's body is a standard measure of the "cool" needed for peer acceptance among schoolchildren. Yet, again, formal curriculum outside of the physical education class does not place much classroom value on "body knowledge." The incorporation of movement into the curriculum promises to reach more students and seem "more relevant" to children growing up in a culture that stresses it elsewhere.

Interpersonal: This intelligence is absolutely fundamental to the success of team learning and, quite possibly, is the key ability to the lifetime success of adults in Western culture (Goleman, 1995). The ability to share ideas, form relationships, enlist others into a common project, and build interactive structures effectively is fundamental to everything from running a fast food restaurant to coaching football to managing a corporation to living in a satisfying family situation. Every human relationship is directly related to this intelligence. Of course, every properly designed cooperative learning activity builds this intelligence and increases the respect schools show for students who possess it. Interestingly enough, until cooperative learning boomed in the late 1980s, this was a valued school intelligence *but* it only existed in extracurricular activities, such as sports, drama, glee club, Honor Society, and the Model U.N. Now, it is respected enough to be found in the regular activities of the school day (but, of course, is not measured on IQ or other standardized tests).

At the present time, interpersonal intelligence might be the third most likely intelligence to find itself used, developed, and respected in the contemporary classroom. This in itself is quite a change in school structures during the past 20 years, and represents something of a victory for Gardner's approach to schooling.

Intrapersonal intelligence: It is hard to read very much of the contemporary educational literature without stumbling across the concepts of metacognition and reflection. As typically used, reflection is the process used by learners to reconstruct and analyze a previous experience. The processes of redefining the moment and planning for a future similar event are also involved. Thus, one who reflects is the one who has the most to make out of an experience and should gain the most from every opportunity.

Metacognition, defined as thinking about thinking, shows an awareness and a control over one's cognitive processes, an ability that also allows one to make the most out of an experience.

Simply put then, self-dialogue (or self-analysis) is evidenced in the reflection and metacognitive processes. This activity is more often found in today's classrooms than previously. For example, a great deal of emphasis has been put on journal writing in language arts activities for the K–12 grades. Social studies has seen the rise of critical thinking strategies that take advantage of metacognitive research. This intelligence says that the ability to learn from all experiences (not just mistakes) is a valuable and helpful skill; it is also one that can be developed and improved in a school situation.

Gardner has offered us these seven intelligences, seven different prisms from which to look at the classroom lessons we have planned for our cooperative learning teams.

Application of MI Theory

Return to the original set of tasks you evaluated a few pages ago. Here is how I see the teachers applying MI theory.

Examples 1 and 6, the billboard and the board game, utilize visual/spatial intelligences. Example 7 forces students to work with their body/kinesthetic intelligence and example 4 "invites" (but does not necessarily require) them to do so. Examples 1 and 3 utilize students' musical intelligence and others could also have done so. Intrapersonal intelligence is utilized in example 10, because the students need to reflect on their metacognitive processes used to stay in role. Logico-mathematical intelligence is used in many classes, notably in examples 5 and 9, and to a large degree in producing the sequenced patterns called for in the dialogue of example 7 and in the planning of example 3. Verbal linguistic intelligence, the historical basis of school learning, is involved in every one of the tasks through the oral processes used to articulate and communicate ideas. It is the primary intelligence used in several items, including example 7, the script writing, and example 2, the oral exchange. Finally, because of the nature of cooperative team learning, every single group activity utilizes the interpersonal intelligence of all the students. The ability to interact effectively is more than good communication skills; it involves the abilities to empathize with the receiver of messages, to see different viewpoints, and to relate to other people's needs. These can be found operating in every single task listed.

The potential for using MI theory as a planning taxonomy for cooperative learning activities is enormous. The set of tasks given next has been used in a college level class that has been reading a very fine book about an effective, but overwhelmed high school English teacher named Jessica Siegel. The book, *Small Victories* by Samuel Freedman (1990), is used at the outset of an education course that I teach. The students have been paired and work on these tasks during an 80-minute class period a day before they are tested (individually, with a bonus based on the partner's score). As you read through them, try to identify the intelligence(s) being "awakened" and "amplified" (using Lazear's words) in the learners:

Freedman, S. G. (1990). *Small victories*. Harper Perennial, New York.

Introductory Chapters

1. Draw an illustration of an important event in each of the first few chapters. Be prepared to have others analyze it and offer modifications. Describe the results of this process to your partners.
2. A study of Jessica Siegel provides many insights into the complexities of a teacher's job; mainly, it says that her roles are varied, difficult, fluid, and

important. Which of these do you, your partner, *and* Siegel feel are important?

a. adult model

b. counselor

c. advisor

d. chaperon

e. driver

f. colleague

g. planner

h. evaluator

i. disciplinarian

j. student

k. curriculum designer and instructor

l. motivator

m. parent "soother"

n. confidante

3. From what you have read in the book, and experienced in life, do teachers take "liberties" with students? Explain.

4. Siegel gave the students two clear assignments very early in the semester: (a) Write an autobiography and (b) write an essay about "the good teacher." Evaluate these assignments. Describe two others that would have been productive for these classes.

5. We get to know a lot about Siegel's life and the history of the school in the first few pages. The importance and/or relevance of this information is debatable. Please reflect on this question by doing the following:

   a. If movies were made of the school's history *and* Siegel's childhood, what music would be played in the soundtrack? Why?

   b. What metaphors evolve from the two realities presented?

   c. If you were teaching at Seward Park now, and had been there 25 years, what kinds of assignments would you *no longer* give these students?

   d. Make a pie chart that shows Siegel's life split up by its various dimensions.

   e. Name two actresses whose physical styles seem appropriate for your image of Siegel. Explain *and* demonstrate.

   f. Siegel is the kind of teacher who says things in class like "I don't know a lot about this, but . . . , " or "one idea that I'd like to have you think about is. . . . " Evaluate that approach for both you and your partner.

   g. Be ready to articulate all of your responses to another pair.

6. A lot is said about adolescence in this book: "writing reveals their naked-ness," "teachers need to be grown up; set standards," "a huge chasm of ado-lescent insecurity." What do these phrases mean?

7. Siegel's planning takes 3 hours a day, plus she carefully grades papers. Many teachers say they "wing it." What is going on here? What would Siegel say in an interview?

8. The first four chapters have most interesting titles. What do they mean? What would have served as a better title in each case?

9. Be prepared to act out Siegel telling Freedman, "I'm always on . . . it never ends." What are the logical consequences of this statement?

10. Death exists in school life; Siegel receives a warning about a suicide and experiences one.
    a. What do these say to the teacher's roles and responsibilities?
    b. Practice what you would say to a student suspected of suicidal intentions and act it out.
    c. Is death a proper subject for teenagers to study? Explain.
    d. Death has racial overtones in New York City. Should these overtones be explored?
    e. What teen music deals with this topic?
    f. How does *death* relate to your subject area?

11. Make predictors about the following, based on what you have read so far:
    a. the success of Seward World (newspaper)
    b. Jessica and Bruce's relationship
    c. Mary Tam's education
    d. the population makeup of the school

Answer Key

Without belaboring the issue, note that if the pairs completed all of these activities during the session, all the intelligences would have been used. In doing so, students would have modeled to their partners talents that may have not been recognized or appreciated and all actors would have gained in self-esteem and in peer recognition. More importantly, the students would have been engaged in the deep processing needed for understanding and long-term recall of the content.

Every activity required interpersonal intelligence; that is a given in any group, team, or pair activity.

Other intelligences were also required. Some examples follow: Musical intelli-gence is touched on in example 10e about suicide and in example 5a about a sound-track; intrapersonal awakening is asked for in example 2 by its references to feelings about roles; logico-mathematical is built into example 11, which asks students to make (logical) inferences called predictions; verbal/spatial is used in the drawings called for in example 1; body/kinesthetic has been slipped into example 10b by calling for practice, a task that most likely results in some kind of role play or acting out; and, finally, because it is school, verbal/linguistic talents are dominant in every task.

Note, carefully, however, example 5, which has seven parts. That alone may have been a hint that each item has a focus on one particular intelligence. Good tasks (and projects) generally utilize combinations of many of the seven, but frequently *one intelligence dominates* an activity. On a separate sheet of paper, identify which of the seven intelligences the lesson planner *tried* to "awaken" and "amplify" in the seven parts of example 5, then consider my answers. (Here is the way I attempted to incorporate a dominant intelligence into my paired assignment: a, M; b, V/L; c, L/M; d, V/S; e, B/K; f, intrapersonal; g, interpersonal).

To reiterate, the use of multiple intelligences as a planning taxonomy is in its infancy. It is powerful, motivating, relevant, and, by using diversity as a positive, democratic in spirit. The future will see many teachers begin to utilize its beauty as a planning vehicle for their cooperative learning activities.

Mention should be made here of Elizabeth Cohen's Complex Instruction model. As you may recall from Chapter 1, Cohen (1994) is concerned that all students become engaged in the teamed work, despite unequal statuses within a group. She calls for the assigning of complex projects, "larger than any one member" of any group could do alone. She wants her students to rely on each other, to utilize all of their various strengths and weaknesses, and to produce something that is unique to them as a team. One can easily see how nicely all of this dovetails with Gardner's views of the complexity of intelligences and the need to have instructional tasks challenge many human abilities.

Thus, Cohen's projects all require complex use of many talents and can easily be built with an eye for the seven intelligences. Examine the following assignment with those ideas in mind:

> So, teams, here is your task. You are to produce a videotape of a play that you have written and performed about the subject of the American Revolution. It should be historically accurate, but also use inventive fiction. Your characters must act convincingly and logically; your sets should look as good as they can and serve a purpose. The music you include should make sense, even if it isn't contemporary. Your teams each have a budget of $27.50 raised from the bake sale—that is *all* you can spend! All team members must have a part and at least one part of the play must involve a soliloquy, which, as you remember, is a self-talk dialogue by a character. The tapes will last twenty-five minutes . . . we'll begin showing them two weeks from Friday. After a showing, your team will be given six minutes to share thoughts and insights you have about your own product. . . . No one of you can do anywhere near as good a job as all of you can do as a team. The books and materials are over there and in the library. Get going!

Dan Johnson, a Wilson, New York, middle school teacher, invented a project very similar to this several years ago and now it is a staple of the entire seventh-grade teaching team. It has produced wonderful results, with students working very hard to produce videos that are played on local cable TV. The students regard the Colonial Unit videotape to be their favorite unit of the year.

CREEEPP Categorization

For the past few years, several of my colleagues at Niagara University, Dr. Jerry Carpenter (history), Dr. Burt Thompson (psychology), Dr. Tom Sheeran (education), and Dr. Deborah Erickson (counseling), have been examining and experimenting with cooperative learning techniques. From that basis, and from the consequent experimentation in the classrooms of student teachers, has come this final planning taxonomy. Nicknamed *CREEEPP,* it offers a thoughtful and differentiated approach that allows teachers to plan quickly and carefully a series of lessons that call on different strategies and different skills of learners. As I describe these next seven activities from my teacher's college classroom, try to imagine them in your mind and then rate them as simply "good" or "not good" as you wish:

_____ 1. The students are constructing the outline of an interdisciplinary unit plan for a middle school based on the concept "weather."

_____ 2. Teammates are helping each other memorize the sentence "Little Lori sorts biblical masks inside igloos," which is a mnemonic for the Gardner's seven intelligences.

_____ 3. Teammates are looking at two lesson plans, identifying similarities and differences from a Hunterian perspective.

_____ 4. In their small groups, students are busy completing two challenges. First, they are inventing anticipatory sets for three lessons and, second, they are explaining how they would use their bulletin boards over the 2-week period.

_____ 5. The groups are given four tests for a third-grade math unit so they can rank order their utility.

_____ 6. The teams are given four lesson plans so they can identify where discipline problems are most likely to occur.

_____ 7. After reading several pages of Freedman's book, the teammates are interviewing each other about how they would feel, given the reality faced by Siegel.

Compare your ratings of the college class activities you just finished with the fourth-grade activities that follow:

_____ 1. The cooperative groups are busy designing a business, using their knowledge of money and economics.

_____ 2. The students are helping each other master the steps in setting up a corporation listed in their textbooks.

_____ 3. The students are comparing various business slogans from fast food restaurants and from TV commercials aimed at their age group.

_____ 4. The students are given a short article from *USA Today* that tells of a major corporate lion's latest project; they are asked to invent a bibliography about him or her that would account for current successes.

_____ 5. Teams are presented with a series of slogans about certain products; they are asked to rank order them by their appeal to certain age groups.

_____ 6. Teams are given charts showing sales for three different companies over the past 5 years; they are asked to guess what will happen in this year and in the next two.

_____ 7. The teammates are asked to interview each other about what they would like or dislike about working at various jobs in a corporation. (The list includes mailroom clerk and president and was produced yesterday in small groups.)

Review your ratings across the similarly numbered item, 1 with 1, 2 with 2, and so on.

These activities were generated by the use of CREEEPP, and the numerically matched items reflected similar categories on the taxonomy. Let us take a look at each of the seven groups and the activities planned for college and grade school teams.

C is for construction activities, my personal favorite, and one that requires the teams to produce something new while using information and content being learned. These are almost always motivating, since there is always a need for invention and challenge and they are seldom limited by existing teacher structures. In the preceding examples, the college class is completing a task that calls for producing an outline and the fourth grade is generating a business, something that may take awhile (and may turn into a project).

Some key verbs that signal a task being a construction are as follows: (1) make, (2) construct, (3) design, (4) build, (5) invent, (6) produce, and (7) generate. The outcomes produced are almost always tangible and innovative.

As with the synthesis level of Bloom, this is perhaps the key level for cooperative learning groups. Being challenged to come up with a unique product sets in motion all the best features of cooperative learning and has the greatest chance of tapping cognitive potential. Here is a sampling of other classroom activities that belong in this category: (1) making newspaper ads, (2) writing stories, (3) designing brochures, (4) building sets for a play (and writing the script), (5) making a puppet show, (6) making a TV commercial, (7) generating a newspaper or magazine, (8) writing epitaphs, and (9) inventing a comic strip.

R is for rehearsal, which is the *least* useful of the seven CREEEPP categories and is offered next because it provides a stark contrast to the construction category. Recall that in the first category, students are engaged in creating some novel combination of content, individuality, and ideas, working at deep cognitive levels and in an interactive manner. In rehearsal activities, the emphasis is on the opposite, seeking almost pure mastery or memorization; ironically this is often thought by laypeople (and some teachers) to be "learning." Most of the time, these activities are incredibly dull, result in a sort of a peer tutoring focused on verbal regurgitation, and do little for long-term understanding or growth. However, there are times when teachers need students to recall something, so the use of rehearsal or memory activities may be justified.

In our previous examples, the college class is learning a mnemonic, knowledge that may be helpful later. In the fourth grade, students are memorizing the steps in a process, a task that often makes little sense to me (see the discussion of elaboration later).

Picture for a minute the French classroom of Ms. Didier. She does a great deal of "tout le monde," which means that she says something in French ("Bonjour") and then *all* the classmates chorally chant it back ("Bonjour"). If they need to memorize this statement, they would be better served practicing it within an interdependent team in which each person gets help or reinforcement and in which each person is heard. A set of such mastered responses could be the focus of a rehearsal activity for a student team.

Every memorized task would be better served by having small groups practice interactively, thus the rehearsal category exists.

Finally, it must be said that most cooperative learning teachers offer *no* rehearsal type tasks during a school year. They are too boring, uncreative, and deadly to use in class. Most of what is remembered by students is not through pure memory; instead, it is gained from using information in many ways so that understanding is developed. For example, as you may know, $a^2 = b^2 + c^2$. That could be learned through (1) a thousand chantings (like a mantra), (2) a hundred writings, or (3) by using it in a dozen problems. This third activity is not rehearsal and it does affect memory in a positive way.

E is for examination, a process that asks students to analyze, compare, and contrast material. In examining lesson plans and commercials, the students in our examples were dissecting the subject matter in a thoughtful and analytical way. Identification of key ideas is another examination activity, a task often used when students are exposed to new information. The process of comparing the new to the old (a Piagetian necessity) in a teamed setting makes these useful tasks. Here is a brief list of examination activities for the K–12 classrooms: (1) finding propaganda in ads, (2) finding clues in mysteries, (3) finding Waldo!, (4) comparing the obituaries of three prominent people, (5) identifying examples of sexism in the newspaper or the text, (6) identifying the colors used in a painting, (7) completing a crossword puzzle, (8) comparing the forms of "d'etre" in four sentences, (9) identifying patterns in the various Greek fables being read, (10) counting syllables in several poems, (11) examining the eating patterns of two different animals, (12) contrasting three kinds of mammals (lions, tigers, and bears), and (13) looking for mistakes in spelling, punctuation, and verb tense in a piece of prose.

Note that the examination activities seem to be shorter and briefer than the construction activities. They are, in fact, because they are essentially analytical procedures and often lead to a next step, either solving an identified problem (elaboration) or creating something different (construction). However, they provide an important step for the teams, because they bring together diverse abilities, skills, and interests providing necessary motivation and expertise. During the course of a year, I believe that groups do these important cognitive activities more effectively than do individuals and they result in much better understanding for everyone in the long run.

Note, too, that this extensive list is adaptable for all grade levels K–12. Finding the colors in a painting, for example, can be done with the youngest of students and with those older ones taking advanced art. Likewise, finding mistakes is a process that is universally done (it is called *proofing* or *editing* in language arts).

Teachers who concentrate on memory activities lose all the potential good that examination and analysis can provide; in fact, memorizing a definition is a poor way to learn a concept, and true mastery of a concept requires the identification of novel examples (Vermette, 1983). Thus, restating the definition of a "verb" is not nearly as powerful as is identifying the verbs in this sentence: "I will arrive before the clock strikes three, but I will not eat until five." Likewise, the verbs in the sentence "The money lies on the table, twitching like sleeping dogs' paws after a hard day hunting" are not necessarily clear. Any reader who wishes to show these sentences to someone else, either to (1) find verbs or (2) to critique the writing, has just felt the natural motivational pull of cooperative learning.

Thus, analysis and examination are powerful and important cognitive tasks and are best done in a shared setting.

E is also for elaboration. This is an all-purpose category that includes all activities in which students are asked to use information either to solve a problem, provide new examples, explain an understanding, or extend a learning to a new idea. Elaboration activities call on the students to use logic and creativity to make the content real, meaningful,. and useful.

In our original examples, the college teams are explaining their plans for the bulletin board and the fourth grade is building a biography for a person. Both attempt to extend their knowledge logically to a new situation that requires a connection between what is known and what is related. Elaboration activities are not totally creative, because they begin with a given set of data (or knowledges). They are more convergent than construction activities and yet allow for deep processing. Many times in class, they exist as teacher questions, which result in a 1-minute paired sharing (Kagan, 1989) and then an answer. These can also be complex activities that require somewhat longer class time or can be used in combinations of time structures. For example, if the arithmetic teacher wanted the students to solve eight problems, she could give them all eight at one time, allowing 15 minutes for work. Or, she could give them one problem at a time and give the teams 1 minute to solve it. She could start with one, debrief it, then give three problems and 5 minutes, and so on. In all cases, she could allow the teams to work together to elaborate on their knowledge by applying it to the new problems.

Here are some interesting elaboration activities that require differential amounts of class time:

1. Third graders have several comic strips, each missing the final box. They have to complete the strip by drawing that last entry.

2. Ninth graders are given the 1994 Regents test items 1 through 10 and get in their teams to answer the items.

3. After viewing a 10-minute film on Thomas Jefferson, the seventh-grade students are given the front page of today's paper and asked to find four articles and tell what Jefferson would have said about each.

4. The 12th graders are given pages of a trial transcript (different pages to different teams). Many lines have been crossed out such that they cannot be read, and the teams have to generate replacement sentences that make sense and help the lawyers case. (*All* "cloze" activities are elaborations, but these do not require the necessity of having to have an exact match of the missing word; conceptually correct is good enough.)

5. The fifth-grade teams are given brief descriptions of eight Greek gods of mythology and are told that two more are missing; they have to invent those two missing gods.

6. Second graders are asked to draw pictures of at least three scenes in the story they are reading and be ready to explain their sequence in the story.

7. The sixth graders are rewriting history, an activity that has the teams read a paragraph from the text and then rewrite it without using any of the same words except proper names.

E is also for evaluation, activities that call directly for the teams to judge, rate, rank, choose, or defend something. This category is a perfect analog to the Bloom level of the same name, but in this taxonomy, it is not considered a higher skill, simply a different task. In our first examples, the college class is selecting the "best" test for students and the fourth graders are ranking slogans. Done in teams, evaluations are fascinating activities because they require carefully articulated explanations, logically built assertions, and the careful interfacing of diverse value structures. Because they tap into strongly held personal opinions they can teach students how to disagree democratically. They should not, however, be used too early in a particular team's existence. They can be most effective in a team that has learned to exchange ideas, respect each other, and see the value of different opinions.

All content that involves two or more of something is ripe for the use of evaluation. For example, if a team has three endings for a story, it can determine the best one. If a team is given a budget and two choices for a house pet, it can choose the better one. If there are five new cars on the market, students can rank order them on several criteria. Teams can rate solutions to poverty, opening lines of a poem, or options for a class trip.

Here is a sampling of tasks and projects that teams could engage in within their teams:

1. Teams of eighth graders are producing a booklet entitled "The Ten Best U.S. Presidents" with clear explanations for their selections.

2. Teams of first graders are looking at all the drawings of the school made by last year's class. Each team will pick five good drawings for their collage called "Our School."

3. The ninth graders have been given a list of foods served in the 27 countries that they have studied. They are to choose 8 based on a specified criteria (category favorites) and design a cookbook.

4. The 11th-grade business students have been generating a series of sales pitches for a new product. Other teams are going to rank order the pitches based on their estimates of probability of success.

5. Third-grade teams are reading and discussing plays so that they can choose one to perform at the Winter Carnival.

6. Twelfth graders have been given pictures of modern stamps and are choosing the five that best describe their view of history.

7. Fourth-grade math teams have been given three approaches to solving a problem. They are ranking them for their usefulness.

8. The fifth-grade language arts teams have articles about a local drowning from three different newspapers. They are determining which one did the best job covering the event.

Evaluation is also built into many cooperative learning projects. As the teams begin their work on a project, they often generate several possible alternatives and need to make a *joint decision* about the best one to follow. When they engage in this decision-making task, they are engaging in the evaluation task and they are doing it as it is really done in the adult world.

P is for prediction, another component of the taxonomy that usually focuses on brief in-class teamwork. This category simply involves all tasks in which student teams are asked to tell what they think will happen in a particular sequence; they discuss options and then make a prediction about the future. These are very handy tools since they offer the students a change of pace by demanding a discovery/hypothesizing approach. This forces students to examine the previous information they have and offers students a chance to use intuition as well as logic.

In our initial examples, the college class was trying to hypothesize about weak points in a lesson that may result in discipline problems and the fourth graders were predicting a future trend. Analogs for these can be found in every discipline and include the following: (1) Teams read and discuss the first three pages of a story and then predict the ending, (2) poems lacking final *words* are studied and predictions made about that final word, and (3) a graph or table is left incomplete so that students can make predictions about the missing data.

A hypothetical example is shown in Figure 6.1. In this example students are to "guess" about the productivity of the years 1940 and 2000. Note that data can be retrieved that will allow a test of the prediction for the earlier time frame, but *not* for the second gap (2000), thus illustrating two kinds of prediction activities: (1) those that can be immediately tested and (2) those that call for a look to the future.

As another example, compare the following questions, and if you are a football fan, generate an answer (I ask your indulgence on the football orientation!):

1. Will O. J. Simpson be in the Hall of Fame in 2010?

2. Will the Tampa Bay Bucs ever win a Super Bowl?

3. The Bills went to the playoffs in 1990, 1991, 1993, 1994, and 1996. Do you think that they went in 1992?

FIGURE 6.1   Prediction Example

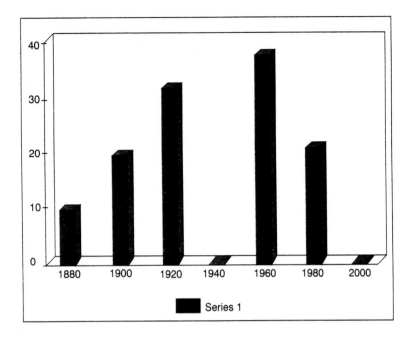

4. Will Dan Marino go to the Hall of Fame?

5. Do Super Bowl winning teams draw more people during their winning year or in the season following the year that they actually won?

6. Will Dallas's number one choice in the college draft become a star?

Note that items 1, 2, 4, and 6 call for predictions that can only be answered in the future. The prediction can be checked when the future provides the necessary data.

The other two items, 3 and 5, call for predictions (hypotheses) that can be tested against existing data. If students became engaged in generating such guesses, they would most likely search out the data to establish truth as quickly as they could.

The sciences well taught take great advantage of this prediction/testing category of activity. Good science challenges teams to make logical and intuitive guesses about reality and equips them with a process to evaluate their answers. As disclosed earlier, this process can also help students determine what data is of value. Bad science, on the other hand, often becomes the memorization of useless facts (and frequently uses the desperate application of the bell curve as a motivator). In fact, schooling has been referred as to as the "memorization of lists nobody needs" and teaching as the "telling of answers to questions nobody asked." The essence of this prediction category is that the student interaction leads to a genuine estimate of some behavior, the generating of an answer to a question, a process which almost always leads the students to seek confirming (or disconfirming) data—namely, the answers to their own questions.

Imagine some third graders watching four tropical fish in a tank. Teams have generated a list of questions and are now working together to make observations that will help them answer their questions. Among the questions are these:

1. How does the fish breathe?

2. How long will it live?

3. How big will it grow?

4. How do fish communicate?

5. How does the fish eat and go the bathroom?

6. Under what conditions will it stop swimming?

7. What are the rules of space these fish follow?

8. What do the fish see?

Now, many of these questions will not be answered by the observation, but predictions can be generated from the student team discussion. Certainly, some may be "wild guesses" ("I think it lives for a hundred years"), but others will be interesting ("I don't think they communicate . . . they seem to ignore everything").

Testing of these hypotheses can be done through observation, interviewing, reading, or film watching. But the *desire* to gain the answer has been built by students' joint generation of an expectation.

It is always amazing to me that teachers do not use analogous processes more often. Mystery writers keep the readers on the edge of their seats, actively anticipating or expecting developments, yet literature teachers do not do anything similar. History is seldom taught by offering a scenario and then asking for predictions about what happened. For example, a partial biography could be given and students could be asked to fill in the missing parts. Answers could be discovered later, or particular conditions could be given and students asked to make predictions about the future.

All in all, incorporating prediction activities into the daily flow of classroom events is both a great motivator of thinking among students and an effective process that forces students to think deeply and logically about the content that they are facing.

P is also for personalization, the seventh and final category in the CREEEPP taxonomy. Personalization tasks ask students to think about and disclose their beliefs, feelings, and emotions about the topics at hand and also asks them to place themselves in other people's situations and describe their reactions. This category attempts to get students to make and share personal insights into dilemmas and aims to help learners empathize with various perspectives and to see the world in its complexity, while retaining great respect for individual differences.

In our initial examples, the college students were asked to role-play Jessica Siegel in an interview, trying to feel her pressures. The fourth graders were discussing preferences for various jobs and careers and explaining their perspectives.

Some interesting and brief personalization tasks that teammates could engage in include the following:

1. Pairs have been asked to interview and write up their partners' reactions to [topic].
2. Teams generate a good news/bad news list of events in the previous history chapter (say, perhaps, the Great Depression).
3. After learning about a historical figure, teams write journal entries from various perspectives (including their own).
4. Teams write pro and con editorials about a topic in the news (or they generate political cartoons).
5. Teams write a letter describing what they would like to see or avoid if they visited [a country].
6. Small groups discuss how a poem or film made each of them "feel."
7. Students build a team collage showing their individual reactions to a particular event.

Although personalization appears to focus on the students' self-reflections, it does so with an interpersonal twist. Often, personal thoughts are recorded in a diary or a journal, but are lost because they never become part of a truly engaging discussion. Making an event meaningful often involves sharing it with someone else, thus the call for using it as the focus of a small, secure, and protected group discussion. Real self-disclosure almost *never* happens in large classroom settings. Most students over the age of 8 have learned to (1) shut up, (2) give the teacher what is perceived to be wanted, or (3) act provocatively, but seldom to really share one's thoughts and feelings in a large group setting.

Second, the role-playing skills called for in taking another's perspective are important for human cognitive and emotional growth. In small groups, students are freer to try to see someone else's perspective: "If I had been Truman, I would have said that . . . " or "The Indians felt that it was their land and that . . . " or maybe "us women have waited over a hundred years. . . . " These are harder comments to make in class than most adults realize: Youngsters do not decenter easily and they do not automatically see the other side of the story. Activities that encourage students to share their own feelings and to imagine and evaluate other people's thoughts and feelings stimulate creativity and memory and promote human tolerance.

Back in Chapter 1, I offered a long list of activities for small group work. It may be interesting for you to go back and analyze that list, using the CREEEPP taxonomy as a guide (an examination activity), perhaps pulling out several that you particularly like (a personalization activity). Do not attempt to memorize the list (a rehearsal) because that makes no sense, but you may wish to add nine more to bring it to an even 100 (an elaboration). You might see a pattern in that list, noting which ones will probably work best for your class this year (a prediction) or combining them to form a neat unit plan for a particular topic (a construction). If you do these things interactively with another reader, you will have a great idea of the benefit of these categories and of the utility of CREEEPP as a planning device. (In this case, my planning your activities.)

Finally, you may wish to go back through the plethora of examples offered in this chapter, selecting those items that you think are sound and those that are not. Please realize that if you do this, you will have done an evaluation activity, the only category left out of the tasks suggested in the previous paragraph.

In closing, recall that CREEEPP is not a theory predicting differential levels of achievement for each "level." It is simply an acronym for seven different types of classroom tasks and projects for cooperative groups and one that has become very useful to its users. It offers diverse types of challenges to learners and it offers a tool for setting up classroom activities of different lengths and different formats. It is easy to recall, comprehensive in nature, and useful as a self-reflection tool for teachers. In my own teaching, about 50% of my tasks are construction, 1% rehearsal, with quite a bit of personalization and elaboration taking up the rest of my class time. It also helps teachers vary the activities and structure them as they use more and more cooperative learning activities in class.

CHAPTER 6 SUMMARY

This chapter was designed to provide two services to the reader. First, it described dozens of real classroom activities that teachers have used with their cooperative learning groups during the past few years. This compendium offers numerous choices and models for teachers to use as they begin to develop effective implementation of their own team programs.

Second, it provided conceptualizations of four distinct planning taxonomies to help organize the planning of teachers. Each of the four taxonomies was described, examples of activities were provided, and analyses of examples were offered.

The first taxonomy, project versus task, is a simple dichotomous system that compares activities that are short, brief, debriefed, and totally in class (tasks) with more complex, long-term, and complicated assignments that often involve outside work (projects). Most cooperative learning should take place in tasks that are completed in class and for which students are held individually accountable.

The second taxonomy defined was the famous Bloom cognitive, which has six stages of learning. The design of activities at the memory, comprehension, application, analysis, synthesis, and evaluation levels has differing implications and suggestions. Paramount was the notion that synthesis activities can be the most useful for team learning, in that they require students to utilize a wide range of skills, knowledges, and abilities and they provoke the greatest cognitive challenge.

The third taxonomy utilized Howard Gardner's multiple intelligences theory, which posits that IQ as represented by a single, immutable, and genetically programmed trait is a flawed concept for understanding learners. Instead, seven intelligences—musical, spatial/visual, body/kinesthetic, verbal/linguistic, logico-mathematical, intrapersonal, and interpersonal—make up the learning potentialities for individuals. Planning lessons for heterogeneous teams involves recognizing and utilizing the potential for each intelligence and many lessons use one of them as a focus. Examples of lessons that "awaken and amplify" the specific intelligences of team-mates were provided for all levels.

Finally, the fourth taxonomy, represented by the acronym CREEEPP, was described. This system is not staged or leveled; instead, it is a simple series of categories that utilize all major types of classroom activities. The seven groups—construct, rehearse, examine, elaborate, evaluate, predict, and personalize—provide a diverse and flexible system that allows variation of planned lessons and provides an analytical tool for a teacher's self-reflection. Examples of activities in each category were provided.

Finally, it was noted that having the three necessary structures in place was not enough to ensure success with team learning. Students must be challenged and engaged in meaningful, interesting, and thoughtfully designed activities for the power of the team strategy to take effect.

REFLECTION QUESTIONS

1. In the middle of the chapter a comment is made that refers to school clubs and organizations as places where students learn the social skills inherent in what Gardner calls "interpersonal intelligence" and which many laypeople call "learning to get along." School organizations and clubs also provide opportunities to develop the seven intelligences in a team framework.

   My son, Matt, attends a small secondary school called Niagara Catholic Junior/Senior High School (NC), and is 1 of 365 students. Under the direction of its principal, Ron Buggs, NC has developed 21 clubs and student organizations, along with 17 sports teams, offering students plenty of opportunities to develop their interests and intelligences in a social setting.

   Here are descriptions of the 21 clubs offered to my son. Please classify them by the Gardner intelligence that most likely forms the focus of the organization (i.e., the drama club's crew requires utilization of spatial/visual intelligence; its actors and actresses also use body/kinesthetic intelligence). Please remember that each club is also a team, a group in which members work together and whose activities probably utilize interpersonal intelligence.

   Art Club: For those students who wish to gain new knowledge of and satisfaction in creating art. Projects would revolve around developing murals and mosaics, providing illustrations for the yearbook, and artwork for the school as needed.

   Calligraphy Club: For students interested in the art of beautiful handwriting. The basic fundamentals will be introduced during meetings. Members will be available for those who need help learning the specialized writing.

Choral Group: Will lead the student body in worship during masses and prayer services. A "great" voice and/or ability to read music are not critical for membership; rather, enjoyment of singing and wishing to honor the Lord are.

Computer Club: For students to exchange ideas about computer programming and games and to improve computer literacy. You do not have to be computer literate to join.

Drama Team: Presents two major productions during the school year, a Christmas play and a spring production. The team needs both "players" (those seen by the audience) and "crew" (those who make it work—sets and planning).

Ecology Club: This club is dedicated to raising the awareness of the student body and the surrounding community with regard to environmental matters and to crusading against wrongful acts that bring environmental harm to our planet. The club also sponsors the NCHS Annual Science Fair for area grade school students.

Instrumental Band: Involves playing music that the membership wants to play. Anyone who has had some experience in playing musical instruments is welcome to join.

Intramurals: Seasonally organized athletic competitions for student-organized teams throughout the school year. Trophies are awarded to the winning groups.

Key Club: A service (sharing and caring) organization affiliated with Kiwanis. Activities include volunteering (soup kitchens), fund-raising (winter sleepout for the homeless), and integrating with other area high school Key Clubs for leadership workshops and social and team events. The club also assists the Kiwanis fund-raising efforts.

Language Club: Promotes the study of foreign languages and cultures. Sponsors Foreign Language Week with poster displays, PA announcements, and an international potluck dinner. Organizing trips to foreign countries is also a goal of this club. Meetings during language classes.

Liturgy Committee: Helps to prepare and to implement the many religious events held at the school every year. These would include masses, prayer services, and the traditional Thanksgiving, Christmas, and Easter events.

Media Club: Concentrates on the audiovisual aspects of school life. Members will prepare photographic displays of major school events and will also plan such video chronicles as the yearbook and class histories.

National Honor Society: A "by invitation only" society that recognizes those students who have demonstrated outstanding achievements in the areas of academics, leadership, character, and service. Students inducted into this society offer tutorials for those in need of academic assistance.

NC Recruitment Club: Dedicated to the recruitment of prospective students. Members will make presentations to junior high school students, participate in the "shadow" program, and develop strategies for promoting the continued excellence of a Catholic education.

Newspaper: The NC newspaper is published quarterly and provides many insights into all aspects of school life. The newspaper staff welcomes any student who wishes to be an artist, an editor, a writer, or a photographer.

Peer Ministry: Student teams are trained to help counsel fellow students in need of assistance. It is akin to a Big Brother/Big Sister program.

Peer Ministry (for retreats):   After a training session, junior and senior students will serve as retreat team members for grades 7 through 9. Since this commitment involves service to the school, participants would earn one-half of their required service hours.

SADD: Students Against Drunk Driving is an organization committed to the reduction of alcohol abuse among students. Activities include attending conferences to become aware of the problem and events to heighten the awareness of the entire student body as to the consequences of drug and alcohol abuse.

Ski Club: Provides those students interested in downhill skiing with a chance to ski at Kissing Bridge for an 8-week period (3 hours per week). Lessons and rentals are part of the package. The approximate cost is $300. A minimum of 20 members is necessary to participate in the program. Parents are welcome.

Student Council: Serves as the student government body. It acts as a liaison between the administration and the student body. It also raises monies to fund the school's other clubs and organizations and plans major school events such as Homecoming Week and the Thanksgiving Food Drive. Its membership includes class and club leaders and a representative and an alternate from each homeroom.

Yearbook: Prepares the NC yearbook. This is a very important and time-consuming operation. For it to be successful, it needs the help of many students in all areas—fund-raising, artwork, editing, writing, photography, and so on.

2. Imagine that you are teaching the first grade. What could teams or pairs of students do together to help them learn each of the following?

    a.   the words to a song

    b.   how to build a house out of "mini-bricks"

    c.   the steps to a dance

    d.   how to spell five new words correctly

    e.   the similarities between certain kinds of leaves

    f.   to listen without talking

    Analyze your plans using the various taxonomies described in the chapter.

3. Imagine that you are teaching the 11th grade. What activities could you have teams of students do in class to learn the following?

    a.   the rhythm and meter of Shakespeare's sonnets

    b.   the proper conjugation of a French verb

c. the five steps in a geometry proof

d. the concepts "metaphor" and "simile"

e. how to conduct a spellcheck on the classroom computer

f. value of options open to a president in a crisis

Reflect back on your answers to these inquiries. Did you create projects or tasks? Did you use upper-level or lower-level Bloom activities? Which intelligences were embedded in the demands of the task? What level of CREEEPP did you use? If you did not use any of these planning taxonomies, what did you use? Now that you have been reminded of the various taxonomies, do new activities come to mind?

4. Glasser (quoted in Lazear, 1991) says that we learn

10% of what we read

20% of what we hear

30% of what we see

50% of what we both see and hear

70% of what is discussed with others

80% of what we experience personally

90% of what we teach to someone else

a. Draw a bar graph showing this data.

b. Compare and contrast it to this old Chinese proverb: "I hear and I forget; I see and I remember; I do and I understand."

c. Redesign parts (a) and (b) so that they require a teamed task.

5. Recall that I said CREEEPP is a useful planning tool because it gives us a nice set of categories of common practices. I also suggested that its use gets better with time and practice. To help you increase your time with it, Figure 6.2 is a brief instrument for keeping a record of various lessons. Use it in a class you take or teach or observe and keep track of activities that fit the categories. In a short time, patterns will appear. Moreover, opportunities for changing categories will also appear and your insights will help you produce better and more effective lessons for your teams.

6. Rehearsal tasks are best thought of as practice opportunities that concentrate on having students memorize material or transform the subject matter into their own understandings. Such tasks do *not* require the adding of anything new to the content, combining it with other content, or picking out specific ideas. In many contexts, rehearsals are thought of as "learning," although they are limited by their focus on simple comprehension.

Incredibly, then, more than 80% of test items on U.S. teacher-made tests are thought to be simple memory or comprehension tasks, which reduces learning

FIGURE 6.2   CREEEPP Activities Check Sheet

<u>C</u>onstruct:
  Make, construct, design, build, etc.   _____

<u>R</u>ehearsal:
  Memorize, practice, etc.   _____

<u>E</u>xamination:
  Compare and contrast, identify, etc.   _____

<u>E</u>laborate:
  Solve, extend, explain, give examples, etc.   _____

<u>E</u>valuation:
  Judge, choose, defend, rank, etc.   _____

<u>P</u>rediction:
  What do you think will happen, etc.   _____

<u>P</u>ersonalize:
  What do I think, what would I do, how do I feel, etc.   _____

to memory for meaningless and unconnected facts. (If they were "connected," learning them would require different types of tasks.) Successful students often create their own applications or contexts for new knowledge, which means that students have had to invent the tasks that help them use the knowledge and learn. The development and assignment of those tasks ought to fall into the professional's duties and perhaps it ought to be seen as the key teacher role.

In this chapter, rehearsal has been stressed as simple memorization because that is how it will be received by students *if* teachers are not careful about the wording of their assignments. For example, Smith asks her teams to "get together and go over the basic functions of the pituitary gland until everybody has it down." I would expect most students to attempt to memorize whatever the documents say about the pituitary gland, or allow only the slightest deviation into what teachers have forever called "in your own words."

If Smith had said, "In five minutes I want everyone in the team to be able to describe the pituitary gland in his or her own words," we might have had a better rehearsal but most students would have still tried for the safe memorization route.

If she had asked, "Describe a person whose pituitary gland has gone bad," she would have been asking an interesting and useful elaboration question. If she had said, "Compare the pituitary gland with the hypothalamus," she would have been presenting an examination category item. In both of those cases, the students would have had to understand the gland but do so in the context of completing a more motivating and/or cognitively challenging context than is found in simple rehearsal.

Several rehearsal tasks for students follow. *Change them* so that they either require or allow a transformation (not a memorization) *or redesign them* to a different, more productive, category of CREEEPP:

a. First graders are mastering the three steps in crossing the street safely.

b. Eleventh graders are mastering the 10 steps surrounding the subject of "a bill becomes a law."

c. Seventh graders are being asked to master the five steps in the whole-language writing process. (There is an irony embedded in this one!)

d. The kindergartners are busy learning the names and favorite "hobbies" of their assigned teammates.

e. The fifth graders are mastering the important events of 1853, 1857, 1860, and 1861 that lead to the Civil War.

7. What do you think of the following social studies activities? As you read each of these activities, which are drawn from the American history curriculum, ask which Gardner intelligence is at the core of the teamed task.

Topic: *End of World War II and Bombing of Japan*

_____ a. The students are to review the various textbook illustrations of the event and generate a song that captures their reaction. They may use existing music as a base, but must write their own words.

_____ b. Using either Hiroshima or Nagasaki as the center, students are to produce a diagram showing the effects—physical, political, social, moral, economic, and psychological—across the globe of the atomic bombing.

_____ c. One criticism of President Truman was that the U.S. military gave the Japanese no warning of the impending bombing raid. This was explained by the fear that "cross-cultural communication" would *not* have functioned well. Imagine that your team had been challenged to generate an explanatory warning to the Japanese that involved *only* gesture and nonverbal communication. Be ready to act it out.

_____ d. The students are asked to construct a dialogue between three people about the decision. The first is Father Lopez, a Catholic priest who was visiting elsewhere in Japan when the bomb went off. The second is Mrs. Tanaka, a Japanese-American living in Los Angeles whose son is a U.S. Marine fighting in the East. The third is Dr. Roller, a pediatrician who has studied both Japanese and American medical practices. They have found themselves together in a train station in Los Angeles the day after the second bomb was exploded.

_____ e. Imagine the scene in the plane moments before the first bomb is dropped. Identify the likely thoughts of the various men as they approach their mission.

_____ f.   Write two Haiku poems about the event, one from President Truman's perspective and the other from a survivor's.

_____ g.   Make a list of 30 adjectives that could be properly used in a long essay about the event. As a team, reach consensus about which 12 would have to appear in an essay that was balanced, accurate, and interesting. Be ready to describe the process that was used to reach a friendly consensus.

Author's note: Each of the seven activities was designed with a Gardner intelligence in mind. Here are the author's classifications: a, M; b, V/S; c, B/K; d, L/M; e, intrapersonal; f, V/L; g, interpersonal.

8. Here are some more sample activities for the Bomb unit introduced in Reflection Question 7. Using information from the chapter, classify the following activities as to their CREEEPP category (also, note the intelligences used). Please try to determine if you are starting to develop patterns of liking certain taxonomies better than others. Please note that all of these are designed as in-class tasks and are not projects. Also note that as schools transform from 40-minute chunks called classes to 80-minute pieces in "block" scheduling (which is already standard fare in Ontario), teachers will begin to utilize more and more tasks each day. Having a systematic approach to planing would help in such a transition.

_____ a.   The students are to design a collage that illustrates the moral, legal, military, political, racial, and economic consequences of the dropping of the atomic bombs on Japan.

_____ b.   The students are to design a Japanese postage stamp commemorating the events of August 1945.

_____ c.   The teams are to master the facts of the situation: dates, bomb tonnage, deaths, and injuries.

_____ d.   The teams are to compare four newspaper headlines from various cities in the United States and identify similarities and differences in their treatment of the story.

_____ e.   The students are to create an outline for an essay entitled: "Hiroshima and Nagasaki: Bombing Warranted?"

_____ f.   The students are to write a 100-word press release from the president's office that explains the decision to bomb Nagasaki.

_____ g.   The students are to write 100-word diary entries for the day after Hiroshima from the perspective of each of the following:

a doctor living 80 miles from Hiroshima

a Shinto priest living in New York City

the bombardier on the *Enola Gay*

a Russian politician living in Moscow

a black U.S. soldier preparing for the invasion of Japan

Hirohito, emperor of Japan

_____ h.   Teams are to produce a series of estimates regarding the likelihood of the world witnessing a future use of atomic/nuclear weapons.

_____ i.   Students imagine that they are members of a CBS press team allowed to interview one of the following: President Truman, a 38-year-old female survivor in Hiroshima, or Mrs. Homoto, a Japanese-American living in Brooklyn and a native of the United States. (She had been in an internment camp in 1944.) They are to generate a list of 10 questions to be asked.

Author's Note: Activities a, b, and i were meant to be construction tasks; c was rehearsal (and useless); d was examination; e was evaluation; f was an elaboration; g was a personalization, and h involved prediction. Again, note that CREEEPP is a taxonomy of categories, not levels: Altering the categories allowed for differentiation of the demands on the teams of students.

REFERENCES

Allen, W. H., and Van Sickle, R. L. (1984). Learning teams and low achievers. *Social Education, 48,* 60–64.

Amabile, T. M. (1989). *Growing up creative: Nurturing a lifetime of creativity.* New York: Crown.

Ames, C. (1981). Competitive versus cooperative reward structures: The influence of individual and group performance factors on achievement attributions and affect. *American Educational Research Journal, 18,* 273–287.

Arends, R. I. (1994). *Learning to teach* (2nd ed.). New York: Random House.

Armstrong, T. (1994). *Multiple intelligences in the classroom.* Alexandria, VA: Association for Supervision and Curriculum Development.

Aronson, E., Blaney, N., Stephan, C., Sikes, J., & Snapp, M. (1978). *The Jigsaw classroom.* Beverly Hills, CA: Sage.

Atwell, N. (1987). *In the middle: Writing, reading, and learning with adolescents.* Portsmouth, NH: Boynton Cook.

Ausubel, D. P. (1968). *Educational psychology: A cognitive view.* New York: Holt, Rinehart and Winston.

Bargh, J., & Schul, Y. (1980). On the cognitive benefits of teaching. *Journal of Educational Psychology, 72,* 593–604.

Bennett, N., & Cass, A. (1988). The effects of group composition on group interactive processes and pupil understanding. *British Educational Research Journal, 15,* 19–32.

Benware, C. A., & Deci, E. L. (1984). Quality of learning with an active versus passive set. *American Educational Research Journal, 21,* 755–765.

Blaney, N. T., Stephan, C., Rosenfield, D., Aronson, E., & Sikes, J. (1977). Interdependence in the classroom: A field study. *Journal of Educational Psychology, 69*(2), 121–128.

Bloom, B. (1984, May). The search for methods of group instruction as effective as one-on-one tutoring. *Educational Leadership,* 4–17.

Chambers, B., & Abrami, P. C. (1991). The relationship between student team learning outcomes and achievement, causal attributions and affect. *Journal of Educational Psychology, 83,* 140–146.

Chernick, R. S. (1990). Effects of interdependent, coactive and individualized working conditions on pupils' educational computer program performance. *Journal of Educational Psychology, 82,* 691–695.

Clarke, J., Wideman, R., & Eadie, S. (1990). *Together we learn.* Englewood Cliffs, NJ: Prentice Hall.

Cohen, E. (1994). *Designing groupwork: Strategies for the heterogeneous classroom* (2nd ed.). New York: Teachers College Press.

Cohen, E. G., & Lotan, R. A. (1995). Producing equal-status interaction in the heterogeneous classroom. *American Educational Research Journal, 32,* 99–120.

Cooper, L., Johnson, D., Johnson, R., & Wilderson, F. (1980). Effects of cooperative, competitive, and individualistic experiences or interpersonal attraction among heterogeneous peers. *Journal of Social Psychology, 111,* 243–252.

Crabill, C. D. (1988). Small group learning in the secondary mathematics classroom. In N. Davidson (Ed.), *Small group cooperative learning in mathematics: A handbook for teachers.* Reading, MA: Addison-Wesley.

Cuban, L. (1983). Persistence of the inevitable: The teacher-centered classroom. *Education and Urban Society, 15,* 26–41.

Dansereau, D. F. (1987). Transfer from cooperative to individual studying. *Journal of Reading, 30,* 614–619.

DeVries, D. L., & Slavin, R. E. (1978). Teams–Games–Tournaments: Review of ten classroom experiments. *Journal of Research and Development in Education, 12,* 28–38.

DeVries, D. L., Slavin, R. E., & Edwards, K. J. (1978). Biracial learning teams and race rela-tions in the classroom: Four field experiments using Teams–Games–Tournaments. *Journal of Educational Psychology, 70,* 356–362.

Dunn, R., & Griggs, S. A. (1988). *Learning styles: Quiet revolution in American secondary schools.* Reston, VA: National Association of Secondary School Principals.

Ellis, A., & Fouts, J. T. (1993). *Research on educational innovations.* Princeton, NJ: Eye on Education.

Erickson, D. E., & Vermette, P. J. (1997). Personality type and preference for cooperative learning. Manuscript submitted for publication.

Erickson, D. E., Vermette, P. J., Cheshire, L., & Sheeran, T. (1996, April). Intervention strategies for sensitizing people to potentially sexually harassing behaviors. Research presentation at the American Educational Research Association Conference, New York City, NY.

Fantuzzo, J. W., Riggio, R. E., Connelly, S., & Dimoff, L. A. (1989). Effects of reciprocal peer tutoring on academic achievement and psychological adjustment: A component analysis. *Journal of Educational Psychology, 81,* 173–177.

Fraser, S. (Ed.). (1995). *The bell curve wars: Race, intelligence, and the future of America.* New York: Basic Books.

Fraser, S. C., Diener, E., Beaman, A. L., & Kelem, R. T. (1977). Two, three, or four heads are better than one: Modifications of college performance by peer monitoring. *Journal of Educational Psychology, 69,* 101–108.

Freedman, S. G. (1990). *Small victories.* New York: Harper Perennial.

Gallagher, J. J., & Coleman, M. R. (1994). Cooperative learning and gifted students: Five case studies. *Cooperative Learning, 14,* 21–24.

Gardner, H. (1983). *Frames of mind: The theory of multiple intelligences.* Cambridge, MA: Harvard University Press.

Gardner, H. (1993). *Multiple intelligences: The theory in practice.* New York: Basic Books.

Gardner, H. (1995, November). Reflections on multiple intelligences: Myths and messages. *Phi Delta Kappan,* 200–209.

Glasser, W. (1986). *Control theory in the classroom.* New York: Harper and Row.

Glasser, W. (1990, February). The quality school. *Phi Delta Kappan, 425–435.*

Goleman, D. (1995). *Emotional intelligence.* New York: Bantam Books.

Good, T. L., & Brophy, J. (1994). *Looking in classrooms* (6th ed.). Harper Collins.

Goodlad, J. (1984). *A place called school.* New York: McGraw-Hill.

Grabowski, B., Birdwell, D., Snetsinger, W., Lui, J., Hong, N., & Harkness, W. (1995). Generative learning activities in a large lecture class: A longitudinal study from multiple perspectives. Paper presented at the Northeastern Educational Research Association Conference, Ellenville, NY.

Grant, C., & Sleeter, C. (1986). *After the school bell rings.* Philadelphia, PA: Falmer Press.

Harris, A. M., & Covington, M. V. (1993). The role of cooperative reward interdependency in success and failure. *The Journal of Experimental Education, 61,* 151–168.

Hertz-Lazarowitz, R. (1993). Using group investigation to enhance Arab–Jewish relationships. *Cooperative Learning, 13,* 26–28.

Humphreys, B., Johnson, R., & Johnson, D. W. (1982). Effects of cooperative, competitive and individualistic learning on students' achievement in science class. *Journal of Research in Science Teaching, 19,* 351–356.

Hunter, M. (1994). *Enhancing teaching.* New York: Macmillan College Publishing.

Hwong, N. C., Caswell, A., Johnson, D. W., & Johnson, R. T. (1992). Effects of cooperative and individualistic learning on prospective elementary teachers' music achievement and attitudes. *Journal of Social Psychology, 133,* 53–64.

Johnson, D. W., & Johnson, R. T. (1981). Effects of cooperative and individualistic learning experiences on interethnic interaction. *Journal of Educational Psychology, 73,* 444–449.

Johnson, D. W., & Johnson, R. T. (1985). Classroom conflict: Controversy versus debate in learning groups. *American Educational Research Journal, 22,* 237–256.

Johnson, D. W., & Johnson, R. T. (1987). *Learning together and alone.* Englewood Cliffs, NJ: Prentice Hall.

Johnson, D. W., & Johnson, R. T. (1989). *Cooperation and competition: Theory and research.* Edina, MN: Interaction Book Company.

Johnson, D. W., & Johnson, R. T. (1995). *Reducing school violence through conflict resolution.* Reston, VA: Association for Supervision and Curriculum Development.

Johnson, D. W., Johnson, R. T., Buckman, L. A., & Richards, P. S. (1986). The effect of prolonged implementation of cooperative learning on social support within the classroom. *Journal of Psychology, 119,* 405–411.

Johnson, D. W., Johnson, R. T., & Holubec, E. J. (1984). *Circles of learning: Cooperation in the classroom.* Alexandria, VA: Association for Supervision and Curriculum Development.

Johnson, D. W., Johnson, R. T., & Holubec, E. J. (1994). *The nuts and bolts of cooperative learning.* Edina, MN: Interaction Book Company.

Johnson, D. W., Johnson, R. T., & Maruyama, G. (1985). Interdependence and interpersonal attraction among heterogeneous and homogeneous individuals: A theoretical formulation and a meta-analysis of the research. *Review of Educational Research, 53,* 5–54.

Johnson, D. W., Johnson, R. T., Stanne, M. B., & Garibaldi, A. (1990). Impact of group processing on achievement in cooperative groups. *The Journal of Social Psychology, 130,* 507–516.

Johnson, D. W., Maruyama, G., Johnson, R., Nelson, D., & Skon, L. (1981). Effects of cooperative, competitive, & individualistic goal structures on achievement: A meta-analysis. *Psychological Bulletin, 89,* 47–62.

Johnson, D. W., Skon, L., & Johnson, R. T. (1980). Effects of cooperative, competitive, and individualistic conditions on children's problem-solving performance. *American Educational Research Journal, 17,* 83–93.

Johnson, R. T., & Johnson, D. W. (1981). Building friendships between handicapped and non-handicapped students: Effects of cooperative and individualistic instruction. *American Educational Research Journal, 18,* 415–423.

Johnson, R. T., & Johnson, D. W. (1983). Effects of cooperative, competitive and individualistic learning experiences on social development. *Exceptional Children, 49,* 323–329.

Johnson, R. T., Johnson, D. W., DeWeerdt, N., Lyons, V., & Zaidman, B. (1983). Integrating severely adaptively handicapped seventh-grade students into constructive relationships with non-handicapped peers in science class. *American Journal of Mental Deficiency, 87,* 611–618.

Johnson, R. T., Johnson, D. W., & Rynders, J. (1981). Effect of cooperative, competitive and individualistic experiences on self-esteem of handicapped and non-handicapped students. *The Journal of Psychology, 108,* 31–34.

Johnson, R. T., Johnson, D. W., Scott, L. E., & Ramolae, B. (1985). Effects of single-sex and mixed-sex cooperative interaction on science achievement and attitudes and cross-handicap and cross-sex relationships. *Journal of Research in Science Teaching, 22*(3), 207–220.

Johnson, R. T., Johnson, D. W., & Stanne, M. B. (1985). Effects of cooperative, competitive and individualistic goal structures on computer-assisted instruction. *Journal of Educational Psychology, 77,* 668–677.

Johnson, R. T., Johnson, D. W., & Stanne, M. B. (1986). Comparison of computer-assisted cooperative, competitive and individualistic learning. *American Educational Research Journal, 23,* 382–392.

Kagan, S. (1989, December). The structural approach to cooperative learning. *Educational Leadership,* 12–15.

Kagan, S. (1992). *Cooperative learning resources for teachers.* Riverside, CA: University of California.

Kagan, S. (1995, May). Group grades miss the mark. *Educational Leadership,* 68–71.

Katstra, J., Tollefson, N., & Gilbert, E. (1987). The effects of peer evaluation on attitude toward writing and writing fluency of ninth grade students. *Journal of Educational Research, 80,* 168–172.

King, A. (1990). Enhancing peer interaction and learning in the classroom through reciprocal questioning. *American Educational Research Journal, 27,* 664–687.

Kohlberg, L. (1963). The development of children's orientations toward moral order: Sequence in the development of moral thought. *Vita Humana, 6,* 11–33.

Kohn, A. (1994). *No contest: The case against competition* (2nd ed.). Boston, MA: Houghton-Mifflin.

Kourilsky, M., & Wittrock, M. C. (1992). Generative teaching: An enhancement strategy for the learning of economics in a cooperative group. *American Educational Research Journal, 29*(4), 861–876.

Larson, C. O., & Dansereau, D. (1986, March). Cooperative learning in dyads. *Journal of Reading,* 517–520.

Lazarowitz, R., Hertz, R. L., Baird, J. H., & Bowlden, V. (1988). Academic achievement and on-task behavior of high school biology students instructed in a cooperative small investigative group. *Science Education, 72,* 475–487.

Lazear, D. (1991). *Seven ways of knowing: Teaching for multiple intelligences* (2nd ed.). Palantine, IL: IRI/Skylight.

Leming, J. S. (1992). Ideological perspectives within the social studies profession: An empirical examination of the "two cultures" thesis. *Theory and Research in Social Education, 22,* 293–312.

Little Soldier, L. (1989, October). Cooperative learning and the Native American Indian student. *Phi Delta Kappan, 71,* 61–66.

Lockheed, M. (1986). Reshaping the social order: The case of gender segregation. *Sex Roles, 14*(11), 617–628.

Lockheed, M. E., & Harris, A. M. (1984). Cross-sex collaborative learning in elementary classrooms. *American Educational Research Journal, 21,* 275–294.

Logan, T. (1986, May). Cooperative learning: A view from the inside. *The Social Studies,* 123–126.

Louth, R., McAllister, C. E., & McAllister, H. A. (1990). The effects of collaborative writing techniques on freshman writing and attitudes. *Journal of Experimental Education, 61,* 215–224.

Luczkiw, G. (1995). Personal communication about the Institute for Enterprise Education, St. Catharines, Ontario, Canada.

Lyman, F. T. (1987). The think-trix: A classroom tool for thinking. *Reading: Issues and Practices,* Westminster State of Maryland International Reading Association Council, 15–18.

Marzano, R. J., Pickering, D., & McTighe, J. (1993). *Assessing student outcomes: Performance assessment using the dimensions of learning model.* Alexandria, VA: Association for Supervision and Curriculum Development.

McAuliffe, T. J., & Dembo, M. H. (1994). Status rules of behavior in scenarios of peer learning. *Journal of Educational Psychology, 86,* 163–172.

McDonald, B. A., Larson, C. O., Dansereau, D. F., & Spurlin, J. E. (1985). Cooperative dyads: Impact on text learning and transfer. *Contemporary Educational Psychology, 10,* 369–377.

Melothe, M. S., & Deering, P. D. (1994). Task talk and task awareness under different cooperative learning conditions. *American Educational Research Journal, 31,* 138–165.

Mesch, D., Johnson, D. W., & Johnson, R. (1987). Impact of positive interdependence and academic group contingencies on achievement. *Journal of Social Psychology, 128,* 345–352.

Mevarech, Z. R., & Susak, Z. (1993). Effects of learning with cooperative-mastery method on elementary students. *Journal of Educational Research, 86,* 197–205.

Miller, N., & Harrington, H. J. (1992). Social categorization and intergroup acceptance: Principles for the design and development of cooperative learning teams. In R. Hertz-Lazarowitz & N. Miller (Eds.), *Interaction in cooperative groups: The theoretical anatomy of group learning.* New York: Cambridge University Press.

Moskowitz, J. M., Malvin, J. H., Shaeffer, G. A., & Schaps, E. (1983). Evaluation of a cooperative learning strategy. *American Educational Research Journal, 20,* 687–696.

Moskowitz, J. M., Malvin, J. H., Shaeffer, G. A., & Schaps, E. (1985). Evaluation of Jigsaw, a cooperative learning technique. *Contemporary Educational Psychology, 10,* 104–112.

Mulryan, C. (1989). A study of intermediate-grade students' involvement and participation in cooperative small groups in mathematics. Unpublished doctoral dissertation, University of Missouri–Columbia.

Newman, F., & Thompson, J. A. (1987). Effects of cooperative learning on achievement in secondary schools: A summary of research. Madison, WI: National Center on Effective Secondary Schools, Wisconsin Center for Educational Research.

Nichols, J. D., & Miller, R. B. (1994). Cooperative learning and student motivation. *Contemporary Educational Psychology, 19,* 167–178.

Novak, J. D. (1990). Concept mapping: A useful tool for science education. *Journal of Research in Science Teaching, 27,* 937–949.

O'Donnell, A. M., & Dansereau, D. F. (1992). Scripted cooperation in student dyads: A method for analyzing and enhancing academic learning and performance. In R. Hertz-Lazarowitz & N. Miller (Eds.), *Interaction in cooperative groups: The theoretical anatomy of group learning.* New York: Cambridge University Press.

O'Donnell, A. M., & Dansereau, D. F. (1993). Learning from lectures: Effects of cooperative review. *Journal of Experimental Education, 61,* 116–125.

O'Donnell, A. M., Dansereau, D. F., Hall, R. H., & Rocklin, T. R. (1987). Cognitive, affective and metacognitive outcomes of scripted cooperative learning. *Journal of Educational Psychology, 79,* 421–437.

O'Donnell, A. M., Dansereau, D. F., Rocklin, T., Lambiotte, J. G., Hythecher, V. I., & Larson, C. O. (1985). Cooperative writing. *Written Communication, 2,* 307–315.

Okebukola, P. A. (1984). In search of a more effective interaction pattern in biology laboratories. *Journal of Biological Education, 18,* 305–308.

Okebukola, P. A. (1985). The relative effectiveness of cooperative and competitive interaction techniques in strengthening students' performance in science classes. *Science Education, 69,* 501–509.

Okebukola, P. A. (1986). The problem of large classes in science: An experiment in cooperative learning. *Journal of Science Education, 8,* 73–77.

Okebukola, P. A. (1992). Concept mapping with a cooperative learning flavor. *The American Biology Teacher, 54,* 218–221.

Palinscar, H. S., Brown, A. L., & Martin, S. M. (1987). Peer interaction in reading comprehension. *Educational Psychologist, 22,* 231–253.

Piaget, J. (1963). *Origins of intelligence in children.* New York: Norton.

Popkewitz, T. S. (1981). The social contexts of schooling, change and educational research. *Journal of Curriculum Studies, 13,* 189–206.

Qin, Z., Johnson, D. W., & Johnson, R. T. (1995). Cooperative versus competitive efforts in problem-solving. *Review of Educational Research, 65,* 129–143.

Ross, J. (1988). Improving social-environment studies problem-solving through cooperative learning. *American Educational Research Journal, 25,* 573–591.

Ross, J. A., & Cousins, J. B. (1994). Intentions to seek and give help, and behavior in cooperative learning groups. *Contemporary Educational Psychology, 19,* 476–482.

Sadker, M., & Sadker, D. (1994). *Failing at fairness.* New York: Macmillan Publishing.

Scott, K. (1985). Social interaction skills: Perspectives on teaching cross-sex communication. *Social Education, 47,* 610–615.

Semb, G. B., & Ellis, J. A. (1994). Knowledge taught in school: What is remembered? *Review of Educational Research, 64,* 253–286.

Sharan, S. (1980). Cooperative learning in small groups: Recent methods and effects on achievement, attitudes and ethnic relations. *Review of Educational Research, 50,* 241–271.

Sharan, S. (Ed.). (1994). *Handbook of cooperative learning methods.* Westport, CT: Greenwood Press.

Sharan, S., Ackerman, Z., & Hertz-Lazarowitz, R. (1980). Academic achievement of elementary school children in small-group versus whole-class instruction. *Journal of Experimental Education, 48,* 125–129.

Sharan, S., & Sharan, Y. (1976). *Small group teaching.* Englewood Cliffs, NJ: Prentice Hall.

Sharan, Y., & Sharan, S. (1992). *Expanding cooperative learning through group investigation.* New York: Teachers College Press.

Sirotnik, K. (1983). What you see is what you get—consistency, persistency, and mediocrity in classrooms. *Harvard Educational Review, 53,* 16–29.

Skon, L., Johnson, D. W., & Johnson, R. T. (1981). Cooperative peer interaction versus individual competition and individualistic efforts: Effects on the acquisition of cognitive reasoning strategies. *Journal of Educational Psychology, 73,* 83–92.

Slavin, R. E. (1978). Student teams and achievement divisions. *Journal of Research and Development in Education, 12,* 39–49.

Slavin, R. E. (1983). *Cooperative learning.* New York: Longman.

Slavin, R. E. (1986a). Best-evidence synthesis: An alternative to meta-analytic and traditional reviews. *Educational Researcher, 15,* 5–11.

Slavin, R. E. (1986b). *Using student team learning* (3rd ed.). Baltimore, MD: Johns Hopkins University, Center for Research on Elementary and Middle Schools.

Slavin, R. E. (1991a). Synthesis of research on cooperative learning. *Educational Leadership, 48,* 82–89.

Slavin, R. E. (1991b). Are cooperative learning and untracking harmful to the gifted? *Educational Leadership, 48,* 68–71.

Slavin, R. E. (1995). *Cooperative learning* (2nd ed.). Needham Heights, MA: Allyn and Bacon.

Slavin, R. E., & Karweit, N. L. (1981). Cognitive and affective outcomes of an intensive student team learning experience. *Journal of Experimental Education, 50,* 29–35.

Slavin, R. E., Madden, N. A., & Leavey, M. (1984). Effects of cooperative learning and individualized instruction on mainstreamed students. *Exceptional Children, 50*(5), 434–442.

Slavin, R. E., & Oickle, E. (1981). Effects of cooperative learning teams on student achievement and race relations: Treatment by race interactions. *Sociology of Education, 54,* 174–180.

Smith, R. (1987, May). A teacher's views on cooperative learning. *Phi Delta Kappan, 68,* 663–666.

Snyder, T., & Sullivan, H. (1995). Cooperative and individual learning and student misconceptions in science. *Contemporary Educational Psychology, 20,* 230–235.

Stevens, R. J., Madden, N. A., Slavin, R. E., & Farnish, A. M. (1987). Cooperative integrated reading and composition: Two field experiments. *Reading Research Quarterly, 22,* 433–454.

Stevens, R. J., & Slavin, R. E. (1995a). The cooperative elementary school: Effects on students' achievement, attitudes, and social relations. *American Educational Research Journal, 32,* 321–351.

Stevens, R. J., & Slavin, R. E. (1995b). Effects of a cooperative learning approach in reading and writing on academically handicapped and non-handicapped students. *Elementary School Journal, 95,* 241–262.

Stevens, R. J., Slavin, R. E., & Farnish, A. M. (1991). The effects of cooperative learning and direct instruction in reading comprehension strategies on main idea identification. *Journal of Educational Psychology, 83,* 8–16.

Stevenson, C. (1992). *Teaching ten to fourteen year olds.* White Plains, NY: Longman.

Talmage, H., Pascarella, E. T., & Ford, S. (1984). The influence of cooperative learning strategies on teacher practices, student perceptions of the learning environment, and academic achievement. *American Educational Research Journal, 21,* 163–179.

Tannen, D. T. (1990). *You just don't understand; women and men in conversation.* New York: Ballantine Books.

Tannen, D. T. (1994). *Talking nine-to-five.* New York: Morrow and Company.

Udvari-Solner, A., & Thousand, J. S. (1995). Promising practices that foster inclusive education. In R. A. Villa and J. S. Thousand (Eds.), *Creating an inclusive school* (pp. 87–109).

Alexandria, VA: Association for Supervision and Curriculum Development.

Vermette, P. J. (1983, October). A generalized model for high school concept instruction. *The High School Journal, 67,* 20–24.

Vermette, P. J. (1994a). The letter home: A rationale for using cooperative learning for the first time. *The Social Science Record, 31,* 12–15.

Vermette, P. J. (1994b, February). Four fatal flaws: Avoiding the common mistakes of novice users of cooperative learning. *The High School Journal,* 255–265.

Vermette, P. J., & Erickson, D. E. (1996). Cooperative learning in the college classroom: Three structures and seven activities. *The College Student Journal, 30,* 203–211.

Vermette, P. J., Wisniewski, S., Janssen-O'Leary, S., Kenny, C., Colman, P., Johnston, G., & Bromberg, H. (1993). *Inside a middle school base group: A case study of cooperative learning.* Paper presented at Northeastern Educational Research Association Conference, Ellenville, New York.

Vygotsky, L. S. (1962). *Thought and language.* Cambridge, MA: The MIT Press.

Warring, D., Johnson, D. W., Maruyama, G., & Johnson, R. (1985). Impact of different types of cooperative learning on cross-ethnic and cross-sex relations. *Journal of Educational Psychology, 77,* 53–59.

Webb, N. M. (1982). Peer interaction and learning in cooperative small groups. *Journal of Educational Psychology, 74,* 642–655.

Webb, N. M. (1984). Sex differences in interaction and achievement in cooperative small groups. *Journal of Educational Psychology, 76,* 33–44.

Webb, N. M., Ender, P., & Lewis, S. (1986). Problem-solving strategies and group processes in small groups learning computer programming. *American Educational Research Journal, 23,* 243–261.

Webb, N. M., & Farivar, S. (1994). Promoting helping behaviors in cooperative small groups in middle school mathematics. *American Educational Research Journal, 31,* 369–395.

Webb, N. M., Troper, J. D., & Fall, R. (1995). Constructive activity and learning in collaborative small groups. *Journal of Educational Psychology, 87,* 406–423.

Weisfield, C. C., Weisfield, G. E., Warren, M. A., & Freedman, D. G. (1983). The spelling bee: A naturalistic study of female inhibitions in mixed-sex competitions. *Adolescence, 18,* 695–708.

Widaman, K. F., & Kagan, S. (1987). Cooperativeness and achievement: Interaction of student cooperativeness with cooperative versus competitive classroom organization. *Journal of School Psychology, 25,* 355–365.

Wiegel, R. H., Wiser, P. L., & Cook, S. W. (1975). Impact of cooperative learning experiences on cross-ethnic relations and attitudes. *Journal of Social Issues, 31,* 219–245.

Wiggins, G. (1994, October). Toward better report cards. *Educational Leadership,* 28–37.

Yager, S., Johnson, D. W., & Johnson, R. T. (1985). Oral discussion, group-to-individual transfer and achievement in cooperative learning groups. *Journal of Educational Psychology, 77,* 60–66.

Ziegler, S. (1981). The effectiveness of cooperative learning teams for increasing cross-ethnic friendship: Additional evidence. *Human Organization, 40,* 264–268.

NAME INDEX

Abrami, P. C., 56–57
Ackerman, Z., 44–45
Allen, W. H., 62
Amabile, T. M., 118
Ames, C., 56
Arends, R. I., 198
Armstrong, T., 130, 200
Aronson, Eliot, 17, 19, 37–38,
    43, 72, 150, 175–176
Atwell, N., 143
Ausubel, D. P., 55

Baird, J. H., 62
Bargh, J., 9, 104
Beaman, A. L., 119
Bennett, N., 77
Benware, C. A., 104
Birdwell, D., 63
Blaney, N., 19, 37–38, 43, 72,
    150, 175–176
Bloom, Benjamin, 6, 18, 198–200

Bowlden, V., 62
Bromberg, H., 104
Brophy, J., 77, 112
Brown, A. L., 57, 62
Buckman, L. A., 120–121

Carlson, Brian, 77–78
Carpenter, Jerry, 207
Cass, A., 77
Caswell, A., 63, 121
Chambers, B., 56–57
Chernick, R. S., 50–51
Cheshire, L., 63
Clarke, J., 77, 151, 157, 181
Cohen, Elizabeth, 22, 25, 62, 70,
    79, 101, 157, 181, 206
Coleman, M. R., 104
Colman, P., 104
Connelly, S., 22
Cook, S. W., 63, 101
Cooper, L., 39, 85

Cousins, J. B., 59, 172
Covington, M. V., 62, 90
Crabill, C. D., 35
Cuban, L., 3

Dansereau, Donald F., 20–22,
    48–49, 52, 57, 72
Deci, E. L., 104
Deering, P. D., 57
Dembo, M .H., 62
DeVries, D. L., 19, 37
DeWeerdt, N., 39–40, 85
Diener, E., 119
Dimoff, L. A., 22
Dunn, Rita, 85

Eadie, S., 77, 151, 157, 181
Edwards, K. J., 37
Ellis, A., 85
Ellis, J. A., 191
Erickson, D. E., 63, 188, 207

SUBJECT INDEX